Pocahontas and Sacagawea

Interwoven Legacies in American History

Cyndi Spindell Berck

Commonwealth Books of Virginia
www.commonwealthbooks.org
e-mail: info@commonwealthbooks.org
Alexandria, VA 22307
703-307-7715

Library of Congress Control Number: 2014948527
ISBN (Paperback): 978-0-9909592-5-0
ISBN (Ebook - EPUB): 978-0-9904018-8-9
ISBN (Ebook - PDF): 978-0-9904018-9-6
ISBN (Ebook - Kindle): 978-0-9909592-8-1

American History/Biography

Printed in the United States of America

Dedication

To my parents, William and Arline Spindell, who drove a station wagon
with three whining kids around the great American West.

Contents

Preface and Acknowledgements

This is a work of non-fiction, and my first goal is accuracy. Notes on sources can be found at the end of the book.

I would like to thank Joyce Appleby, Anna Snow Berck, Arica Coleman, Keith Gilless, Michael Hittman, Landon Jones, Robert Snow, Eric Walquist and Eden Welker for sharing their knowledge and perspectives. I thank Kate Harrison for Spanish translation assistance. Several members of my family helped with comments and proofreading: thank you, Mom, Peter, Anna, Joe, Glenn, Mitch, and Stephen. I also thank the patient, cheerful and knowledgeable staff at the Virginia Historical Society, Bancroft Library (University of California, Berkeley), Mission San Luis Rey museum, Pamunkey Reservation museum, Smithsonian Institution/Art Resource, Wisconsin Historical Society, Santa Bárbara Mission Archive-Library, and Cumberland County Historical Society (Carlisle, Pennsylvania). Finally, I thank James Thompson of Commonwealth Books of Virginia for his enthusiasm and support, and Betsy Hodges for production assistance that went far beyond my expectations.

And what would I do without Peter? He has patiently explained which way rivers flow to his directionally-impaired wife, has always been willing to drive a little farther, and has kept the dishes and laundry from piling to the ceiling.

Thanks to everyone who helped me avoid errors of fact, interpretation, and omission. All opinions are my own. Those errors which remain are my responsibility.

Migration and Enlightenment

*I*n 1919, a direct descendant of Pocahontas stepped into an unexpected role. She was Edith Bolling Wilson, First Lady of the United States. When President Woodrow Wilson suffered a stroke during the crucial year following the end of World War I, the First Lady unofficially took over his duties. These included unsuccessfully lobbying the U.S. Senate to join the new League of Nations. The League of Nations was part of Wilson's Fourteen Points, a vision of the postwar world that included self-determination of peoples. The idea of self-determination issued from a land that had been taken by force from Pocahontas' people.

The straight line from the peacemaker of the 1600s to her descendant in the 1900s illustrates the contradictions inherent in the building of a great nation. The stories of Pocahontas and Sacagawea trace one slice of the migration that built America: from Jamestown in Virginia, across the Appalachian Mountains to St. Louis, up the Missouri River with Lewis and Clark, and to the Pacific.

Self-determination would have been an odd concept to Edith Wilson's Indian ancestors. Pocahontas' father, Chief Powhatan, was consolidating his dominant position over nearby tribes when he was interrupted by the white invasion. Powhatan's hegemony was based on shared culture and mutual defense, but it was backed up by force. For most of history, taking over someone else's territory has been a routine activity.

The first Americans migrated from Siberia to North America over 13,000 years ago, probably in five waves that brought five very different language groups. "The complicated geographical diffusion of tribes with a common ancestral language base suggests continual movement, invasion, migration and conquest long before the white man set foot on the continent." By the time of European contact, the original language groups were distributed all over North America. The first Americans explored, traded, and conquered, north, south, east and west. Pocahontas' people raised corn that had been domesticated in Mexico. Sacagawea's Shoshonean language is related to the language of the Aztecs.

Then came European colonialism. With all its evils, it was not a monolithic process; it reflected the variety of the people who crossed the ocean. One face of colonialism was a creative process of migration and cultural mixing, through face-to-face human contact. Personal relationships have been the bridge across cultures in the harshest of times. Pocahontas and Sacagawea stepped across that bridge.

Pocahontas entered history when she saved the life of John Smith in Jamestown. Or did Smith make up the story? What's certain is that she married another Englishman, John Rolfe, who introduced the plantation economy to Virginia. Their descendants became part of the slave-owning elite that gave rise to many of the Founding Fathers. These Virginia plantation owners, as well as poor farmers, crossed the Appalachian Mountains in search of fresh land. This was in direct violation of the Proclamation of 1763 issued by King George III, who tried to prevent English encroachment on lands still held by Indians. The colonists' refusal to stay east of the Appalachians was one reason underlying the American Revolution.

Crossing the Appalachians put settlers in conflict with southeastern tribes, such as the Shawnees and Cherokees, but also opened the door to personal and cultural contacts. Daniel Boone, who led settlers across these mountains on the Wilderness Trail, learned much of his famous woodcraft from Indian neighbors, and was once adopted into a Shawnee band. The Cherokee leader Nancy Ward introduced new agricultural methods to her people – including, tragically, black slavery – and sought peace until the white onslaught became overwhelming.

After the revolution, planters and farmers fought their way through the original inhabitants toward the next boundary, the Mississippi River. The Louisiana Purchase brought the land west of the Mississippi under American control in 1804. This was the beginning of the end of an era when French traders coexisted with Indian tribes. The entry point to the new territory was St. Louis, at the meeting of the two great rivers, the Missouri and Mississippi. From St. Louis, Meriwether Lewis and William Clark headed upstream along the Missouri, adding Sacagawea to their party along the way. The kindness shown to the explorers by Sacagawea's Lemhi Shoshone people was later repaid with the theft of their land, despite the peacemaking leadership of Sacagawea's family. Sacagawea herself probably died young, although a tantalizing alternative history suggests a very different end to her story.

Lewis and Clark crossed the great western mountain ranges, reached the Pacific Northwest, and returned to St. Louis. There, William Clark became the guardian of Sacagawea's son, Jean-Baptiste Charbonneau. Baptiste grew up to play his own role in the west, sometimes in the company of his friend James Beckwourth, the famous mountain man. When the wagon trains rolled, and the Mexican War was fought, and gold was discovered, Baptiste and Beckwourth were there.

As Indian superintendent, Clark oversaw the deportation of eastern tribes across the Mississippi. The same fate befell the Cherokees, although not under Clark's direction, over the protests of Chief Justice John Marshall, a distant relative of Pocahontas. As the tide of migration rolled west, the Nez Perce, who had generously hosted Lewis and Clark, were driven from their land. When their flight under Chief Joseph was over, a fair-haired old warrior identified himself as "Clark," son of the explorer.

As the 19th century and the American conquest moved toward their conclusion, a Northern Paiute woman named Sarah Winnemucca struggled to protect her Great Basin people against an invasion that had reached a peak of cruelty. She became known as the Pocahontas of the west. At the same time, Sacagawea's Lemhi Shoshone continued a peaceful struggle to remain on their land, until 1907, when they were forced onto their own Trail of Tears.

Our pride and shame as a nation are intertwined, and many of these contradictions began in Virginia. Londoners of the 1600s called Pocahontas and her people "Virginians." Edith and Woodrow Wilson were Virginians; so were Lewis and Clark; so was John Marshall. One of its most famous sons – Thomas Jefferson, the slave owner who wrote of the inalienable right to liberty – was related by marriage to the descendants of Pocahontas, and was a friend of the families of both Lewis and Clark. Virginia was the home of an American Enlightenment, a vision of human freedom and a thirst for knowledge. Woodrow Wilson was a college president, and one of Thomas Jefferson's proudest accomplishments was founding the University of Virginia. The Enlightenment was the wellspring of Jefferson's ideas about natural rights and, ultimately, Wilson's Fourteen Points. Virginia and its Enlightenment were central to the founding of a republic whose ideals have gradually expanded to include those who were sacrificed in its creation.

Pocahontas and Sacagawea were women of this American Enlightenment. They embraced new ideas and befriended people from different worlds. They weren't naive; they were sensible. Faced with an unstoppable influx, they made the best of it. Their friends, including John Smith and William Clark, were decent people by the standards of a brutal era: men who didn't target civilians and who kept the promises made in hard bargains.

English policy, and later American policy, was never a monolithic plan to exterminate all Indians. It was a schizophrenic mix. Most Anglo-Americans were certain of their God-given right to remake the new land. As a group, they were willing to kill as many Indians as necessary to take their land. However, many whites also felt uneasy consciences, paternalistic responsibility, and genuine appreciation of Indian cultures. Along the way, it was often business as usual, as whites and Indians worked and loved side by side. My goal, then, is not just to write about what people did to each other, but also what they did with each other. Colonizers and conquered alike have common enemies: violence, hunger, disease, ignorance, and short-sighted greed. The struggle against those common enemies is what all people share.

The original inhabitants of North America often called their own tribe or nation the People, the Real People, or the Original People. Their descendants call themselves both Native Americans and American Indians. I use shorthand: Indian, white, black, Mexican. Perhaps someday "Americans" or, better yet, "the people" will be sufficient description for all.

Chapter 1

The Invasion of Virginia

"The warres in Europe, Asia, and Affrica taught me how to subdue the wilde Salvages in Virginia."

Captain John Smith

*A*round 1595, a girl was born among the Powhatan people of Virginia. Her real name was Matoaka. That name is inscribed on a portrait drawn when she visited England as an adult, where she poses with a white feather. Pocahontas was her nickname, meaning playful or lively. It's sometimes translated as "little wanton," in the sense of mischievous, or perhaps wearing less clothing than the English were used to. Pocahontas, wrote John Smith, saved his life twice: throwing her arms around him to prevent his execution, and later warning him of an ambush. With gifts of food, she saved many other lives in Jamestown, the first permanent English settlement in North America. As a married woman and a convert to Christianity, she died as Rebecca, the wife of John Rolfe. But she is remembered by the nickname of a lively child. And the white feather may hold a clue to her story.

The life of Pocahontas was documented by the Englishmen she encountered, and those sources have been mined from many viewpoints. A biographer looks for evidence that Pocahontas had romantic feelings for John Smith. An anthropologist is skeptical that a girl aged 11 or 12 was old enough to rescue a captive. An Indian scholar suggests that Pocahontas was a young medicine woman. An author descended from the Powhatan people is a medicine man in both senses: licensed physician and keeper of sacred oral history. Here is a weave of these stories.

The Spanish invaded the New World over a century before Jamestown. The germs that came with them starting in 1492 traveled so fast that the tribes encountered by later explorers were already decimated. Indians had no immunity to smallpox, measles, influenza, tuberculosis, scarlet fever, or cholera. "Disease was the overwhelming cause for the estimated 90 percent drop in Indian population between 1492 and 1900."

All European explorers claimed territory in the name of their king or queen. The practice of claiming thousands of square miles "by right of discovery" led to conflicting claims. Some of the conflicts were settled by "right of conquest." Treaties followed each war. In the diplomatic process, both "right of exploration" and "right of occupation" (permanent settlement) helped each European country, and later the United States, make its claim. The claims of the original inhabitants counted not at all, a point made in 1971 by Indian activists who occupied Alcatraz Island and claimed it "by right of discovery."

Sir Walter Raleigh claimed the lands we now call Virginia and North Carolina for England in 1584. He named the area for his "Virgin Queen," the unmarried Elizabeth I. Raleigh visited America again in 1584 and planted the "Lost Colony" of Roanoke Island. Two Englishmen, a scientist and an artist, spent time among the Chesapeake Indians in 1585-86. The Roanoke Island colony was on its own for two years and was abandoned when Raleigh returned. The survivors may have been captured or adopted by local tribes, but their fate remains a mystery.

In the 16th century, a number of tribes in the Chesapeake Bay area were coalescing as the Powhatan people. Pocahontas' father, called Powhatan, was a chief of the Pamunkey tribe. He was also paramount chief over the Algonkian-speaking tribes that made up the Powhatan confederacy or alliance. John Smith counted 28 tribes, 36 tribal capitals, and 161 villages under Powhatan's control, each under local and regional chiefs, called *werowances,* and at least one *weroansqua,* or woman leader. These were subordinate to the paramount chief. Some of these subordinates were Powhatan's relatives, including his brother Opechancanough, chief of the family's Pamunkey tribe, and Powhatan's son Parahunt, or Tanx-Powhatan.

As well as the Pamunkey, another of the surviving Powhatan tribes claims Pocahontas as its own. The Mattaponi tribe has an oral tradition that Pocahontas' mother was Mattaponi and that Pocahontas left behind a Mattaponi child whose descendants live on. The Pamunkey and Mattaponi still hold neighboring tracts of land in Virginia.

The Powhatan people called themselves and their land the *tsenacommacah.* They lived in the Virginia Tidewater, the area where several rivers flow into Chesapeake Bay. The rivers were part of an extensive trading network that brought copper from the Great Lakes. Wild food was plentiful: venison and turkey, oysters and mussels, grapes and berries, walnuts and chestnuts, fish and waterfowl, wild rice and a starchy root called tuckahoe. The soil was fertile. Women raised corn, beans, squash, and sunflowers. Men raised tobacco, the sacred crop; they hunted and defended the villages against enemies. The bountiful land supported a population estimated at 8,500 to 15,000 when John Smith arrived in 1607, possibly higher before the impact of European diseases.

About three million people live today in the tsenacommacah. English technology could exploit land more effectively than Indian methods – or Spanish and French, for that matter. With a good deal of land either fallow or used for hunting, much of Virginia looked to the English like a land without a people.

These Algonkian peoples were matrilineal: identity traced through the mother's family. Matrilineal doesn't mean matriarchal, but women in most Indian societies had far more rights than European women. Among agricultural tribes, women were respected as the farmers who grew corn. Their spiritual and leadership insights were respected as well, and there were medicine women as well as female chiefs. In fact, the fact that a father's identity did not determine status in Algonkian society is one red flag for the anthropologist who thinks John Smith made up the story about being saved by "the Kings dearest daughter."

The people of the tsenacommacah called one of the rivers the Powhatan. The English name, "the James," has stuck. The Pamunkey River has kept its original name. On its banks, or on the nearby York River, Powhatan lived in a town called Werowocomoco, about fifteen miles upstream from Jamestown. Still another of these rivers is the Potomac, once home of the Patawomecks, on the edge of Powhatan's control. Now it is the home of another tidewater capitol. The river and town called Appomattox were once home to the "Appamattucks," ruled by a weroansqua who reported to Powhatan.

Powhatan's personal name was Wahunsenacawh. He was called *mamanatowick*, which the English understood to mean "great king" or emperor. It's not clear whether Powhatan gave his name to the confederacy, or took the name of his domain. Although the Powhatan peoples have survived, their language has not. The word Powhatan may mean leader or dreamer, in the sense of dreams from the spirit world. Or it might be a place name, possibly describing the falling water at the tsenacommacah's western edge, the "fall line" at the piedmont, the foot of the mountains, where the tidewater region ends.

When John Smith and his expedition arrived in 1607, the confederacy was new, perhaps better described as a paramount chiefdom with allies on its fringe, still on its way to becoming a fully established confederacy like the famous Iroquois League farther north, or perhaps on its way to becoming something less consensual: an empire. Powhatan had consolidated his control only a few years earlier, adding to territories that came to him by matrilineal inheritance. A number of tribes retained considerable independence, but the paramount chief

Chesapeake Bay and the Virginia Tidewater

The rivers that flow into the tidewater region and the Chesapeake Bay were the homeland of Pocahontas' people, and later the Cradle of the American Republic.

clearly hoped that would change over time. In exchange for accepting Powhatan as paramount chief, members gained peace within the confederacy and defense against raids by enemy Iroquoian tribes, who were armed with metal hatchets purchased from the French, and by the Siouan-speaking Monacan tribe. The Powhatans and Monacans raided each other every summer or fall. There were peaceful borders with other Iroquoian tribes. To the enemy tribes, the Powhatan hegemony must not have been cause for celebration.

To "insure domestic Tranquility" and "provide for the common defence." There's a reason for this echo in the Preamble to the Constitution of the United States. The Iroquois League of New York and the Great Lakes, also known as the Six Nations or Haudenosaunee, influenced the American Founding Fathers' ideas about federalism. However, the Iroquois federation was created by diplomacy, not conquest. Powhatan used both. His commanding presence was remarked on by more than one English writer. "[S]uch Majestie as he expresseth," wrote the English colonist William Strachey, "which oftentimes strykes awe and sufficient wonder unto our people." When that wasn't enough, Powhatan resorted to force, and even to genocide on one occasion, if the English writer's hearsay report is true.

William Strachey, arriving in 1610, reported that Powhatan had recently destroyed an entire tribe because of a prophecy that strangers would invade the tsenacommacah three times and overthrow it the third time. The first threat had been a group of Spanish missionaries, defeated a generation earlier. The second threat came from nearby: "from the Cheasapeak Bay a Nation should arise, which should dissolve and give end to his Empier, for which not many years synce...he destroyed and put to sword...all the Inhabitants, the weroance and his Subjects of that province and so remayne all the Chessiopeains at this daie, and for this cause extinct."

The prophecy predicted a third invader. And so it happened. On April 26, 1607, the *Discovery, Susan Constant,* and *Godspeed* entered Chesapeake Bay, commanded by Captain Christopher Newport. They sailed in the name of the British crown and the investors of the Royal Virginia Company, with the goal of establishing a permanent colony. The Virginia Company was a joint stock company; the expedition, a hybrid political, military, and commercial venture. King James appointed the board of the company, and the board appointed a council of seven men to oversee the colony. Captain Newport may have visited the New World before; he knew the sign language that tribes used to communicate with each other, and understood werowance as the word for king or chief. And, of course, there was Captain John Smith.

John Smith was in his late 20s, a soldier of fortune with ten years of hard living behind him, a veteran of England's wars with Spain and the Holy Roman Empire's fight against the Ottoman Turks. By age 25 or so, he had been captured and sold as "a slave to the Turks," befriended by a "faire Mistresse," escaped from her cruel brother, lived by his wits as he journeyed through Russia (helped by another "good Lady") and raided with a French privateer in North Africa. This was one of the men who was sent with instructions from the Virginia Company "not to offend the Naturals, if you can eschew it." Smith's later assessment of his role was much more blunt: "The warres in Europe, Asia, and Affrica taught me how to subdue the wilde Salvages in Virginia...."

Yet there was a degree of respect between Smith and the Indians, as there would be with William Clark two centuries in the future. Smith was "a man of his word, whether the word was a threat or a promise." Smith and Clark were soldiers as much as explorers, facing Indian warriors in times and places where the odds were closely balanced. Both men often got their way without shedding blood, reminding us that, when our gorilla cousins beat their chests, the point is to avoid actual violence.

This tough character, John Smith, was his own biographer, and was never shy of singing his own praises. We should be skeptical of self-promoting adventure tales, especially from an era when the line between fact and fiction was blurry. John Smith didn't mention Pocahontas saving his life until years after the fact. Each time, he was the only witness. Any of his tales of being saved by kind ladies might have been more boastful than real. So the famous rescues have to be taken with a grain of salt. But the rest of the Pocahontas story played out in front of many witnesses.

The English landing party stepped ashore on April 26, 1607. As they returned to the ship, "the Salvages" shot arrows, wounding two Englishmen. This was not in keeping with the warm welcomes reported by the earliest explorers, but Spain had introduced itself to the Powhatans around 1560 by kidnapping one of their youth. The boy was baptized Don Luis, taken to Spain and Mexico, and eventually returned to Chesapeake Bay with a group of missionaries. Luis eventually led a party to kill the missionaries, sparing only a youth named Alonso. The Spanish sent a punitive mission, rescued Alonso, and killed a number of Indians. English invaders were also guilty of killing, kidnapping, and enslavement, although these crimes were more common among the Spanish. By the time Captain Newport brought his men ashore in 1607, Indians had learned to be wary of light-skinned men in large boats.

Captain Newport's next encounter with the Powhatans, a few days later, went better. Seeing a group of Indians, the English captain placed his hand on his heart. The Indians responded with an invitation to eat and smoke. Additional friendly meetings followed. The two shouts of greeting, the feast of corn and meat, the speeches in the longhouse, the dancing by the fire – Indian diplomacy displayed wealth and ritual as both welcome and warning.

To choose a site for the colony, the English sent a party up a river that they named for their king, James. On the James River, on May 14, the newcomers chose a site for James Town or James Fort. This area would come to be called the Cradle of the Republic. At the moment, it was an English outpost and a challenge to the Powhatan confederacy. In fact, the site that appeared uninhabited to the Virginia Company was the traditional hunting ground and fallow farmland of the Paspahegh, a tribe within the confederacy.

The Powhatan leadership was watching the English, and the English knew it. Powhatan took a wait and see attitude. What did it mean – invasion and conquest, or alliance and trade? It was a nuanced set of responses from a society that was politically sophisticated but uneasily united.

The English explorers were as disunited as could be when it came to power struggles in the colony's leadership. But they expected hierarchical governance. When it came to supreme authority, there was one king of England; when it came to military discipline, there was one commander. From 1607 forward, English and then Americans tried to deal with "the chief," when Indian political structures were more diffuse. For the next three centuries, whites would negotiate with one tribe and try to hold another tribe to the treaty, or kill members of one band in retaliation against a different band, or fail to understand factional politics and shifting alliances. Unable to believe that "simple savages" were so politically complex, whites became convinced that Indians were changeable, childlike, treacherous. This tragic confusion began with the mixed reception in 1607. Either Powhatan was unable to enforce a uniform policy among all the tribes, or he decided to let them act independently.

The English reported that they were under surveillance and that smoke and drums transmitted intelligence to Powhatan's base at Werowocomoco. The tribes that made up the confederacy, as well as the individual leaders, were divided in their responses. Trade, fishing, and alliance were acceptable, even desirable. Also, the Powhatans and the English had a mutual enemy, Spain. Permanent settlement was a different matter. Powhatan took his time to determine the intentions of the newcomers.

The English set to work in May, building a fence, simple structures, and a church in Jamestown. The defenses were minimal, in keeping with the instructions "not to offend the Naturals." The Paspahegh, who traditionally hunted on the site, made a show of both force and friendship, sending a hundred armed warriors carrying "a Fat Deare as a gift." As the parties tried to communicate about land rights, an Indian picked up a hatchet. Was he just curious or did he mean to steal it? The English reached for their weapons and the Paspahegh warriors left in anger.

Concepts of theft and property would lead to frequent clashes between whites and Indians. Most Indian tribes had notions of property that were communal to some degree. In addition, making away with an item was almost a game, a test of cleverness, for some tribes. Accusations of theft would be a constant source of conflict on the Lewis and Clark journey as well.

Smith was part of a party that explored the James River later in May. The Virginia Company had directed the explorers to look for the Northwest Passage, gold and silver, and any survivors of the Lost Colony. They found none of this, but they found America's real wealth: acre upon acre of corn growing on fertile land.

The tribes that had not yet been alienated were friendly to the river travelers. They were greeted "with many signes of love," wrote Smith, "the people in all places kindely intreating us, daunsing and feasting us...." Gifts were exchanged: "Bels, pinnes, Needles, beades, or Glasses" for corn, tobacco, "a Deare roasted," "basketes full of Dryed oysters." Like the tribes that Lewis and Clark would meet two centuries later, these Powhatan tribes provided guides and mapped out the route upriver. Why not? After all, the newcomers were not Monacans.

They met Powhatan's son Parahunt at the fall line, near present-day Richmond. By then, the English had heard of the paramount chief, and apparently thought they had found him. They introduced him to "beere, Aquavite, and Sack." Parahunt complained the next day about the "hott Drynckes" that "caused his greefe." This was a harbinger of disaster. The Asian heritage brought over from Siberia was not set up to process alcohol. "Hott Drynckes" would help defeat many tribes.

Parahunt's people helped themselves to a knife and a few other items, but the chief ordered them returned when Captain Newport "made knowne unto them the Custome of England to be death for such offense." The English also demonstrated the firing of a musket, a sound frightening in its unfamiliarity to warriors who prided themselves on personal courage.

Then the English started lying. The colonists were under orders from the Virginia Company to hide the fact that "you mean to plant [settle] among them." A group of Indians objected when the English staked King James' claim to the head of the river by erecting a cross inscribed "Jacobus Rex 1607." Captain Newport explained that "the two Armes of the Crosse signified king Powatah and himself, the fastening of it in the myddest was their united Leaug...." Smith told a similar lie when he met Powhatan the following year. "Hee asked mee the cause of our coming." Smith made up a storm at sea and a battle with the Spanish. Powhatan was skeptical. The "politick salvage...demaunded why we went further with our Boate." Just looking for the Northwest Passage to the "backe Sea," the Pacific. No wonder Pocahontas' final verdict in 1616 would be "your Countriemen will lie much."

On the way back down the James River, Captain Newport and his party met Opechancanough. Because his usual base was with his own tribe on the Pamunkey River, he might have been assessing the invaders. The English did not realize that he was next in succession to the supreme chief. Even when they figured out that Parahunt was not Powhatan, they would have assumed that the king's son would inherit the throne.

In fact, the appointment of a chief's son was an exception to the usual practice of matrilineal succession. Chiefly succession ran from brother to brother, or to sister if brothers ran out, and then to the sisters' sons. As Powhatan explained to John Smith, "my brethren, namely Opitchapam, Opechancanough, and Kekataugh, my two sisters, and their daughters, are distinctly each others successors." Thus, a chief expected his nephews rather than his sons to inherit his role.

As leader of the war faction, Opechancanough would soon have allies in the aggrieved Paspaheghs. The Paspaheghs attacked the fort one day before the river party returned to Jamestown. They killed a man and a ship's boy and wounded several others. The council president was "shott cleane through his bearde, yet scaped hurte...." The English responded by putting up palisades around Jamestown. Now James Fort was a fort, and the first Indian war was on. One man was shot full of arrows while "going out to doe the naturall necessity." The first cross-cultural ally was there too: an Arrohattoc Indian who had guided them along the James River now joined the English in the fort. He insisted that there could be peace with the English and alliance against the Powhatans' enemies.

In June, Captain Newport led the transport ships home across the Atlantic, leaving behind John Smith as part of the governing council – marooning them, essentially, taking with them the ship's stores of "bisket." It was summer, time for humidity and mosquitoes and foul standing water, time for dysentery and other diseases to take their toll on the invaders. There were about a hundred men when the summer began – fifty when it ended, and forty by the end of 1607.

Some were picked off by Paspahegh arrows. Far more died of hunger and disease. These common enemies of humankind, more than bullets and arrows, were the main killers among all peoples in the centuries of upheaval in the New World.

The settlers were left with "halfe a pinte of wheat, and as much barly...for a man a day; and this having fryed some 26 weeks in the ships hold, contained as many wormes as graines," wrote Smith. With neither bread nor beer, he added with dark humor, "Had we been as free from all sinnes as gluttony and drunkenness, we might have bin canonized for Saints...." They buried the casualties in secret, sneaking out at night, fearful of advertising their dreadfully weakened state to the Paspaheghs, who would have made short work of them.

Successes in agriculture and technology would soon allow England to outpopulate Indians, French, and Spanish in the New World, but at the moment surplus population was a problem back home. Colonization was an outlet for people who did not know how to make their way in either the Old World or the New. There were two problem groups: too rich and too poor. Among the landed class in England, the oldest son inherited the property, leaving younger sons at loose ends. These gentlemen thought it beneath their dignity to work with their hands. Among the landless were those displaced when common lands in England were fenced so that landowners could profit from wool used in the textile industry during the Industrial Revolution. This "enclosure" process uprooted countless farmers, who flooded English cities, unskilled in new technologies and desperate enough to risk the gallows – or the colonies.

The quality of settlers would not improve much over the next few years. "When you send againe," Smith wrote to the Virginia Company in 1608

"I intreat you rather send but thirty Carpenters, husbandmen [farmers], gardiners, fisher men, blacksmiths, masons... then a thousand of such as we have...." The 1610 contingent would be described as "the very excrements of a full, swelling State." These were the people expected to live by their wits in a new land, and they got off to a bad start.

"[A]s yet we had no houses to cover us, our tents were rotten, and our Cabbins worse than nought," wrote Smith the summer of 1607. Most of the men were "in such dispaire, as they would rather starve and rot with idlenes, then be perswaded to do any thing for their owne reliefe." Smith, at least, was willing and able to work hard and to convince others to do the same. As starving men accused the council president of hoarding rations, harsh discipline and internal power struggles divided the survivors. Captain John Smith emerged as a leader among the colonists still alive late in 1607.

Throughout the summer and fall of 1607, colonists begged and bartered for corn from those Indians who were not yet hostile. Smith could negotiate because he had learned some Algonkian words, possibly even before setting foot in the New World, as there were Indian captives in England. The Indians' own supplies were limited until their crops ripened. Then they opened their hands to the desperate survivors at Jamestown. It was November "when God...so changed the harts of the Salvages, that they brought such plenty of their fruits and provision, as no man wanted," Smith reported. "[N]ow they were no lesse desirous of our commodities then we were of their Corne...."

The corn surplus near Jamestown quickly ran short. Smith was chosen by lot as one of the men who would take two boats up the Chickahominy River. One goal of that trip was corn. Another was to meet Chief Powhatan face to face. And there was always the hope of the Northwest Passage. The boats encountered the Chickahominies, a tribe that was loosely allied with the Powhatans. They willingly traded food for goods. After delivering these supplies to Jamestown, Smith set out again up the Chickahominy in December. At the very end of 1607, Smith was on his way to his immortal encounter with Pocahontas.

Chapter 2

The White Feather

"I am the daughter of the king,
And I claim the Indian right!"

William Makepeace Thackeray

*J*ohn Smith sailed up the Chickahominy River, through the territory where he had successfully traded. The river became impassable for the barge. Leaving seven men with the barge at the last Chickahominy village, Smith took two of his men, hired a canoe and two Chickahominy guides, and proceeded upriver. When even a canoe could not pass, Smith left his two men in the boat with one Indian, with instructions to fire a warning shot if other Indians were seen, and set out on foot with the second Indian as a guide. There was no warning shot; instead, within fifteen minutes, a party of Pamunkeys was firing arrows. Suspecting his guide of treachery, Smith used him as a human shield, and fought his way back to the canoe, where he lost his footing and was captured. One of the colonists left behind was dead, and the other was never seen again. Smith later learned that one of the men left on the barge was captured, tortured for information, and then killed. That wasn't special treatment; torturing captives to death was the norm in Powhatan warfare. The survivors on the barge returned to Jamestown.

Smith was now a captive of the Pamunkeys, Powhatan's own tribe, the core of the alliance. The warriors took him to their chief Opechancanough, whom Smith had met the previous summer on the James River. Smith was fed well, given warm clothes, and stared at. Then, accompanied by Opechancanough, he was taken on a tour throughout the confederacy. The purpose of the trip was probably to survey opinions among the tribes. The tour also gave witnesses a chance to identify Smith as a white captain who was wanted for murder and kidnapping some years earlier. The conclusion was that the wanted man was tall and Smith was short. Of this particular crime, the Jamestown colonists were innocent.

The journey featured a ceremony of prophecy and divination, "the meaning whereof they told him, was to know if he intended them well or no." (Smith often wrote in the third person). To a Christian Englishman of Smith's era, a literate global traveler, the rites must have seemed superstitious. He seemed almost sympathetic to their limited knowledge when they arranged concentric

These are the Lines that shew thy Face; but those
That shew thy Grace and Glory, brighter bee:
Thy Faire-Discoueries and Fowle-Overthrowes
Of Salvages, much Civilliz'd by thee
Best shew thy Spirit; and to it Glory Wyn;
So, thou art Brasse without, but Golde within.

Captain John Smith

Pocahontas' friend, shown late in life, was not the worst of the colonizers.

circles around a great fire: "the Circle of meale signified their Country, the circles of corne the bounds of the Sea, and the stickes [Smith's] Country. They imagined the world to be flat and round, like a trencher [slab of bread]; and they in the middest." Of course, it was not many years earlier that Europeans had believed the earth was flat.

In the first week of January, 1608, Smith was finally taken to Werowocomoco. In a great longhouse, with hundreds of people watching, Smith was brought face to face with the supreme chief. Powhatan, about 60 years of age, was seated before a fire, surrounded by men and women, young and old. Among the women – who apparently included Pocahontas – "many of their heads [were] bedecked with the white downe of Birds...." Powhatan was "a tall, well-proportioned man," reported Smith, "...of a very able and hardy body...." The crowd, the spectacle, and especially the chief impressed the captive: "Such a Majestie as I cannot expresse," wrote Smith, "nor yet have often seene, either in Pagan or Christian."

"[H]aving feasted him after their best barbarous manner they could," wrote Smith, "a long consultation was held but the conclusion was, two great stones were brought before Powhatan; then as many as could layd hands on him, dragged him to them, and thereon laid his head, and being ready with their clubs, to beate out his brains, Pocahontas the Kings dearest daughter, when no intreaty could prevaile, got his head in her armes, and laid her owne vpon his to saue him from death...."

Was it true? What did it mean? And what was Pocahontas' role?

Our anthropologist raises two good points. One, being the "Kings dearest daughter" didn't count for much in a matrilineal society. Two, pre-pubescent children don't have a lot of authority in any society. So, how old *was* Pocahontas? English observers guessed that she was between ten and fourteen years old when she met John Smith. She was "in the 21st year of her age" late in 1616, according to the inscription on the portrait made in London during the last winter of her short life, meaning 21 or approaching 21. That would make her 11 or 12 when she met Smith. In 1608, she was young enough to turn cartwheels with the ship's boys of Jamestown, wearing the minimal clothing of an Indian child. "Pochohuntas, a well featured but wanton young girle Powhatans daughter, sometymes resorting to our Fort, of the age then of 11. or 12. yeares, gett the boyes forth with her into the markett place and make them wheele, falling on their hands turning their heeles upwards, whome she would follow, and wheele so her self naked as she was all the fort over...." If she was close to adolescence in the winter of 1607-08, then she was barely old enough to make an important decision.

There's another glaring problem. When Smith wrote "A True Relation of Such Occurrences and Accidents of Noate as Hath Hapned in Virginia..." later the same year, 1608, he didn't mention a word about that brush with death. Did he want to downplay the colonists' problems? Or did he make up the story much later, deciding to write himself into another dramatic rescue by a noble lady, and eager to emphasize his friendship with a woman who had become famous?

The story first shows up years after the fact. In 1624, in his *Generall Historie of Virginia, New-England, and the Summer Isles,* Smith claims that he wrote a letter about Pocahontas to Queen Anne, the wife of King James, on the occasion of Pocahontas' 1616 visit to London. "[S]ome ten yeeres agoe being in Virginia, and taken prisoner by the power of Powhatan their chiefe King, I receiued from this great Saluage exceeding great courtesie, especially from... Pocahontas, the Kings most deare and wel-beloued daughter....," Smith wrote to the queen. "[A]t the minute of my execution, she hazarded the beating out of her owne braines to saue mine...." The letter itself is gone, but Smith reported its contents in the 1624 book and took credit for introducing the princess to the queen – or at least providing a glowing reference to accompany the Virginia Company's promotional efforts.

My conclusion is that John Smith was much too attached to his head to lie to the queen while Pocahontas was in England to contradict the story, or to lie later on about having written to the queen. Queen Anne died in 1619 but King James was still alive when the *Generall Historie* was published. Smith's survival instinct is the strongest indication that the story is true.

The best guess is that the Powhatans, acting through Pocahontas, decided that Smith's life should be spared so that he could be adopted as one of their people. His story was consistent with later reports of adoption rituals in some eastern tribes. In much of North America, when Indians took a captive, the likely fate was either execution or adoption. If the captive's life was to be spared, there could be a mock execution with a ritual rescue, or a last-minute reprieve from a real execution. Then the captive would undergo a ritual rebirth as a member of the tribe.

Until that moment, Powhatan had not settled on a definite policy toward the newcomers. The capture of John Smith forced a decision. Powhatan's advisors included matrilineal kin, subordinate chiefs, and shamans ("priests," as the

English called them), who would later be called medicine men. Pocahontas, despite her youth, might have been one of these shamans, suggested the late Paula Gunn Allen, a renowned Native American scholar. As such, she would have the power to redeem a captive, the poet's famous "Indian right."

"Medicine man" (or woman) comes from *midewewin*, an Algonkian word for the spiritual world, according to Professor Allen. In her view, Powhatan was a "priest king" whose leadership was based not only on his matrilineal inheritance but also on his ability to discern the spirit world through dreams and visions, and Pocahontas was a Beloved Woman based on the same gifts. Insight, we might now call these qualities. Whether or not Pocahontas was actually Powhatan's daughter, their relationship might have been based on this shared role. Pocahontas the medicine woman, Pocahontas of the Enlightenment – perhaps they are just different ways of recognizing Pocahontas the visionary.

John Smith's presence of mind in noticing that the women surrounding Powhatan were "bedecked with the white downe of Birds" has left us with a clue. "…Matoaka or Matoaks is thought to mean 'white (or snow) feather,'" wrote Professor Allen. "Since a white feather, or numerous white feathers, always signifies a Beloved Woman and is carried or worn by such women most of the time, it is likely that she did indeed have that 'calling,' or vocation, from birth." Years later, Pocahontas would wear white feathers when her portrait was drawn in London, but this was the fashion in the English court at the time. Gravely, the mature Pocahontas stares from that portrait, leaving us to wonder whether the white feathers meant the same thing in her first and last appearance in history.

Pocahontas' high status, obvious in every interaction she had with the English, might have reflected this role of Beloved Woman, her relationship with the ruling family, or both. The *nonpareil* of Virginia, the English would come to call her, the one without parallel. When others carried burdens, she walked unencumbered, wearing a fine deerskin dress and a mantle of blue feathers. Other ladies waited on her, handing her jewelry of copper, pearls, and coral, spreading mats so that she could recline in the shade. To the English, these were the trappings of royalty: if Powhatan was a king, Pocahontas must be a princess. To Smith, she was "Lady Pocahontas." When she visited London, she would be called "lady," despite her commoner husband, John Rolfe. Later, white Americans would speak of "the Powhatan princess" and her "royal red blood." It is possible, however, that Smith was not spared simply as an indulgence to a beloved royal daughter, but as the prerogative of a medicine woman.

Adoption played an important role in Indian societies. When disease or warfare reduced populations, captive women and children from other tribes (and later white captives) were often adopted to replace those who were lost; Sacagawea would be kidnapped and adopted by the Hidatsa. Later, white Americans would take care of Indian children; in that way, Sacagawea's child would become "a son of Captain Clarke." Adoption also wove existing bonds tighter; Sacagawea would adopt an orphaned nephew when she returned to her Lemhi people. Time and again, the rituals of adoption transformed enemies into kin; of the many white women and children who would be captured and adopted before the Indian wars were over, some waited for rescue, but others embraced their new lives. In the case of capture and adoption of one leader by another, an alliance could be formed. That, apparently, was what Pocahontas and Powhatan had in mind for Smith.

Kinship ties, literal and figurative, were important in Europe as well, but with enough differences to rationalize European convictions about childlike savages. Two hundred years later, when Sacagawea helped William Clark bring the greetings of the "Great Father" to his "red children," condescension would blend with linguistic confusion. Among Indians, however, there was nothing childish about kinship. "Father" was a metaphor for leader, while "child" could describe age difference or adoptive kinship. When the adult Pocahontas was reunited with John Smith in England, she would remind him that Powhatan was a father to Smith and that Smith was a father to her. This is further evidence that the dramatic rescue was part of an adoption ritual.

All in all, we will never be certain whether Powhatan's relationship with Pocahontas was biological, adoptive, or symbolic. But it appears true that she influenced a great chief who held the power of life and death over a captive Englishman. When she cried out and embraced John Smith's head, she might have been motivated by childlike compassion, adolescent attraction, or maturing wisdom that saw the benefits of allies who brought new ideas.

So, as 1608 began, Smith became an adopted son of Powhatan, expected to act as Powhatan's sub-chief and ally. The adoption ceremony took place two days after the near-execution. "Powhatan more like a devil then a man, with some two hundred more as blacke as himself, came unto him and told him now they were friends, and presently he should goe to James towne, to send him two great gunnes, and a gryndstone, for which he would give him the Country of Capahowosick, and for ever esteeme him as his son Nantaquoud." He returned home with an escort (or guard): "So to James towne with 12 guides Powhatan sent him." As Smith must have expected, he didn't have to make good on the great guns; the cannons were too heavy to move.

Together with the parent-child metaphors of Indian society, the Indians' interest in manufactured goods contributed to the image of childlike savages. Lewis and Clark would travel with a boat load of trade goods, and Lewis would remark of Sacagawea, "if she has enough to eat and a few trinkets to wear I believe she would be perfectly content anywhere." John Smith, looking back on his captors' change of heart after Pocahontas threw her arms around him, focused on the trinkets. "Whereat the Emperour was contented he should live to make him hatchets, and her bells, beads, and copper..." It made sense for the Powhatans to want manufactured goods. Every tribe did. Who wouldn't appreciate an innovation that makes life easier? If there were conservatives who had the foresight to worry about dependence on foreigners or about social structures unraveling, they were probably in the minority, like the holdouts today who refuse to use microwave ovens or smartphones. Trade came to dominate Indian interactions with whites in the way that oil now dominates world politics. Whites saw this fascination with "trinkets" as further evidence of the childlike simplicity of natives. When John Smith returned safely to Jamestown in January 1608, he sent his guides home with "toyes" and "presents."

Back at Jamestown, the colonists were dissolving into backstabbing and mutiny. Smith himself was marked for execution, saved again when Captain Newport returned on the *Susan Constant,* bringing supplies, manpower, and trade goods. While Smith was away, some colonists had plotted to take a boat and escape. Shortly after the resupply ship landed, Jamestown caught fire. "[I]n that extreame frost" many men "for want of lodging perished."

But they would not starve. Every few days, a delegation of Powhatans brought cornbread, venison, turkey, and fish to the colony. "[H]ad the Salvages not fed us, we directly had starved," Smith wrote to Queen Anne in 1616. "And this reliefe, most Gracious Queene, was commonly brought us by this Lady Pocahontas." Pocahontas, having raised her voice to bring the invaders into Powhatan society, and Powhatan, having ratified that decision, were making good on their commitment. This time, all were witness to her "compassionate pitifull heart." If she was too young to claim a captive, she was also too young to be the organizer of these lifesaving delegations, but she was part of them. Either way, the presence of a woman or a child was a sign of peace, as it would be when Sacagawea and her baby accompanied a party of armed men two hundred years later.

In February, Smith brought his "father," Captain Newport, to meet Powhatan. The new allies were received with feasting and dancing, "great Platters of fine bread," "signes of great joy," and promises of "a perpetuall league and friendship." Powhatan accepted a red suit, a white greyhound, and a stovepipe hat. A 13-year-old English boy, coincidentally named Thomas Savage or Salvage, was instructed to live with the Powhatans to learn their language, and a young Powhatan named Namontack was sent to Jamestown for the same purpose.

The honeymoon didn't last. Having seen weapons that the English were reluctant to supply, and metal tools that the settlers could not afford to part with, Indians began stealing from the settlers. Sporadic fights erupted in the spring of 1608, and two Englishmen were captured. John Smith responded with severe chastisement, as William Clark would say, capturing and beating warriors, burning houses, and holding seven Indians hostage. It is not clear how much of the hostility was condoned by Powhatan, but the "perepetuall league and friendship" quickly deteriorated as the scale of the English incursion became clear.

The Englishmen were released, but the Powhatans remained captives. Powhatan "sent his messengers, and his dearest daughter Pocahontas with presents to excuse him of the injuries done by some rash untoward Captaines his subjects, desiring their liberties for this time, with the assurance of his love for ever." The men were freed for her sake only, wrote Smith. Then he acknowledged the diplomat with trinkets: "Pocahuntas also we requited with such trifles as contented her."

With all his capacity for brutality, there was something genuine in Smith's relationship with the young woman who had spared his life. Whether there were romantic feelings between Pocahontas and John Smith is a matter of speculation. Theirs was a diplomatic relationship with a warm, even fatherly, tone. They worked to learn each other's language: "Bid Pokahontas bring hither two little Baskets, and I will give her white Beads to make her a Chaine," appeared in both English and Algonkian in a vocabulary book that Smith compiled. In this inevitable reference to trinkets, respect mingled with condescension, foreshadowing Meriwether Lewis' comments about Sacagawea (a woman of "fortitude" who was content with trinkets).

In early June, Smith took a party to explore more of the Chesapeake Bay, encountering tribes friendly and hostile, Algonkian and Iroquoian speakers, and tribes with copper wares obtained from the French. The English marked crosses in trees, claiming the banks of rivers in places that would become Maryland and Delaware. They saw "woodes extreame thick, full of Woolves, Beares, Deare, and other wild beasts." There were rivers full of "Otters, Beavers, Martins" and "an abundance of fish lying so thicke with their heads above the water, as for want of nets we attempted to catch them with a frying pan." It didn't work. Smith caught a stingray with his sword; he was stung and swelled so badly that he picked out a burial site, but he recovered and ate the stingray for supper. His leadership was formalized in September 1608 when he was chosen president of the governing council.

If the rescue of Smith was an adoption ceremony designed to cement political bonds through kinship, another misunderstanding was brewing over which side of the parent-child relationship the English were on. In October 1608, Captain Newport brought instructions from London: Powhatan was to be crowned as a vassal of King James. A coronation robe and copper crown had been sent along, a bed and furnishings, impressive trinkets to turn the supreme chief into a vassal. Smith wrote back to the Virginia Company that he was "directly against it," but followed orders and traveled with a small group to Werowocomoco to invite Powhatan to Jamestown for the ceremony.

Powhatan was away, hunting or governing, and messengers were sent for him. "In the meane time Pocahantas and her women entertained Captaine Smith in this manner: In a fayre plaine field they made a fire.... [S]uddainly amongst the woods was heard such a hydeous noise and shreeking, that the English betooke themselves to their armes....But presently Pocahontas came, willing him to kill her if any hurt were intended.... Thirtie young women came naked out of the woods, onely covered behind and before with a few greene leaves, their bodies all painted, some of one colour, some another, but all differing, their leader had a fayre payre of Bucks hornes on her head, and an Otters skinne at her girdle, another at her arms, a quiver of arrows at her backe...." . After singing and dancing, after the fire died down, the women reappeared in their usual dress, and then "solemnly invited him to their lodgings, where he was no sooner within the house, but all these Nymphes more tormented him than ever...most tediously crying, Love you not me?...."

Again, this is Smith's version. Mattaponi oral tradition suggests that Powhatan women said "take me" in order to deflect the invaders' lust from helpless children. However, Smith's story fits in with Indian traditions of Corn Maidens celebrating the fertility of the land and the people. In addition, sexual hospitality was common among many tribes; a matrilineal society has different requirements for chastity and fidelity than a society where property rights are passed from father to legitimate children.

By then, Pocahontas was 12 or 13 years old. If love or lust between the Indian princess and the English captain had its moment ... on this point, Smith is silent.

There was still the problem of the coronation. Powhatan came back to Werowocomoco and declined the invitation to Jamestown. "I also am a King, and this is my land," was his reply. "Your Father [Captain Newport] is to come to me, not I to him...." So Smith returned to Jamestown, and he and Newport had to transport the gifts upriver, bed and all. They were accompanied by Namontack; the Indian youth had traveled to England and back with Newport.

Powhatan refused to kneel to receive the crown. The best the English could do was to lean on the shoulders of the tall king until he stooped a little.

Powhatan sent them home with less than a dozen bushels of corn. The settlers needed much more, but no one would trade. The harvest was not yet in, but scarcity was not the only problem. The English were wearing out their welcome. Two more boatloads of settlers had arrived in 1608, including the first two English women in Jamestown. Opechancanough's hard line was prevailing. No longer did Pocahontas appear with gifts of food. As the fall of 1608 wore on, it appeared that Powhatan had directed his people to starve the invaders out. With winter coming, Captain Smith – now President Smith – resorted to threats and destruction to get food for his two hundred colonists.

One year after Smith's first meeting with Pocahontas, an English delegation struggled through snow and ice to Werowocomoco to demand corn from their sovereign, or their vassal. It was January 1609. After the shouts of greeting and the generous spread of food, Powhatan asked his adopted son "when would we be gone." The Virginia Company's intention "to plant among them" had become clear. "[S]ome doubt I have of your comming hither, that makes me not so kindly seeke to relieve you as I would," Powhatan told Smith, "for many doe informe, your comming hither is not for trade, but to invade my people, and possesse my Country."

Face to face, the leaders sought accommodation. "I know the difference between Peace and Warre better than any in my Country," said the old chief. "What will it availe you to take that by force you may quickly have by love, or to destroy them that provide you food?...Thinke you I am so simple not to know it is better to eate good meate, lye well, and sleepe quietly with my women and children, laugh and be merry with you, have copper, hatchets, or what I want being your friend: then be forced to flie from all, to lie cold in the woodes, feede upon Acornes, rootes, and such trash; and be so hunted by you, that I can neither rest, eate, nor sleepe...." For his part, Smith promised not to "dissolve that friendship we have mutually promised...except you constrain me by our bad usage."

For a copper kettle, Powhatan promised eighty bushels of corn, but it was his turn to practice deception, at least according to Smith's account. Later that day, the supreme chief put into action a drastic decision: he removed himself and his family thirty miles away to the remote village of Orapaks. "My countrie is large enough to goe from you," Powhatan had once boasted. So began a pattern of white encroachment and Indian withdrawal – until, as the mountain man Jim Beckwourth would write in the 19th century, there were "no more Mississippis to drive him beyond."

As Werowocomoco emptied out, English guards waited with their boat for the promised corn. Smith realized that his lodging was surrounded and rushed for the boat, but the water ebbs and flows in the tidewater rivers, and the Englishmen were stranded. On that cold night, wrote John Smith, Pocahontas saved his life again.

"For Pocahontas his dearest jewell and daughter, in that darke night came through the irksome woods, and told our Captaine great cheere should be sent us by and by: but Powhatan and all the power he could make, would after come kill us all...," Smith, again the only witness, reported in his 1624 *Generall Historie*. "The darke night could not affright her," said the 1616 letter to Queen Anne. The *Generall Historie* goes on to explain how Smith tried to reward her: "Such things as shee delighted in, he would have given her: but with the teares running downe her cheekes, shee said shee durst not be seene to have any: for if Powhatan should know it, she were but dead, and so she ranne away by her self as she came."

If the story is true, there are several possible interpretations. Was she again playing a role, perhaps giving the English a stern warning that they were going too far? Was she acting on behalf of the peace party, perhaps as its young leader? Or was she acting on her own? In the last two scenarios, her personal courage is astonishing: a girl of 12 or 13 defying her powerful father and traveling thirty miles alone through a forest at night. Maybe she was unwilling to accept the ambush of people she had fed. Maybe she was in love. Maybe insight told her that the English brought the future. John Smith believed, or chose to believe, that she felt "extraordinarie affection to our Nation." All of these possibilities suggest such serious purpose that she must have been deeply insulted when Smith tried to thank her with…trinkets.

Still stranded by the tide, Smith and their men were on high alert when "eight or ten lusty fellowes" came bearing "great platters of venison and victuall," the "great cheare" intended to lull them. Around midnight, the tide came in, and the men escaped with their lives but without the corn. Still desperate for winter supplies, the party continued upstream – away from Jamestown – only to run into the militant Opechancanough and hundreds of hostile men. Smith managed to seize the warrior chief by the hair, shove a pistol to his chest, and force him to personally load the boat with corn. Years later, Opechancanough would take harsh revenge for this humiliation.

Extortion continued, although Smith grudgingly left the tribes something for their own winter supplies, faced with "such complaints and teares from the eyes of women and children, as he had beene too cruell to have beene a Christian, that would not have been satisfied and moved with compassion." And so the colonists at Jamestown survived another winter. "Men may think it strange," Smith reflected, "that there should be such a stirre for a little corne, but had it been gold with more ease wee might have got it, and had it wanted, the whole Colony had starved."

Back at Jamestown in the spring of 1609, Indians who were still friendly taught the newcomers how to hunt, farm, and fish in their new world. Some Indians lived at the fort; some were captives. To ease pressure on supplies at the fort, some colonists boarded with local tribes. Some stayed – defected, from the English point of view. There was occasional fighting but no all-out war.

The complexities of these relationships are illustrated by the fate of three English youths placed with Powhatan in 1608 and 1609 as a hybrid between hostages, exchange students, and adoptive sons. At some point after Powhatan's departure from Werowocomoco to Orapaks, the lads tried to escape. Samuel (last name unknown) was killed. Thomas Savage decided to return to Powhatan, who apparently was fond of him. Henry Spelman escaped into the forest, and chanced upon Pocahontas, who guided him to a distant subchieftancy, where he "lived many yeeres after," according to an anonymous historian, "amongst the Patawomekes" (Potomacs).

In Jamestown, the weak links continued to exasperate their leader. Too many were lazy gentlemen, hard luck cases, or both. They included criminals one step ahead of the gallows, giving rise to future wisecracks about the First Felons of Virginia. They inspired John Smith to issue his famous command: "he that will not worke shall not eate." Work they did, if reluctantly, planting and building farther away from the original fort.

Credit Smith. Jamestown under his presidency was not a death trap and, even in his roughest dealings with the Powhatans, he knew that the two peoples needed each other. All this was about to change.

A supply ship in the summer of 1609 brought food, wine, and news. Seven ships with hundreds of men, women, and children were on the way. A governor named Lord De La Warr would be sent the following year, and a new high council was already on the way. This crossing, the Third Supply, was deadly for many, even before the ships were beset by a hurricane. Six of the seven made it to Jamestown, with considerably fewer passengers than they started with. The seventh was the flagship, the *Sea Venture,* carrying the high council. It was believed lost in the hurricane.

The situation at Jamestown collapsed in short order. The new governing structure was ripe for infighting. The newcomers turned straight to violence against the native people. Negotiating as a father to a son, a brother to a brother, Smith made a proposal. The English would help the Powhatans fight the Monacans if the Powhatans would help the new arrivals survive the winter. Some of the new arrivals were worse than the Monacans, replied the Powhatans. Even so, Powhatan's son Parahunt – Smith's adoptive brother – offered the emigrants an entire village, complete with houses and cleared fields. Smith's political rivals rejected the deal.

Then the kinship bond was broken; the bridge across cultures was burned, literally. A spark ignited the gunpowder pouch around John Smith's waist. When the transport ships returned to England in the fall, the badly injured leader went with them. He sent no message of farewell to Pocahontas, and she believed him dead. There were no more gifts of venison and cornbread. The policy of starving out the colonists prevailed again. This time, it almost succeeded.

It was the Starving Time. Winter set in. Once again, Indian arrows picked off those who ventured out of the fort to hunt or fish. Hunger, cold, and disease killed the rest. The colonists ate "dogs Catts Ratts and myce." There were reports of cannibalism; one man was executed after killing and eating his wife. There were about 500 men, women, and children in Jamestown in September 1609. By spring, only sixty were alive.

The emaciated, heartbroken, and traumatized survivors of Jamestown in 1610 saw what happened next as evidence that God "would not this Countrie should be unplanted...."

Chapter 3

The Tempest

*"But God that would not
this Countrie should be unplanted,
sent Sir Thomas Gates,
and Sir George Sommers
with one hundred and fiftie people...
to preserve us...."*

Anonymous Chronicler

*T*he *Sea Venture* was no more, but its passengers and crew had survived. The hurricane had shipwrecked the flagship on Bermuda Island. Their deliverance may have inspired Shakespeare to write *The Tempest*. With the resourcefulness for which their new land would became famous, the men of the *Sea Venture* had built two replacement ships. The sixty starving survivors of Jamestown, including the anonymous chronicler, greeted the new ruling council and colonists on May 23, 1610.

One of the new arrivals was John Rolfe. During their stay on the island, his daughter Bermuda was born and buried. The date of Mistress Rolfe's death is not known, but John would be a widower when he met Pocahontas a few years later.

Facing the despair in Jamestown, the council decided to abandon the colony. On June 7, the two ships sailed away, arriving at the mouth of the James River and anchoring for the night before entering Chesapeake Bay to begin the sad journey across the Atlantic.

But one more act of Providence was in store. In the early dawn, who should sail through Chesapeake Bay but Lord De La Warr himself. The ships turned around, and the first permanent English colony in the New World was saved. Lord De La Warr stayed long enough to give his name to a river, a state, and an Indian tribe, and to help England keep its foothold against its Spanish and French rivals in their contest to take over the Indians' world.

The Powhatans sought to contain the damage. They maintained their refusal to sell corn to the latest batch of "Gentlemen, whose breeding never knew what a daies labour means" and their social opposites, "the scumme of England." The newcomers put some effort into "bowling in the streets," said John Rolfe's friend Ralph Hamor, but were "so improvident as not to put Corne in the ground for their bread," while "their houses [were] ready to fall on their heads."

The English sought to encourage trade by destroying villages. In response, Powhatan sent word to De La Warr "that either we should depart this country, or confine ourselves to Jamestown only." Otherwise, "he would give a command to his people to kill us." But there was no more direct contact with the paramount chief, who had moved permanently away from Werowocomoco.

And what of his daughter? Her first marriage was within her own society. "[Y]oung Pocahunta," Strachey reported in 1612, "is now marryed to a private Captayne called *Kocoum* some 2 yeares synce." Her availability to marry John Rolfe a few years later can be explained by dissolution (easily accomplished in a matrilineal society), polyandry (not common but not unheard of), or Kocoum's death.

With the personal bonds shattered, violence bred violence. The English captured a Paspahegh weroansqua and her children, throwing the children into the water and then shooting them to death. De La Warr had the hand of a Paspahegh man cut off and sent the mutilated man to Powhatan to demand the return of English captives and weapons. Indian arrows flew. Settlers burned Indian towns to the ground. Indians captured and tortured settlers.

Lord De La Warr got sick and sailed home. Sir Thomas Dale arrived in May 1611 with another 300 colonists and the title of marshal. Exasperated with the lack of progress in the four years since the original settlement, Dale imposed martial law on gentlemen and scum alike. The "Lawes of Blood" included the death penalty for insubordination and desertion. "And some which robbed the [common] store, he caused them to be bound fast unto trees and so starved them to death." A far harsher version of John Smith's "he that will not worke shall not eate," Dale's crackdown accomplished the same result: building, cultivation, and expansion.

Dale was equally brutal in raiding the Indians, although he remained open to alliance. "I should leave [Powhatan] either no room in his country to harbor in," Dale wrote to London, "or draw him to a firm association with ourselves." Indian tribes started to make common cause against the invaders; the Powhatans and their former enemies, the Monacans, formed an alliance in 1611.

Pocahontas came back into the lives of the colonists when she was about 17 years old, possibly a married woman or a widow, possibly a mother in the natural course of things, no longer a child herself. In 1613, she was living on the river ruled by the "great King Patawomeck" (Potomac), far from her home. The Potomacs were on the edge of the Powhatan hegemony and defied the paramount chief by continuing to trade with the English. "Patomack," reported Lord De La Warr in 1611, was "a King as great as Powhatan...." No doubt the comfortable distance from Jamestown made the Potomacs more tolerant of the English. They remained a source of lifesaving corn for colonists still unable to sustain themselves. On a trading mission in April 1613, Captain Samuel Argall heard a rumor that Pocahontas was nearby. Here was a chance to take a hostage that Powhatan could not sacrifice, and to achieve the alliance that Dale hoped for.

A Potomac chief named Japazaws had long been friendly with the English and agreed to lure Pocahontas into a trap. Some say it was for the price of a trinket; others that he was protecting his people by going along with the English, and carefully negotiated for the young woman's safety. Pocahontas, always interested in new ideas, "was easily by her friend Iapazaws perswaded to goe abroad [aboard] with him and his wife to see the ship: for Captaine Argall had promised him a Copper Kettle to bring her but to him, promising no way to hurt her, but keepe her till they could conclude a peace with her father." After a tour and a meal, Argall told Pocahontas "she must goe with him, and compound peace betwixt her Countrie and us, before she ever should see Powhatan." All three Indians began wailing. "[U]pon the Captaines faire perswasions, by degrees pacifying her selfe," she bid farewell to the chief and his wife.

This formidable woman submitted calmly to her fate, whatever was in her heart. Captivity could be the fate of any Indian woman or child, who would be taught to compose herself and prepare to be adopted into a new tribe. In this case, Pocahontas might have guessed what would happen if she boarded the ship. The romantic explanation is that she had turned her heart to the English. Another possibility is intelligence gathering. Whether her tears were genuine or contrived, she was soon to resume her role as a bridge between cultures. As for her husband, Kocoum, Mattaponi oral tradition holds that the English killed him after the kidnapping, leaving a young son to be raised in the Mattaponi tribe. However, some parts of Mattaponi tradition don't square with well-known facts, and there is no other evidence of this murder.

Negotiations now began for Pocahontas' return. "A messenger forthwith was sent to her father, that his daughter Pocahontas he loved so dearely, he must ransome with our men, swords, peeces [guns], tooles, &c. hee treacherously had stolne." So a ship's ensign told the story to Ralph Hamor. The English also wanted to retrieve their "men who had runne away...," some preferring Indian hospitality to Dale's harsh rule. Powhatan responded to Argall's ransom note, "That he desired me to use his Daughter well, and bring my ship into his River, and there he would give mee my demands; which being performed, I should deliver him his Daughter, and we should be friends." As requested, the captive princess received "extraordinarie curteus usage." The negotiations were slow.

This could mean that Powhatan wanted Pocahontas to spend some time with her eyes and ears open, or – conversely – that the chief had become distanced from his daughter because of her leanings toward the English. "[Y]et it was three moneths after," picks up Hamor, "ere he returned us any answer: then ... he returned seven of our men, with each of them an unserviceable Musket, and sent us word, that when wee would deliver his daughter, hee would make us satisfaction for all injuries done us and give us five hundred bushels of Corne, and for ever be friends with us."

While the negotiations dragged on, Pocahontas entered deeply into the life of the colony. Both the colonial governor, Sir Thomas Gates, and the notoriously harsh Thomas Dale treated her as a member of their own ruling class, with Dale in particular assuming a role as friend and guardian. She was escorted to a new town in the growing colony: Henrico, upriver from Jamestown on the James River.

There, Pocahontas was entrusted to a Puritan clergyman. Dale was as unforgiving about matters of religion as he was about work. Church attendance twice a day was required by law. A man who skipped church too often was subject to the usual penalty: death. Pocahontas, however, would be brought into the fold by persuasion. Allowing for the possibility that it was a ruse to gain information, or a strategy to survive, Pocahontas drank in all there was to learn. Building on the English vocabulary she had gained as a girl, she improved her fluency and learned to read. Whatever her motivations, her intelligence and curiosity were undeniable. Willing or feigning, brainwashed or shown the light, she was convincing. All who met her spoke of her sincere faith. One of these admirers was the devout John Rolfe.

Not all gentlemen in Virginia were lazy. Rolfe was an entrepreneur. His economic contribution to the colony was high-quality tobacco. North American tobacco was sacred but harsh. It was used in small doses for ceremonial purposes. On Caribbean islands, Spaniards were working slave laborers to death to raise a South American species of tobacco that is said to have a smooth taste, if you like that sort of thing. Those enslaved plantation workers, first Indians, then Africans, were among the early casualties of this epidemic of addiction. Autopsies were already revealing the dangers of smoking. King James despised the habit, and even wrote a *Counter-Blaste to Tobacco*. But the English monarchy was not absolute.

Rolfe, a smoker himself, got his hands on some Spanish seeds and planted his first crop a year or two before he met Pocahontas. Soon, he would have Indian relatives to give him advice on local techniques for cultivation and curing. The struggling colony finally had a profitable export crop and plantation agriculture in the south had its start. The seeds of the slave economy and the American Civil War were planted at the same time. The tobacco industry flourished in Virginia, and still does, sustaining a regional economy and killing people for four centuries.

Before John Rolfe courted Pocahontas, he was one of her religious mentors. As 1613 turned to 1614, and the two spent time together in study and worship, the growing attraction must have been spiritual as well as physical. By all accounts, it was mutual. That is how Ralph Hamor saw it. "Long before this time," said that good friend, who would present Rolfe's petition to marry Pocahontas to the colonial governor, "...maister John Rolfe had bin in love with Pocahuntas and she with him." She was in her late teens, he was in his late 20s. Rolfe wrote of his "inthralled" feelings for her and "her greate apparence of love to me...." Love had bridged the cultural divide.

Or had it? Some Indian writers reject the idea. Pocahontas could have suffered the Stockholm syndrome: bonding with one's captors. Rolfe could have been nothing more than an intelligence source. The truth may be more complicated. What about coming to Jamestown as a captive or a spy but falling in love? What about mixed motives, such as fascination with a new culture?

There were certainly mixed motives on John Rolfe's side, or so he said in preparing his suit for presentation to Governor Dale. The marshal who executed people for insufficient piety and for desertion to the Indians was Rolfe's superior as well as Pocahontas' caretaker. Rolfe made his case in almost 2,000 cautious words. His caution was justified; recent research suggests that the letter may have been written after the marriage, in response to some who wanted to charge him with treason.

"[T]o avoide teadious preambles," Rolfe wrote in the middle of a tedious preamble, "....Lett therefore this my well advised ptestacon [petition or protestation]...be a sufficient wyttnes...to condemne me herein yf my chiefe intent & purpose be not to stryve with all my power of boddy and mynde ... for the good of the Plantacon [Plantation, the colony]...and for the Cnvertinge to the true knowledge of God and Iesus Christ an vnbeleivinge Creature, namely Pohahuntas To whome my hart and best thoughts ... have byn a longe tyme soe intangled & inthralled....."

Godly people weren't supposed to marry heathens. "Woe am I ignorant of the heavy displeasure wch Almighty God Conceyved against the Sonnes of

Leuie [Levy] and Israell for marrienge of straunge wyves...." He wondered whether he was being tempted by Satan, but decided that his motives were pure. "[S]hall I be of soe vntoward a disposicon [disposition] to refuse to leade the blynde into the right waye? ... [I]f I ... were soe sensually inclyned...I might satisfie suche desire...with Christians more pleasinge to the eye and lesse fearefull in the offence vnlawfully Comytted." He would risk his soul in order to bring a convert into the fold. Anyway, it wasn't about the physical attraction.

Perhaps Pocahontas, with one foot in the world of her people, and one foot in the world of her beloved, was torn in her own heart. Perhaps that shared experience was part of their bond. As Rolfe drafted his plea to Dale, and Dale waited for Powhatan to send the ransom, Pocahontas stood in the middle – between tradition and change, love and hate, peace and war.

A year had passed since the king's dearest daughter had been lured aboard an English ship. In April 1614, Governor Dale, Captain Argall, John Rolfe, Pocahontas, and 150 men traveled up the Pamunkey River in search of Powhatan. The great chief directed the English messengers to Opechancanough, but Governor Dale refused to see anyone lesser than Powhatan. Dale sent out soldiers to burn houses and kill Indians. Finally, Pocahontas herself went ashore, and stated that "if her father had loved her, he would not value her lesse then old Swords, Peeces, or Axes."

Powhatan finally sent a message agreeing to Dale's terms, but the ransom of the hostage took a different twist than envisioned a year ago. The chief's daughter "should be my child [Dale's child], and ever dwell with mee [Dale], desiring to be ever friends...." Whether by stratagem or acceptance of the change that had come to his daughter, Powhatan did not try to bring her home. At any rate, home was now with the English. That very day, John Rolfe and Pocahontas were engaged to be married. The Peace of Pocahontas was sealed.

Pocahontas was baptized into the Church of England in preparation for her marriage, and took the name Rebecca. John Rolfe married Rebecca in April, 1614, in a new Jamestown church, which has been recently located and excavated. Powhatan didn't attend; he sent other family members instead. The supreme chief apparently gave a gift of land to the couple, possibly in Henrico. There, John and Rebecca Rolfe raised tobacco. Rolfe was fortunate to have priestly men among his new in-laws; they knew how to raise and cure the sacred crop.

According to Governor Dale, the newlyweds lived happily together. Their only child, Thomas, was born in late 1614 or early 1615. Mattaponi oral tradition insists that Pocahontas became pregnant with Thomas before she married John, the result of rape by another Englishman, but this is inconsistent with all other accounts.

Sadly, the example set by the Rolfes was the exception. Unlike the French and Spanish, English men seldom married Indian women. An Anglo-American *woman* marrying an Indian man provoked outrage. Only three Powhatan-white marriages were recorded in Virginia in the 17th century, including the Rolfes. There were unofficial relationships, and Americans paid lip service to peace through marriage, but Virginia and other states would soon outlaw interracial marriage. These laws included a "Pocahontas exception" for the distinguished descendants of the Powhatan princess. It was Virginia's ban on interracial marriages that was before the U.S. Supreme Court when it struck down state miscegenation laws in the aptly named case of *Loving v. Virginia*. That was in 1967. The Indians of Virginia, not to mention blacks, were in for a long and terrible spell of racism. But the Peace of Pocahontas marked a brief age of tolerance.

The Peace of Pocahontas was marked by occasional fighting, but for the most part the Powhatans and English lived side by side for a few years. Englishmen hired Indian hunters and trained them in the use of firearms. Trade went on without coercion. In 1615, the English had adequate supplies flowing from home, and the Indians came to buy food because their own harvest was poor. Indians also bought iron hatchets, knives, hoes and shovels, as well as cloth and beads. Indians came and went freely in English settlements.

Among the Indians who worked for the whites, some became friendly enough to be torn in their loyalties when war erupted in earnest in 1622. Similarly, Thomas Savage, the man who had been placed with the Indians to learn their language and ways, was serving as an interpreter for the English when the Peace of Pocahontas broke down, and came under suspicion of disloyalty. He probably was torn, for, like many before and after him, he had come to see the enemy as human.

In 1616, Governor Dale brought the Rolfe family to England for an extravagant and dangerous real estate promotion. The Indian princess and devout convert would give a much-needed boost to the Virginia Company, convincing would-be colonists and investors that the future was in Virginia. So it was, but its most famous native daughter would never return.

The size and prestige of the Indian delegation reflects Pocahontas' status in both societies, and also hints that the Powhatans had some goals of their own:

reconnaissance and diplomacy. The young family was attended by Pocahontas' sister Matachanna, her husband Uttamatamakin, and a dozen young men and women, "to be educated here," according to a court official in London. Uttamatamakin had the shamanic gift; he was a priest, a counselor to the paramount chief. Except for the young Christian mother, the Indians were in native dress. The Virginia Company footed the bill for travel and lodging.

Seven weeks at sea – seven weeks of increasingly stale food and water. Uttamatamakin couldn't understand at first why they didn't anchor at the shore at nightfall. During storms, the seasick passengers were confined below the deck, where it was fairly safe but stinking and stuffy. No wonder most of the Indians arrived in London in a weakened state, ready to fall ill.

London was filthy. Powhatans bathed daily; Londoners, hardly ever. London was crowded, reeking of open sewers. Smoke from hearths and industry combined with fog to make every breath dangerous. All the European diseases were there. Half of the Indian delegation would die.

The Virginians – so the Londoners called the colony's original residents – arrived in England in late May or early June. They completed their journey up the Thames River in London on June 22. By wonderful coincidence or clever plan, they were lodged in the Belle Sauvage Inn, which had been given that name long before Jamestown was planted.

These weren't the first Indians in England. As well as earlier kidnapping victims, there was Namontack, who had visited with Captain Newport. There had even been a native canoe demonstration in the Thames in 1603. It was all still a sensation.

Pocahontas lived the remaining ten months of her life as a celebrity. This was the occasion for John Smith to write a letter introducing her to the queen. The court was fascinated with the New World and entertained itself with Indian-themed pageants. Here was the real thing, and royalty, no less. The Lady Rebecca was formally presented to King James – without her commoner husband – and more than once visited Queen Anne.

Pocahontas' childhood nickname doesn't appear in the famous engraving made in London. She poses in court dress, wearing the plumed hat and feather fan favored by English nobles of the era. These were the white feathers: perhaps symbols of her station as a Beloved Woman, perhaps a sign of assimilation into English society, perhaps both. The border of the portrait is a short biography: "Matoaka als Rebecca Filia Potentiss Princ: Powhatani Imp: Virginiae." Inscribed

"No fair lady."

That was the comment of a Londoner about this engraving of Pocahontas, made during her visit to London. Ever since then, she has been painted as lighter-skinned, with delicate features, rather than dark, strong and regal.

within the border is "Aetatis suae 21 A[nno]" – in the 21st year of her age. Under the border, there is a translation and more: "Matoaks als Rebecka daughter to the mighty Prince Powhatan Emperour of Attananoughskomouck [tsenacommacah] als virginia converted and baptized in the Christian faith, and wife to the worff. [worthy] Mr. John Rolff." Subsequent portraits made her look paler, softer, and less regal. "[N]o fair lady," scoffed an Englishman who saw the portrait. Indeed not: the face is strong and determined.

John Rolfe was not by the Lady Rebecca's side when she met King James, but Uttamatamakin was. Uttamatamakin was the lady's opposite: no Christianity, no lace collar, no assimilation. Uttamatamakin greeted the king wearing paint and feathers, a leather apron around his waist, his bare chest decorated with beads and copper, snake and weasel skins on his head as a priestly symbol. The princess and the priest were later the royal couple's guests of honor, at a Twelfth Night Celebration on January 6, 1617. John Rolfe was invited this time but given an inferior seat.

The Church of England was not going to claim the soul of Uttamatamakin. With Dale translating, Uttamatamakin debated with the most learned souls and pious men of England. The hosts were interested in his world view, the better to convert the heathen, and were impressed with his intelligence, but despaired at his stubborn rejection of their truth. The Indian holy man "bid...us teach the boys and girls which were brought over from thence, he being too old now to learn," wrote a frustrated Anglican holy man, the Reverend Samuel Purchas. An Anglican minister in Virginia would come to the same conclusion, in chilling terms. "[Till] their Priests and Ancients have their throats cut," wrote that servant of the gentle Savior in 1621, "there is no hope of bringing them to conversion."

The contest between Old World and New would come down to material advantage. As Powhatan's eyes and ears, Uttamatamakin saw it for himself. "Hee is said also to have set up with notches on a stick the numbers of men, being sent to see and signifie the truth of the multitudes reported to his Master," wrote Reverend Purchas. "But his arithmetike soone failed, and wonder did no lesse amaze him at the sight of so much Corne and Trees in his comming from Plimmouth [England] to London, the Virginians imagining that defect thereof here had brought us thither." No, the English invasion was backed by wealth, not scarcity, and by population beyond imagining.

The social whirl in London must have been exhilarating but exhausting, and the time was coming for John Rolfe to return to his ventures in the New World.

The young family spent some time in the beautiful countryside. Then, finally, Pocahontas was reunited with an old friend.

John Smith knew perfectly well that the woman who had twice saved his life was in England; he had written to the queen when the Rolfes arrived. Pocahontas had learned that Smith was alive when she arrived in England, but the protocols of rank and gender required the gentleman to seek out the lady. Smith finally presented himself, several months late. The captain's description of her displeasure bolsters his credentials as an honest reporter. She does not sound like a lover scorned; she sounds like a kinswoman betrayed and an ambassador snubbed.

"After a modest salutation," Smith wrote, "without any word, she turned about, obscured her face, as not seeming well contented; and in that humour... we all left her two or three houres." Perhaps she was regaining her composure while choosing her words, and they were reproachful. She "remembered [reminded] mee well what courtesies shee had done: saying, 'You did promise Powhatan what was yours should bee his, and he the like to you; you called him father being in his land a stranger, and by the same reason so must I doe you.... With a well set countenance she said: 'Were you not afraid to come into my fathers Countrie, and caused feare in him and all his people (but mee), and feare you here I should call you father. I tell you then I will, and you shall call mee childe, and so I will bee for ever and ever your Coutrieman....'"

This speech supports Professor Allen's view that Pocahontas carried the burden of maintaining a political bond based on kinship. It also speaks of her character. She did not mince words. There is resolve in the "well set countenance." She was not afraid. There was "feare in ... all his people (but mee)." True, the captain would never have hurt her personally, but she was also the young woman who ran through the forest alone at night. This woman of the Enlightenment did not fear the unknown.

" 'They did tell us alwaies you were dead,' " she went on, " 'and I knew no other till I came to Plimoth [England]; yet Powhatan did command Uttamatamakin to seeke you, and know the truth, because your Countriemen will lie much....' " It is a political reproach, and further evidence of Uttamatamakin's intelligence mission, but it is personal as well. Smith was her friend, maybe more than a friend. He had abandoned her. The whites had lied. If she had made the fateful decision to befriend Smith and save the settlers, if she had opened her heart, she had made a grave mistake.

Pocahontas had little time left for regrets. She was already very ill in early March, as the family began its shipboard journey on the Thames to the sea. The young Indians, those who were still alive, remained behind as students of the Old World, their new world. Matachanna and Uttamatamakin were aboard the ship. Matachanna was sick herself. So was two-year-old Thomas. The expedition stopped at Gravesend on the Thames River, to bring Pocahontas ashore for care, such as existed in those days.

No one knows which disease killed Pocahontas. Indians were vulnerable to every germ in Europe, especially with respiratory systems weakened by the foul air of London. We can only be sure that it wasn't smallpox, for no one with that terrible contagion would have been allowed aboard ship. Both Professor Allen and our Mattaponi chronicler suspect that she was poisoned by the English, possibly by her own husband, because she had discovered their real intentions and outlived her usefulness as a contact. True, Rolfe began a dangerous voyage with an ailing wife, putting his ambitions in Virginia ahead of her safety. But that is scant evidence for this speculation.

Rebecca Rolfe's last recorded words were to comfort her husband, "saying all men must die," and to look to the future: "tis enough that the child liveth." Her calm courage has been seen as Indian stoicism and Christian piety. At about age 21, the nonpareil of Virginia was gone. She was buried on the first day of spring. "Rebecca Wrolfe... A Virginia Lady borne," says the parish burial register for March 21, 1617.

She lives on as a legend: in paintings and books and movies; in Halloween costumes and school plays; in Pocahontas State Park and Pocahontas County in her native Virginia. And she lives on in her white descendants, numbered in the millions, and possibly in the Mattaponi tribe as well.

Was the real Pocahontas the savior of the English colonists and, inseparably, a destroyer of her own people? Almost certainly the whites would have won in the end, with their advantages in population, immunity, and technology. Jamestown's survival helped England in its rivalry with Spain and France, but Jamestown rebounded after the Starving Time without her help.

Was her intuition so very wrong? The goals of the English and Indians were not yet entirely incompatible. England wanted to expand its empire – a desire familiar to Powhatan himself. The English came to "plant," to settle, but not to destroy the native population. After all, the instructions were not to offend the locals. But the disconnect between orders from London and land-hungry colonists would get worse with each passing year until the American Revolution. Pocahontas was right in looking ahead to new ideas. Opechancanough was right in seeing the danger that his niece missed. No one could foresee the whole story. That is why the Powhatan leadership debated long and hard how to deal with the newcomers.

The Peace of Pocahontas soon broke down. Powhatan learned of his daughter's death when John Rolfe arrived in Virginia in 1617. The old chief died the following year. Powhatan's brother Opitchapam was the official successor, but the real power went to Opechancanough. The Virginia Colony ordered its residents not to trade individually with Indians and not to teach them to use firearms. The tribes moved west to get away from the colonists, losing their best farmland. The colonists followed, seeking farmland and tobacco wealth.

There was sporadic fighting from 1617 to 1622. Indians went to work for whites so that they could buy the prized metal tools. Henry Spelman, who as a youth had been directed to live with the Powhatans, now worked as an interpreter, increasingly caught between two cultures. The English leaders complained in 1619 that Spelman spoke too frankly to Opechancanough about colonial politics, and that he had become "more of the Savage then of the Christian." Anglican proselytizing continued, with diminishing interest in saving the souls of those who clung to their old ways and stood in the way of tobacco profits. Opechancanough hosted an English minister who believed that Indians "were of a peaceable & virtuous disposition" and had been driven to violence by malicious acts of settlers. The Virginia Company in 1617 encouraged colonists to adopt Indian children, but few Indian families were willing to part with their children. Epidemics periodically tore through both peoples, but there were about 1,240 English in Virginia in 1622. At that moment, they were still outnumbered by the original inhabitants.

There was an exception to the long-running pattern of uneasy peace and active hostility. Indians and whites, including Thomas Savage, lived in relative harmony on the eastern shore of Chesapeake Bay. An English court even found in favor of the Accomac Indians, who lived there on the edge of Opechancanough's control, when English settlers encroached on land assigned to them by treaty. In 1643, three squatters were ordered to pay compensation to the "greate king of the Eastern Shoare." The Accomacs finally lost this land, the Gingaskin Reservation, in 1813.

This was by no means the only example of coexistence in American history. Others would include the Quaker colony of Pennsylvania, white settlements in Shoshone and Nez Perce territory throughout Idaho and Montana, and peaceful Spanish farming communities among the Pueblo Indians of the Southwest. Coexistence never meant perfect harmony, and greed and violence eventually took over, but warfare was not the only theme in Indian-white relations.

West of the Chesapeake Bay, in the Cradle of the Republic, there was little hope for peaceful coexistence. The militant Opechancanough had been biding his time for fifteen years, watching his initial prediction that the English would take over become a reality. Now he was planning a slaughter. When the time came to communicate his plans to his people, at least one or two young Indians warned English settlers. Those who were warned fought back when the assault was launched on March 22, 1622. In other cases, English settlers were struck down with their own tools by Indians who had been working alongside them. About 300 English men, women and children were killed. The Indians took hostages, mostly women, burned houses, and killed livestock. They captured guns and gunpowder, sowing some of the powder in the settlers' fields.

"[B]efore the end of two Moones there should not be an Englishman in all their Countries," Opechancanough told the ruler of the Patawomecks, the tribe that was semi-independent of his rule and had stayed out of the raid. He was wrong. The English sent replacement colonists. By 1640, the English would out-number the Indians in Virginia. (Virginia became a royal colony in 1624 and the Virginia Company came to an end.)

The English retaliated, of course, but in some sense life went on. The English were still more focused on tobacco than on food production. The Potomacs kept selling them corn. All the warring parties went hungry after the uprising of 1622 because of a bad growing season and damage done by the attack. Supplies were slow in arriving from England, and Powhatan warriors kept picking off settlers when they went out to farm. Opechancanough called for truce talks to allow time for planting. In May 1623, a truce was declared and the English hostages were returned. During the peace ceremony, the English gave the Indians poisoned drinks. This made them sick but didn't kill them, so the English opened fire. Opechancanough himself was shot but survived. Open fighting resumed and continued on and off until a peace treaty in 1632.

Possibly because of the failure of his 1622 attack to stem the tide of invasion, Opechancanough tried to keep the peace of 1632 for a dozen years, despite relentless immigration and encroachment. When an Englishman decided to avenge theft by one Indian by murdering another, the General Court in Jamestown imposed a stiff fine, required a deposit to assure future good behavior, and ordered him to move to another county. Opechancanough actually backed the settler in his appeal, stating that the Englishman had made a mistake.

In 1638, an Englishman married a Christianized woman of the Nansemond tribe of the confederacy, one of the three recorded Indian-white marriages. The descendants of John and Elizabeth Bass maintain a cross-cultural identity as Anglicized Nansemond to the present.

Throughout this period, another child of a cross-cultural marriage was growing to manhood in England. "Tis enough that the child liveth." That Thomas Rolfe grew to manhood was nothing to take for granted. Without immunizations or antibiotics, infant mortality was no respecter of wealth or class. When John Rolfe returned to Virginia in 1617, he left his ailing and motherless two-year-old child in England in the care of an uncle. Father and son never saw each other again. John Rolfe died in 1622 in Virginia.

Thomas Rolfe returned to the New World in 1635, at about the same age that his mother was when she left it. English subjects were required to obtain the colonial governor's permission to go into Indian areas. Pocahontas' son petitioned to visit his uncle, the paramount chief, "Opachankeno [Opechancanough] to whom he is allied" and an aunt known only as "Cleopatra his mother's sister." The young man soon established himself as a planter on land left to him by his father.

Opechancanough launched one more major attack in April 1644. His warriors again killed hundreds of English and took many captives. The English now had superior numbers as well as superior weapons on their side. The Powhatans were beaten by March 1646. Rather than undertake "the great and vast expence" and "the almost impossibility of a further revenge vpon them, they being dispersed," the English sent messengers to seek an "honourable peace." Opechancanough resisted the peace overture. The English took him back to Jamestown as a prisoner. Almost 100 years old, very feeble, but still seen as "that bloody Monster," he was shot to death in prison by an English soldier.

The Powhatan hegemony was broken. The English found a chief, probably a Pamunkey, to negotiate on behalf of the Chesapeake Bay tribes that had been part of the once-mighty confederacy. This "emperor," Necotowance, agreed to a treaty in 1646 and became a vassal of the King of England. Land was set aside for the tribes, soon to be whittled away. Indian access to English settlements was strictly limited, except for children aged twelve and under, who were welcome to live among the English – mostly as servants.

As whites pushed Indians west, Indians pushed other Indians farther west. As Algonkian Indians withdrew from the tidewater to the fall line, they drove their Siouan and Iroquoian rivals out of the piedmont, those who had not joined with them in common cause against the English. As their military power waned, the Powhatans were themselves open to attack by other tribes.

The English moved west too, and clashed with more tribes. The remnants of the Powhatans were only marginally involved in the conflicts leading up to Bacon's Rebellion, which began in 1675, but Nathaniel Bacon's vigilantes turned on them as well. Bacon's Rebellion was one of a number of disputes, culminating in the Revolutionary War, in which one of the frontiersmen's grievances was that the governing elite, safe on settled land, didn't protect the westward pioneers when they encroached on territory that was supposed to be reserved for Indians.

In 1677, the Treaty of Middle Plantation reserved land for some of the Chesapeake tribes. This treaty is with the Commonwealth of Virginia, not with the United States that would come into being a century later. The Indians of Virginia remember this as their own time of hunger. Many went to work as hunters, scouts, and servants for the colonists. Indian slave labor was common in the colonial era. Free Indian-black families faced additional grounds for discrimination by the Virginia aristocracy.

The Powhatans' language disappeared. The English tempest had broken their power. But it never destroyed the people. Although Virginia's 1924 Racial Integrity Act sought to ban the designation "Indian" from birth certificates, on the grounds that black-Indian mixing had created an indistinguishable group of non-whites, the Indian tribes of Virginia have retained their identity. All except the Pamunkey and Mattaponi lost the land promised by the Treaty of Middle Plantation, but several tribes retain active social and political structures.

The Pamunkey and Mattaponi still hold their land in King William County. Every year to this day, just before Thanksgiving, the leaders of these two tribes present the governor of Virginia with a deer or other game killed on their reservations, in scrupulous fulfillment of the treaty obligations of 1677. One year during the 20th century, game was scarce. "My dad was chief then," recalled Pamunkey Chief William "Swift Water" Miles, "and he knew we had to have something to present to the governor; so he went to a turkey farm, bought a live turkey, brought it back to the reservation and killed it. That way we were able to fulfill the terms of the treaty – after all it was killed on the reservation."

In the century between the Treaty of Middle Plantation and the Declaration of Independence, Virginia would mature into one of the most influential colonies. And the descendants of the woman with the white feather would join its most powerful families.

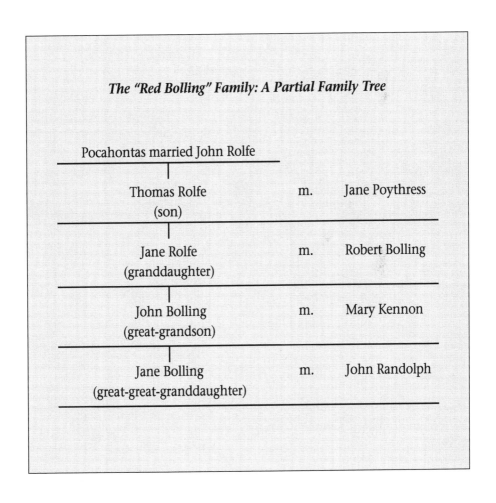

The "Red Bolling" Family: A Partial Family Tree

Pocahontas married John Rolfe

Thomas Rolfe (son) m. Jane Poythress

Jane Rolfe (granddaughter) m. Robert Bolling

John Bolling (great-grandson) m. Mary Kennon

Jane Bolling (great-great-granddaughter) m. John Randolph

Chapter 4

Mother of Presidents

*"He [King George III]...
has endeavoured to bring
on the inhabitants of our frontiers,
the merciless Indian savages..."*

Thomas Jefferson in the Declaration of Independence

*A*lthough the Peace of Pocahontas lasted only five years, the brief marriage of Rebecca and John Rolfe produced two lasting fruits: tobacco and Thomas. Tobacco created a wealthy class of planters in the Commonwealth of Virginia. Thomas helped populate it.

Tobacco gave the planter class its economic foothold. Their wealth increased with other plantation crops: sugar, rice, and cotton. During colonial times, tobacco financed the birth of a class of aristocrats in Virginia, Enlightenment men who placed a high value on education and freedom – for themselves. The plantation economy depended on slave labor. A number of Virginian Founding Fathers were uncomfortable enough to feel the need to justify slavery as a necessary and perhaps temporary evil, and to free some or all of their own slaves. In 1832, the Virginia Assembly seriously discussed a gradual end to slavery.

King Cotton, however, came to rule the south after the American Revolution. In 1793, Eli Whitney invented the cotton gin, which made large-scale cotton growing profitable. Virginia was not a major cotton growing region, but it became the main supplier of enslaved human beings to the Deep South. Southerners came to rationalize slavery as a benign institution – overlooking the vicious whippings and forced breakup of families – and "began to think of themselves as a culture apart from the rest of the nation."

Plantation agriculture called for continuous westward expansion, in part because tobacco exhausted the soil. That expansion displaced one tribe after another, while the question of whether slavery should be allowed in newly settled territories eventually tore the country apart.

Virginia also was a microcosm of the divide between heartland and elite. The Founding Fathers were as insulated from everyday struggles for survival as today's "Washington insiders" are said to be. The Appalachian Mountains of western Virginia were full of white subsistence farmers who were simply too poor to own slaves. During the Civil War, several western counties refused to join the Confederacy and became the state of West Virginia. To the Indians whose lands were overrun, all these whites were "Long Knives," but the aristocrats carried swords while the mountaineers carried hunting knives.

A common denominator between coastal and frontier, rich whites and poor, was racism, then as now. There is a strong argument that rich whites engineered this common denominator to divert attention from their own privileges, then as now. Laws against intermarriage reinforced racial separation. Sex was another matter, with countless slave women impregnated by their masters.

For good and ill, it all began with Jamestown, the first permanent English colony in America. Jamestown was well-established when the *Mayflower* brought the Pilgrims to Plymouth Rock in 1620. The tidewater is the "Cradle of the Republic." The Commonwealth of Virginia is the "Old Dominion." Virginia is the "Mother of Presidents" – eight of them, including George Washington, Thomas Jefferson, and Woodrow Wilson. Slaveholding and the Civil War badly tarnished this proud history, somewhat redeemed now that parts of the New South are more racially integrated than parts of the north. We northerners could add the dispossession of Indians to the list of Virginia's past crimes, but that would make us uncomfortable.

Even the insight of a medicine woman could not have predicted all that would follow the Rolfe family's tobacco farm.

Young Thomas Rolfe settled into this life. He married into a wealthy planter family and had a daughter, Jane. Jane Rolfe married Robert Bolling, an emigrant from the mother country who acquired an estate on the James River. Jane and Robert Bolling had one son, John Bolling. Jane Rolfe Bolling died shortly after John's birth. It was John who gave rise to a clan known as the Red Bollings, numbering at least two million in the late 20th century. First Lady Edith Bolling Wilson was a Red Bolling. The name distinguishes them from Robert Bolling's children by his second wife; those "White Bollings" were half-siblings of Pocahontas' great-grandson.

John Bolling had six children who survived to marry: one son and five daughters. When one of the daughters, Jane, married Richard Randolph, the Red Bollings were joined with one of the most influential families of Virginia. Richard's parents, the wealthy and fertile William and Mary Randolph, have been called the Adam and Eve of Virginia. William and Mary's descendants included Thomas Jefferson and Chief Justice John Marshall. Richard and Jane's descendants – the Pocahontas line – included Thomas Randolph, a governor of Virginia and son-in-law of Thomas Jefferson, as the expanding clan wove together the founding dynasties of the Commonwealth and the Republic. The intermarried families included the Lees, with two signers of the Declaration of Independence, a Revolutionary War general, and an even more famous Civil War general. Meriwether Lewis and William Clark were not Bollings themselves, but they were part of this slave-owning Virginia elite. Thomas Jefferson was a friend of the families of both Lewis and Clark.

In the Red Bolling family, Pocahontas, Powhatan and Matoaka showed up as first and middle names for generations. One of them, Powhatan Bolling, was known as a hot-tempered duelist who lost to John Randolph for Congress by five votes. Red and White Bollings served in the Virginia Assembly during the revolutionary period and fought in the Continental Army during the American Revolution.

These Virginians had a sense of aristocracy. They looked and acted much like the landed gentlemen of the mother country, down to fox chases and satin clothes. Part of that self-image was based on the Bolling family's "royal red blood." In the 19th century, it was still common knowledge that Pocahontas was a founding mother of Virginia. During the Mexican War of 1846, a Virginian lieutenant made a fool of himself by offering a dollar to the plainly dressed General Zachary Taylor to clean his sword. A delighted witness described "that high-toned dignity which the descendants of Pocahontas and other Virginians are so famous for." (The future President Taylor was born in Virginia but raised on the frontier, in Kentucky.)

While Rebecca Rolfe's direct descendants helped build the privileged white aristocracy, Matoaka left Indian and black legacies too. First, Mattaponi oral history holds that there are descendants from her first marriage. Second, there have been countless cousins among Indian communities, often mixed with black as well as white Virginians. In 1844, a former slave named Armstrong Archer published a narrative discussing his "descent from an African King on the one side and from the celebrated Indian Chief Powhatan on the other."

Among the white aristocrats of Virginia, most of the men were military officers at one time or another. That meant they were Indian fighters, for all the wars in North America were Indian wars in one sense or another. Between 1754 and 1763, Britain and France fought for control of North America in the French and Indian War, or Seven Years War. The rival nations sought out Indian alliances, and the tribes had to decide: Britain, France, or neutrality? In 1754, the British population on the Atlantic coast was 1,500,000. In contrast, there were only 100,000 French speakers in Louisiana and Quebec combined. The two empires competed in the areas west of the settled Atlantic region: the Great Lakes region, the Ohio River Valley, and the Mississippi River. Central to that competition was securing Indian allies.

As eastern tribes migrated west to escape the English onslaught, they pushed other tribes out of the way. Tribes regarded Europeans as useful allies against traditional enemies. Some took sides. Others took warning. "If the French claim all the land on one side of the river," a Delaware Indian asked an English surveyor, "and the English claim all the land on the other side of the river, where is the Indians' land?"

The Iroquois League stayed neutral in the French and Indian War. Some of its member tribes had Algonkian enemies, and most Algonkian tribes allied with France. England sent diplomats who persuaded the Iroquois League to stay out of the fight. One of the diplomats married an Iroquois woman. Their son Joseph Brant grew up loyal to the British and fought fiercely on the Tory side during the Revolutionary War.

The Shawnee bands were widely dispersed and there were many opportunities for both love and war. For decades, the Shawnees and their allies fought the English-speaking invaders, first as allies of the French against the British in the French and Indian War, then as allies of the British against the Americans in the Revolutionary War and War of 1812. At the same time, French men often married Shawnee women, and there were peaceful interactions of all sorts between English speakers and the diverse Shawnee communities. On the frontier, an English speaker compiled a list of Shawnee and Delaware vocabulary that included "I love you" and "will you sleep with me?"

The French and Indian War ended with defeat for France in the New World. Under the treaty of 1763, Britain gained control of Canada. France kept New Orleans and the Louisiana Territory, the vast area between the Mississippi River – the "Father of Waters" – and the Rocky Mountains. As part of the negotiations of 1763, France granted the Louisiana Territory to Spain (which also claimed Florida, and, of course, Mexico, California, and the southwest.) Americans and Europeans traded territory regardless of who was living there first. It was the way of nations.

Before the Seven Years War, Britain had a somewhat hands-off approach to North America. After 1763, the mother country took tighter control of the colonies. This produced many of the grievances leading to the American Revolution. One of those grievances was England's attempt to prevent white encroachment on Indian lands.

In 1763, King George III issued a proclamation forbidding "Our loving Subjects" from settling west of the Appalachian Mountains. "And whereas it is just and reationable...that the several Nations or Tribes of Indians...who live under Our Protection, should not be molested or disturbed in the possession of...their Hunting Grounds; We do therefore... declare it to be Our Royal Will and Pleasure, ...that no Governor...grant Warrants of Survey, or pass Patents for any lands beyond the Heads or Sources of any of the Rivers which fall into the Atlantick Ocean from the West and North West...."

The Appalachian Mountains were the first American frontier. This ancient chain includes several ranges, rising in New York and ending in Georgia. In the Virginias, the Blue Ridge and Shenandoah Mountains shelter the Shenandoah River Valley. The Great Smoky Mountains or Alleghenies – the Unakas or White Mountains, the Cherokees called them, for their smoky haze – form North Carolina's border with Tennessee. West of the Blue Ridge and Smokies lies the fertile Ohio River Valley, including the Kentucky bluegrass country. The headwaters of the rivers that flow into the Atlantic, at the crest of the Appalachians, were to form the dividing line between English settlement and Indian tribes.

The Proclamation of 1763 was ignored by investors and farmers alike. The surveyors and land speculators included several Founding Fathers and pioneering legends. Peter Jefferson (father of Thomas), George Washington, and Daniel Boone worked as surveyors, laying the groundwork for private land ownership. The farmers, wrote Virginia's royal governor Lord Dunmore, "do not conceive that Government has any right to forbid their taking possession of a vast tract of country." Competing land companies from Pennsylvania and Virginia fought for control of the western lands, and the two colonies came close to a border war.

Worn down over the ages, the Appalachians are older and lower than the western ranges that Sacagawea would struggle across with a baby on her back. Indians used the mountains as both a boundary and a highway, for migration, trade, and warfare. For the English settlers, they were a barrier to western expansion. Colonists crossed the ranges, one after another, becoming more American and less English with each passage. Each crossing was a feat of human courage, a land grab, and a step closer to war with the mother country.

Decades before the American Revolution, white settlers traveled the Great Wagon Road from Maryland and Pennsylvania. This path took them through the Shenandoah Valley, to North Carolina. Nature also provided a water gap in

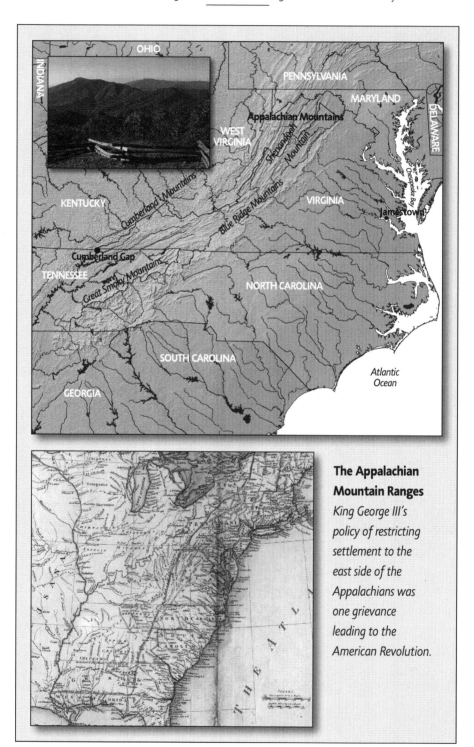

The Appalachian Mountain Ranges

King George III's policy of restricting settlement to the east side of the Appalachians was one grievance leading to the American Revolution.

the Blue Ridge Mountains in today's West Virginia, where the Potomac and Shenandoah rivers meet. There, in the 18th century, a man named Harper started a ferry service, and President Washington directed construction of an armory at Harper's Ferry to take advantage of the water power that was so important in the early Industrial Revolution.

To cross the farthest ranges in violation of the king's decree, one option was river travel, starting in Pennsylvania. George Washington traveled the Ohio River around 1770 to inspect the land grants that he had received for his service in the French and Indian War. The fact that colonial governments were distributing land in violation of the king's proclamation was a sign of the coming revolt. Another Virginian who traveled the Ohio River route was George Rogers Clark, the much older brother of William Clark, heading for Kentucky in 1773.

The most famous route was Daniel Boone's Wilderness Road through the Cumberland Gap. The Wilderness Road began in 1775 with a path called Boone's Trace. The Cumberland Gap, where today's Virginia, Kentucky, and Tennessee meet, is a portal through the westernmost Appalachians. "Stand at Cumberland Gap," wrote the historian Frederick Jackson Turner, "and watch the procession of civilization, marching single file – the buffalo following the trail to the salt springs, the Indian, the fur-trader and hunter, the cattle-raiser, the farmer – and the frontier has passed by."

The Cumberland Gap lies on the Warriors' Path, part of a network of Indian hunting and trading trails through the Appalachian ranges. Along these trails, tribes from the north fought tribes from the south for control of hunting grounds. Until recently, a rock pyramid in North Carolina stood in memory to Cherokee women and children murdered centuries ago by an Iroquois war party.

Daniel Boone wasn't the first white man to see the Cumberland Gap, but it is forever associated with that legendary frontiersman, who sacrificed "two darling sons" on the frontier. Boone first crossed the Gap in 1769 to hunt and explore in Kentucky. His eldest son, James, was killed by Indians while trying to settle in Kentucky in 1773. The second sacrifice, Israel, fell in the Battle of Blue Licks in 1782. Through it all, there was mutual respect between Daniel Boone and Indian tribes, beginning in Boone's youth when his family and Shawnees were peaceful neighbors, and continuing when they were bitter adversaries. In fact, Boone felt a deep attachment to Indian culture, especially its connection to the natural world that this woodsman dearly loved. The wilderness skills that made Boone a Long Hunter, a white who could live off the land, were Indian skills.

Late in his long life, Boone said he had killed at most three Indians. That would be surprising for a crack shot who defended frontier outposts, but his attitude contrasted with both whites and Indians who bragged about their kills. Boone's parents were Quakers who migrated from England to live near William Penn's idealistic settlement, Philadelphia. The City of Brotherly Love was a sincere experiment in coexistence. In Pennsylvania, whites and Indians lived near each other, learned from each other, and befriended each other for decades. As late as 1809, Shawnees in Ohio were writing President Jefferson in praise of a Quaker Indian agent named Kirk, "our friend," "a good man," whose "good advice" helped them produce abundant harvests – until they were forced to move yet again.

Yet the Quakers' son Daniel Boone was instrumental in the dispossession of these one-time neighbors. Land hunger kept whites on the move. Young Daniel's family traveled south to Virginia, then on to North Carolina on the Great Wagon Road in 1750. As a married man, Boone and his wife, Rebecca, a legend of courage in her own right, moved their children back and forth between North Carolina and Virginia before venturing to Tennessee and finally Kentucky. The Boones could have stayed within the line drawn by the king in 1763. But this new people, the Americans, were emigrants and children of emigrants. "Americans" wrote Lord Dunmore "...acquire no attachment to Place: But wandering about seems engrafted in their nature...."

By the time of the American Revolution, 30,000 English-speaking people were settled west of the proclamation line. The settlers were called over mountain men or back water men. "Back water" originally referred to the change in the direction of the rivers, the marker that King George had used as a boundary. The urban elite still use the term to refer to sturdy rural folk, such as a barefoot man Daniel Boone encountered one very cold day. The man didn't have to worry about frostbitten feet, the famous woodsman said. "Even taters wouldn't freeze with that much dirt on them."

The line of white settlement was pushed west through a combination of fighting and negotiation, displacing Cherokees and Shawnees in North Carolina, Virginia, West Virginia, and Kentucky. Each time, Indians pushed other Indians farther west.

Kanta-ke, the Indians called the rich hunting grounds west of the Great Smoky Mountains. Kentucky. The Great Meadow or the Middle Ground, whites called it. In a pair of treaties in 1768, Britain bought much of the Ohio River Valley, including Kentucky, from the Iroquois, while recognizing some Cherokee rights there. The French-allied Shawnees were frozen out. Shawnees and Cherokees had long fought the Iroquois and each other over that land. After the treaties of 1768, however, the Shawnees sent a painted hatchet to the Cherokees to propose an alliance against white settlers.

Perhaps because of the ongoing warfare among tribes, there were few Indian villages in Kentucky. Perhaps because there were few Indians, there was abundant game. These agricultural tribes were not taking full advantage of the fertile soil in Kentucky. To white farmers, it was land waiting for the plow.

In another sense, tens of thousands of Indians depended on that land, for meat to eat and skins to trade. Long Hunters began competing with the Indians for game. A deer hide – "a buck" – was currency. During Daniel Boone's first crossing of the Cumberland Gap in 1769, a Shawnee chief and his warriors confronted the white hunting party. After confiscating their horses, guns, and furs, the chief let them go with a warning: "this is Indians' hunting ground, and all the animals, skins and furs are ours; and if you are so foolish as to venture here again, you may be sure the wasps and yellow-jackets will sting you severely." Boone and a companion waited for their chance, stole the horses back, were captured, escaped, and kept trapping and hunting. Boone came home in 1771 with reports of abundant land and bountiful hunting.

Farther south in the Appalachians, home of the Cherokees, a long and complicated tragedy was unfolding. In 1730, seven Cherokee headmen had traveled to London to accept British sovereignty. A quarter century later, during the French and Indian War, a group of Cherokee warriors demonstrated their loyalty to Britain, and their enmity to the French-allied Shawnees, by fighting alongside white Virginians. As the Cherokee warriors traveled home after the battle, other Virginian frontiersmen attacked them, resulting in the Cherokee War of the late 1750s. Under a custom of corporate responsibility, Cherokees retaliated against random whites. The only unusual thing here was the theoretical basis for group retaliation, a nicety that few Indians or whites bothered with. Whites responded by murdering Cherokee hostages and burning towns, cornfields, and granaries belonging to their former allies. Clashes and truces continued for years.

Daniel Boone crossed paths with the Cherokees in the days when both were frontier hunters. Sometimes he hunted on their lands without permission and occasionally he hunted by their side. Asleep during a solo hunt one winter night in Tennessee, Boone was awakened by a party of Cherokee warriors. "Ah, Wide-

Mouth, I have got you now," exclaimed one of them, pleased to catch the elusive hunter, probably nicknamed for his humor and storytelling. As Boone told the story, he smiled and shook hands. The Cherokees took his pelts and rifle, and left him with his scalp.

"War is their principal study," said a merchant who traded with the Cherokees in those years. The Cherokees fought the Creeks, Shawnees, Iroquois, and Chickasaws and held captives as slaves. They conquered the Catawbas, took some of their land, and sold the defeated warriors in the white man's slave markets. There were 43 Cherokee towns when Daniel Boone first hunted in the Middle Ground, about 12,000 people, settled farmers who hunted too.

White farming methods called on men to do the woman's work of farming. This was distasteful to hunters and warriors. Over time, though, the farming tribes of the southeast adopted the plow, the forge, and the loom. Five southeastern tribes did much the same and came to be called the Civilized Tribes: the Cherokees, Creeks, Choctaws, Chickasaws, and Seminoles. Blacks were enslaved by all five tribes, in very different ways. Cherokees treated slaves as property, while Seminoles essentially adopted escaped blacks.

In response to the white invasion, the Cherokees moved gradually from clan-based to centralized governance, becoming the Cherokee Nation in the process. A national council established a Light Horse Guard, to discourage young warriors from raiding on the frontier, stealing horses, and provoking retribution by settlers.

A few years before the American Revolution, an over mountain man named Nathaniel Gist fathered a child with a Cherokee woman. The child was Sequoyah, also called George Gist, inventor of the written Cherokee language. Sequoyah's grandfather, Christopher Gist, was a neighbor of the Boone family and worked with a young surveyor named George Washington for the Ohio Land Company in the 1750s.

Sequoyah grew up with his mother's people, and could not read English, although he could sign his name. His great accomplishment, completed in 1821, was assigning a symbol to each syllable used in the Cherokee language. Some Cherokees thought the project was a step backward from education in English. Sequoyah's wife at one point threw his "talking leaves" into the fire. But he persisted, and Cherokees embraced literacy, in both English and their own language. When missionaries brought in a printing press, with English and Cherokee typefaces, the Cherokees printed a bilingual newspaper.

Some Cherokees accumulated wealth through the deerskin trade. Others inherited property from white fathers. The Cherokee council decided to allow inheritance from white fathers as a departure from matrilineal inheritance. They welcomed new technology. Sequoyah, for instance, worked as a silversmith. They bought livestock and ran inns, ferries, and trading posts. A tug of war developed between tradition and change. The most visionary Cherokees sought the best of both.

In 1773, the Boones were ready to move west, part of the first party of whites to try to settle in Kentucky. In doing so, they violated orders of their colonial

Sequoyah

The inventor of the Cherokee alphabet would later work for reconciliation among Cherokee factions that were bitterly divided by the events leading up to the Trail of Tears.

governors and their impossibly faraway king, and made their first great sacrifice for the new land. One October night, Daniel's oldest son, 18-year-old James, was camped separately from the main party with a small group. They were watched by a party of Delaware, Shawnee, and Cherokee warriors, now cooperating. The Indians caught James and his group and killed them slowly. James had been shot and stabbed by the time one of the captors started pulling out his nails. First he begged for mercy and then for a quick death. One man, a slave, escaped to tell the tale; another slave was killed. Illegal though the expedition was, the colonial governments pressed tribal leaders to punish the perpetrators, and at least two were executed.

On the Ohio River the same year, a party of whites lured a group of Iroquois to a friendly bout of drinking and target shooting. The whites then massacred the Indians, including the family of Chief Logan, who had been friendly to whites. They hung Logan's pregnant sister by her thumbs before killing her. The heartbroken chief swore revenge and made common cause with the Shawnees. Lord Dunmore's War was on. Daniel Boone and George Rogers Clark served in the Virginia militia, with the Atlantic colonies still providing the political framework for the western lands.

Lord Dunmore's War ended in 1774 with a treaty. Under their principal chief Cornstalk, who was able in war but worked hard for peace, the Shawnees gave up Kentucky for a promise of the land northwest of the Ohio River. The deal quickly fell apart. The Ohio River, like the Appalachian Mountains, came to symbolize a lost opportunity for a negotiated boundary.

A Beloved Woman of the Cherokees also tried the path of giving up land for peace. Her name was Nanye-hi (One Who Goes About), also called the "Wild Rose," or Nancy Ward after her marriage to a white man. Born about 1738, she earned the title of Beloved Woman or War Woman in 1755 in battle against the Creeks, when her husband was killed and she picked up his rifle and rallied the Cherokees to victory. She became a member of the council of chiefs.

In March 1775, a land speculator named Richard Henderson engaged Daniel Boone as a negotiator, taking advantage of the respect between the woodsman and the Indians. The idea was to persuade a group of Cherokees to "sell" 17 million acres of land in Kentucky and Tennessee, including access to the Cumberland Gap. The result was the Treaty of Sycamore Shoals. Cherokees had weak claims to the area relative to other tribes, and the private "treaty" was in clear violation of the Proclamation of 1763. However, the colonists were about

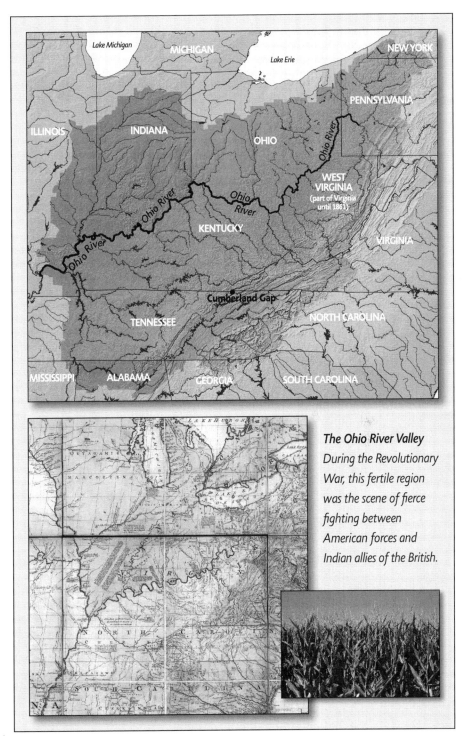

The Ohio River Valley
During the Revolutionary War, this fertile region was the scene of fierce fighting between American forces and Indian allies of the British.

to rebel against the author of the proclamation. The shot heard round the world was fired a few weeks after the Treaty of Sycamore Shoals. The Cherokee war chief Dragging Canoe refused to accept the agreement, prophetically warning his people that there would be more demands for land, until they would "be compelled to seek a retreat in some far distant wilderness." He soon brought in four scalps.

Nanye-hi warned white settlers of Dragging Canoe's war plans and later gave intelligence to American forces "and made an overture in behalf of some of the Chiefs for peace...." She made her reasons clear: "Our cry is all for peace; let it continue. This peace must last forever. Let your women's sons be ours. Let our sons be yours." Before Nancy Ward died in 1822, however, she counseled her people not to cede any more land.

As a Beloved Woman, Nanye-hi had the right to decide the fate of captives. Using this power, she became the first Cherokee to own black slaves. She exercised the same right to rescue a white woman captured by Dragging Canoe's militants. Mrs. Bean was about to be burned at the stake when Nanye-hi intervened. The War Woman nursed the ailing captive back to health and then set her free. Mrs. Bean, in turn, taught her Cherokee friend the whites' methods of weaving and dairy production.

To take advantage of the lands ceded by the Treaty of Sycamore Shoals, Henderson would need a way to get people there. He hired Daniel Boone to hack Boone's Trace, the beginning of the Wilderness Road, through the Cumberland Gap. This time, Boone's party successfully crossed into Kentucky, and established Boonesborough in 1775, under the auspices of Henderson's Transylvania Company. The settlers signed a compact of self-government and built fortifications.

As Dragging Canoe was fighting the Americans, the Americans declared their independence from Great Britain. Some Cherokees took the revolutionary side; others allied with the British. All tribes faced that decision, as they had during the Seven Years War. Back then, many Indians had concluded that they would be better off if the French threw the British out of North America. Now, several tribes concluded that they would be better off siding with the author of the Proclamation of 1763. Iroquois unity and neutrality broke down during the American Revolution, with members of the confederacy choosing opposite sides. For the tribes that chose the losing side, the Americans' revenge earned George Washington the name "the Town Destroyer."

To the south, the Shawnees, Delawares, Dragging Canoe's Cherokees, and Chief Logan's Iroquoians were encouraged by the British to attack frontier settlements, with initial success in driving settlers back across the mountains. "The father has called on his Indian children, to assist him in punishing his children, the Americans...," explained a Delaware chief. "At first I looked upon it as a family quarrel, in which I was not interested. However at length it appeared to me, that the father was in the right; and his children deserved to be punished a little. That this must be the case I concluded from the many cruel acts his offspring had committed from time to time on his Indian children...."

In June, 1776, George Rogers Clark traveled from Kentucky to petition the governor of Virginia for protection against attacks by Indians aligned with the British. Ten days before the Declaration of Independence, the Commonwealth of Virginia took control from the Transylvania Company. In its closing days as a colonial government, Virginia ratified the breach of the Proclamation of 1763 by declaring the frontier "Kentucky County." Responding to George Rogers Clark's petition, they sent him back with gunpowder. In the next several months, a Kentucky militia was organized, and George Rogers Clark was placed in command.

The colonies had been at war with the mother country for over a year when Thomas Jefferson wrote the immortal declaration. By that time, the atrocities on all sides were mounting up. The Redcoats' alliance with "the merciless Indian savages," or some of them, could be added to the list of grievances that justified independence. Jefferson was also voicing a colonial grievance dating back to the Proclamation of 1763, during Britain's half-hearted efforts to keep the colonial frontiers from encroaching on Indian land.

Between 1607 and 1776, a new people had arisen: Americans. Although they defined themselves as civilized people claiming the land from savages, they were more Indian than they cared to admit. They raised corn and wore buckskin, smoked tobacco, hunted deer, and built a confederacy on an Iroquois model. They were a mix of Indian, black, and several European nationalities. They were self-reliant pioneers, determined farmers who freed their descendants from the specter of famine, brave soldiers who have fought for freedom in every generation. They built a democratic republic on a foundation of Enlightenment ideals and English liberties, extending those liberties to more people with each passing generation, finally including the descendants of those enslaved and dispossessed. The achievement was magnificent. The cost to the peoples swept aside was inexcusable.

Chapter 5

Father of Waters

*"The utmost good faith shall always
be observed towards the Indians;
their lands and property
shall never be taken
from them without their consent...."*

The Northwest Ordinance of 1787

*T*en days after the Declaration of Independence, Shawnee Indians kidnapped Daniel Boone's 14-year-old daughter and two friends. The girls were not harmed, out of respect for Boone (or fear of angering a formidable adversary) or because they were candidates for adoption. The woodsman and his friends rescued the girls after a deadly firefight.

Boonesborough was under constant attack by Shawnee allies of the British. Like the Paspahegh outside Jamestown, the Shawnees waited for the invaders to step outside of the fortified areas. Sometimes they picked off livestock, and it was said that the cows were afraid to go out to graze when they sensed Indians watching. Settlers stood guard for others who were plowing and planting. Bullets, gunpowder, and manpower were scarce. Two female sharpshooters protected a neighboring settlement using bullets made of melted pewter dishes.

There was still a peace party among the Shawnees, led by Cornstalk, a man highly respected by whites for both military and diplomatic skill. In the fall of 1777, Cornstalk warned the Americans that war chiefs in his tribe were joining the Redcoats. The American commander took Cornstalk, his son, and two others hostage. A few days later, Virginia militiaman decided to avenge the killing of one of their own by killing Cornstalk and his party. Seeing the results of their attempts at neutrality, Shawnees turned toward the British.

Chief Cornstalk of the Shawnees
Cornstalk, respected by all sides in both war and peace, was trying to keep his people from allying with the British during the American Revolution when he was murdered by a Virginia militiaman.

In 1778, George Rogers Clark led a regiment to engage the British along the Mississippi River. West and south they traveled, along the river systems of today's Ohio, Illinois, Missouri and Kentucky. These backwater militiamen traveled like Indians, some wearing deerskin and moccasins, carrying parched corn and jerked venison, powder horns and tomahawks.

Clark and his men reached Cahokia and Kaskaskia, where the mound builder civilizations were in their decline when the first Spaniards invaded. The mound builders' descendants lived on as the Five Civilized Tribes and other southeastern Indians.

The southern Mississippi River region had been claimed by France, and then ceded to Spain, but was still the land of French traders who married the daughters of their Indian trading partners. Part of George Clark's mission was diplomatic: to discourage tribal alliances with Britain. As his younger brother William would later do, George Clark won the Indians' confidence by speaking bluntly but with respect: "I am a man and a warrior, not a councilor," he said. "I carry War in my right hand and in my left Peace," he told the tribes gathered at Cahokia. He also spoke eloquently about the revolutionary ideals of freedom. Those who heard his words agreed to remain neutral.

George Rogers Clark retained the trust of Indians in negotiations for years to come. It was a trust based on a harsh warrior creed. When Clark captured a group of Indians from British-allied tribes, he had four of them executed to encourage a British surrender. The British surrendered, and George Rogers Clark became a hero of the Revolutionary War, retiring as a general.

In Kentucky, the everyday tasks of pioneering went on in the land that George Clark was fighting to secure. In February 1778, while leading an expedition to make salt, Daniel Boone was captured by the Chillicothe band of Shawnees. He negotiated the safe surrender of the other salt makers, offered to turn over the Boonesborough settlers for mass adoption if the Shawnees would wait for warmer weather, and appeared receptive to proposals by the Shawnees' British allies to turn the fort over to the Redcoats. He insisted later that it was all a ploy to save lives and buy time, not to save his own skin.

"Howdydo, howdydo," said the captive as he recognized the warrior who had warned him about the wasps and yellow-jackets. Boone was adopted by a Chillicothe chief named Blackfish, who addressed Boone as "my son," and shared a sugar cube from his own mouth with this son to show their intimacy. Adoption was a way to replace relatives killed in battle. Boone's men – possibly

Daniel Boone
This son of Quakers had genuine respect for Indians, but was instrumental in dispossessing them. Courtesy of the National Portrait Gallery, Smithsonian Institution/ Art Resource, New York.

Boone himself – had killed a son of Blackfish during the rescue of the kidnapped girls. Boone spoke fondly of his months among the Indians, but he escaped to return to his wife and children and to prepare Boonesborough for the coming Shawnee attack. According to one version of the story, his adoptive mother begged Boone not to go, warning that the warriors would catch and kill him. It seems she did not want to lose another son.

Boone's daring escape, return to Boonesborough, and urgent preparations for its defense support his argument that he had never switched loyalties. When Blackfish led a party of warriors to Boonesborough to make good on Boone's promise to surrender the fort, there were long negotiations between adoptive father and son. The bond was real, but Boonesborough was on Indian land.

The Chillicothe warriors asked to see the beauty of the women of Boonesborough. The women stepped into view and let down their long hair. Then these women prepared a feast for a final round of peace talks, to be held outside the fort. Boone ordered sharpshooters to stand ready inside the fort during the feast. He and Blackfish agreed to a treaty. Then the chief directed his warriors to embrace the white negotiators. This appeared to be a pretext for taking them hostage. With both sides double-talking and on hair-trigger alert, it's hard to criticize Indian treachery.

Boone was slashed with a tomahawk, but he and the other settlers escaped into the fort and defended it until the Shawnees gave up their siege and withdrew. The successful defense of Boonesborough helped George Rogers Clark secure the Ohio River Valley, the western front of the Revolutionary War.

When the fight was over, Boone's rivals accused him of treason, based on his dealings during captivity and his warm relationship with Blackfish. He was quickly cleared. As with so many people in this age of migration and conquest, he lived on both sides but had to choose one.

In a number of states, the Revolutionary War was a civil war, Tories against Patriots. While some whites on the frontier responded to Indian attacks by retreating east, some Tories moved west to get away from the revolutionary fighting, willing to take their chances with Indians. Patriots moved west too, willing to defend the frontier and pursue the dream of a farm of their own. People walked barefoot across the Appalachians, carrying their children and belongings. Daniel Boone guided a man named Abraham Lincoln to Kentucky in autumn 1779. The president's grandfather would fall to an Indian bullet some years later while working the farmland he had cleared.

The Hard Winter, they called the winter of 1779-80. People, livestock, and game froze and starved. Wild turkeys suffocated from the ice of their own freezing breath. The settlers worked in the snow to build cabins at a new settlement, Boone's Station. Guns wouldn't fire reliably, but Boone shared what he caught, in the manner of Indians.

As the Revolutionary War and Indian attacks wore on, attitudes hardened. George Rogers Clark had consciously avoided a fight with Logan's people in 1773 because of the presence of women and children, but during the war he vowed never again to spare a woman or child. Thomas Jefferson wrote to George Clark to suggest "their extermination, or their removal."

Massacre led to massacre. Indians scalped American children, and Americans scalped Indian children. "Infants are torn from their Mothers Arms and their Brains dashed out against Trees," a Kentuckian wrote to Clark. Another white infant was taken from its dead mother's arms and disemboweled. "Hardly a week passes without someone being scalped...." wrote another settler. Whole families were wiped out. But settlers kept coming west.

Virginia militiamen killed Boone's adoptive father Blackfish in 1780. Later that year, George Rogers Clark's men attacked a Shawnee village, burned their cornfields, tortured a woman to death, and killed dozens, including his own cousin who had been captured and adopted.

American independence was assured when Cornwallis surrendered at Yorktown in 1781, but the Indian wars continued. A peaceful group of Delaware Indians were rounded up and slaughtered. Wyandot Indians tortured a captive American officer to death over hot coals. Americans fought Cherokees to the south, and George Clark kept burning Shawnee towns and crops.

An Indian alliance crushed an American force at the Battle of Blue Licks in 1782, killing the American captives by torture, fire, and scalping. There, Daniel Boone sacrificed another son, Israel. Unlike his brother, Israel died quickly, killed in battle.

The Treaty of Paris in 1783 confirmed American independence and granted the Old Northwest territory to the United States. The tribes that had allied with Britain were now at the mercy of the Americans. George Rogers Clark and other revolutionary soldiers were rewarded for their service with land in Indiana, Kentucky, and Tennessee. More Americans flooded across the Appalachians.

A bad case of land fever swept over the Middle Ground. Daniel Boone was licensed as a surveyor in 1783. Sometimes land speculators sold the same tract

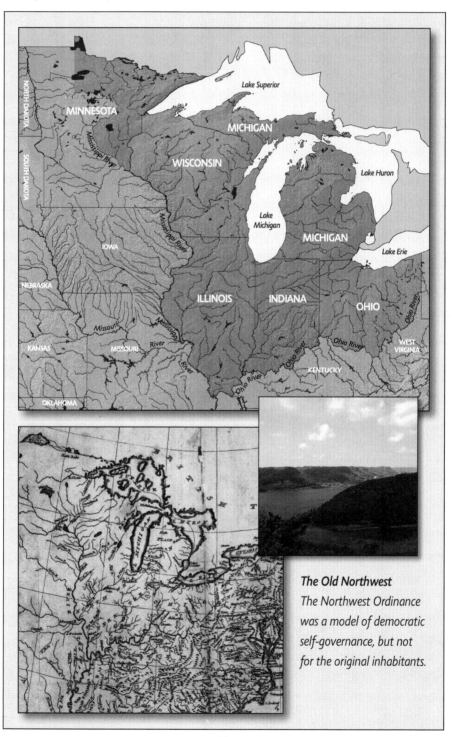

The Old Northwest

The Northwest Ordinance was a model of democratic self-governance, but not for the original inhabitants.

of land to several people. "I am afraid to lose sight of my house lest some invader should take possession," wrote a Kentucky settler, and he wasn't speaking of Indians. As the back water became civilized, the frontier moved farther west. The next generation of explorers and Indian fighters included William Clark.

William Clark was 14 years old in 1784 when his parents took him down the Ohio River to Kentucky, to the land that his older brother had helped win. The Clark family brought its slaves to Kentucky and settled down to raise corn for food and tobacco for profit.

The new nation was faced with the problem that had stumped Britain: regulating settler-Indian relations. The Treaty of Hopewell in 1785 set boundaries on lands for the Cherokees. Nanye-hi was introduced at the treaty council as "one of our beloved women...who has borne and raised up warriors." She spoke hopefully as the treaty was concluded: "I am fond of hearing that there is a Peace, and I hope you have now taken us by the hand in real friendship."

U.S. citizens were required to move out of the reserved areas, and the tribes were given permission to punish trespassers. The Trade and Intercourse Acts of 1790 provided that the federal government would negotiate treaties and pay compensation. Congress passed laws prohibiting Americans from buying land directly from Indians, selling them alcohol, or squatting on territories that were the subject of treaty negotiations. President Washington established a $500 reward for the apprehension of "lawless and wicked persons" who had invaded and burned down a Cherokee town and murdered several residents.

It was mostly lip service. Federal policy was always ambivalent, teetering between the uneasy consciences of whites already in secure possession of land and the hopes, fears, and greed of those who were not. The revolution was fought in part so that every white man would be free to settle on Indian land. Settlers violated every treaty and, sooner or later, the federal government acquiesced. Sometimes, though, federal officials took their jobs seriously. At a peace conference in 1793, when an over mountain militia attacked both Cherokees and white negotiators, the officials regained control and successfully pleaded for the lives of the residents of a Cherokee town.

Along the Ohio River and across the Cumberland Gap, Indians killed whole families, but the settlers kept coming. In 1786, George Rogers Clark extracted a Shawnee concession of land northwest of the Ohio River, contrary to the promises made at the end of Lord Dunmore's War. The new treaty did not put an end to the violence. Whites and Indians continued raiding and murdering on both sides of the river.

When Kentuckians raided Shawnees in Ohio and stole their horses, Boone insisted on returning them. He then led a force across the Ohio River, intending to take Indians hostage to exchange for white captives. Two of the prisoners were leaders of the Shawnee peacemaking faction. One was a sister of Cornstalk. The other was Moluntha. Moluntha surrendered himself and his family while waving an American flag and a copy of the treaty. After chatting pleasantly with his friend Daniel Boone, the old chief extended his hand to Hugh McGary. "Was you in the Battle at Blue Licks?" demanded McGary, who was one of the hotheads behind that ill-conceived military action. Moluntha hadn't been at Blue Licks, but was not fluent in English, and nodded pleasantly. McGary promptly split the chief's head open with a hatchet. Simon Kenton, a close friend of Daniel Boone, had to be restrained from killing McGary on the spot. McGary was courtmartialed and lost his rank, but there was no criminal proceeding.

McGary had been driven by vengeance ever since he found the body of his stepson, murdered by Indians, and watched his wife, the boy's mother, turn inward and die in her grief. Daniel Boone might have chosen the path of blind revenge after the deaths of his sons, but he didn't. He was a militia commander, but he treated prisoners humanely. He still had Indian friends. He wanted control of their land, but respected their cultures and their lives. Boone's humanity foreshadowed William Clark in some ways, but William Clark was no Quaker.

Age 19 in 1789, William Clark took up the fight. He joined the Kentucky militia, becoming an Indian fighter, like so many other American heroes. The militia came upon a group of Indian families. "We fir'd on them," Clark reported. "The other party fired....Kill'd 4 men 4 squaws." In very different circumstances, a squaw named Sacagawea would become Clark's friend fifteen years later. ("Squaw" was often used by whites as a derogatory term, but not always. It was the Algonkian word for woman.)

The land that was being conquered in the name of civilization was already full of Indian corn fields and log cabins. "Cut down all the corn about 50 acres and Burned the Town about 35 houses," wrote William Clark. Throughout the Ohio River Valley, the Americans burned these works of civilization, driving Indians into hunger and poverty.

A number of tribes formed an alliance, including the Shawnees and a young scout named Tecumseh. The Shawnees and Miamis won a bloody and temporary victory in 1791, slaughtering the wounded as the Americans fled. These tribes were led by the Shawnee Blue Jacket, an adopted white who called Daniel Boone his friend, and the Miami Little Turtle, respected in peace and war by all sides. This defeat brought the United States to the bargaining table. Talks failed.

In 1794, at the Battle of Fallen Timbers in Ohio, it was the Americans' turn to defeat the Shawnees. Young Lieutenant Clark fought on one side and young Tecumseh on the other. The Shawnees had British-Canadian allies, as the Great Lakes area was still disputed between the United States and Great Britain. Translation services were provided by a Delaware Indian educated at the College of New Jersey (later Princeton). When the battle turned against the Indians, the British commander locked them out of his fort.

The Indian alliance was defeated. "We raised corn like the whites," lamented Little Turtle, "but now we are poor hunted deer." With their corn fields destroyed, dependent on American rations, Indians moved into temporary buildings outside Fort Greenville in Ohio. "[W]hen Drunk (as they are often)" wrote William Clark, "Cut a number of antick tricks, Such as are verry amuseing to us." Leaders of several tribes came to the fort for a treaty council in 1795.

Little Turtle and Blue Jacket came to negotiate. Little Turtle's wife died during the treaty council, and the commanding general had her buried with military

Chief Little Turtle of the Miamis
After losing the fight to keep his people's land in the Old Northwest, Chief Little Turtle promised that, as the last to sign the treaty, he would be the last to break it.

honors. Then the Americans demanded 25,000 square miles of territory. With their people facing starvation, the chiefs agreed. Little Turtle was the last to sign the treaty, promising that he would then be the last to break it. The Indians were invited to celebrate the Treaty of Greenville with "a little drink."

Little Turtle did not drink. He did accept an invitation to meet President Washington in Philadelphia, the nation's first capital. There, like Uttamatamakin in London, the chief contemplated power that he could not overcome and a world where he did not belong: "One makes shoes, another hats, a third sells cloth....I say to myself, which of all these things can you do? Not one." Years later, Little Turtle met George Rogers Clark. "General, we have met often in war – never before in peace," the chief said to the Revolutionary War hero. "I perceive that you, like myself, are getting old. We must be content that it is so...."

Thus were Illinois, Ohio, and Indiana secured so that white farmers could build a new breadbasket on the ruins of the old. Defeated Shawnees moved west, encroaching on the hunting grounds of the Osage and Kansas tribes along the Missouri River.

These were the strange parallel tracks of federal Indian policy: make treaties, defend the settlers who broke the treaties, and all the while cast about for less bloody solutions, for federal policy was never to exterminate all Indians. In 1787, Congress adopted the Northwest Ordinance to organize the Old Northwest territories and guide them to self-governance and eventually statehood. The ordinance was a model of democratic self-governance. It included the directive that "The utmost good faith shall always be observed towards the Indians; their lands and property shall never be taken from them without their consent...."

Enter a soldier seeking conquest without bloodshed. Henry Knox was known as the Ox for his size, strength, and "fat ass," to quote the Father of our Country. He was one of George Washington's most trusted officers during the Revolutionary War, a husky young bookseller turned military genius. George Washington became president in 1789, and Knox became America's first Secretary of War. With some realism, Indian affairs were considered a matter for the Department of War, and that's what it was called, with the same realism, before it became the Department of Defense.

Knox, like John Rolfe before and William Clark after, believed that Indians and whites could live in peace, provided that Indians became "civilized." Civilization meant farming on private parcels. The farming tribes, no matter how settled, also relied on hunting and, to some extent, regarded land as tribal property. Open hunting land was incompatible with private land sales. Civilized Indians would not hold on to tribal hunting land, Knox reasoned; that land would be surveyed and put on the market. Assimilation but not murder: that defined a decent white man at the time. It was Knox who made sure that the Cherokees had plows and cotton seed, drawing them into the slave-based plantation economy. President Washington embraced his friend's idea of peace through civilization.

"[W]e wish you to live in peace, to increase in numbers, to learn to labor as we do and furnish food for your ever increasing numbers, when the game shall have left you," President Thomas Jefferson would tell a delegation of Old Northwest Indians in 1809, continuing the argument that communal hunting lands were a vestige of a primitive civilization and therefore should be sold to whites. "In time you will be as we are: you will become one people with us; your blood will mix with ours: and will spread with ours over this great island."

What Jefferson really sought was the erasure of tribal identity in order to get rid of tribal land claims. Few members of the Virginia elite after John Rolfe had been willing to mix their blood with Indians. That prejudice existed all over the new nation. In the 1820s, two young Cherokee cousins attending a missionary school in Connecticut would fall in love with two young white women. The young men were John Ridge and Elias Boudinot. The couples married amid an uproar. One bride was derided as a "squaw" – not the neutral use of the word – and the other was burned in effigy by a mob led by her own brother. Much later, these two men would lead the Cherokee treaty party that was ready to escape the empty promise of the civilization policy by moving west, across the Mississippi River.

The Mississippi River would become the gateway to "Indian country" when the Cherokees and other tribes were forced from their homes in the 1830s. In the years of the revolution and early republic, the Mississippi still formed the boundary between land-hungry Americans to the east and French traders to the west. This was the Louisiana Territory that France had traded to Spain in 1763. The French, by and large, did not want to push Indians off their land; they wanted to trade for furs. Louisiana remained under Spanish control until 1804, lightly populated by French traders and lightly garrisoned by Spanish soldiers.

In 1764, two young Frenchmen named Auguste and Pierre Choteau had been sent by their stepfather to build a trading post at the point where the Mississippi River meets the Missouri River. So the city of St. Louis and the Choteau dynasty were born and became part of a long history of migration and commerce on the Missouri River. Local historians in Choteau, Montana, say that one can still see traces of the Great North Trail, where the first Americans traveled south along an ice-free corridor east of the Rocky Mountains during the last Ice Age. The Choteau family would become rich on the beaver fur trade along the Missouri River.

St. Louis would be the starting point for Lewis and Clark's voyage up the Missouri and for Sacagawea's last journey. In St. Louis, William Clark would become guardian of Sacagawea's children. There, as Superintendent of Indian Affairs, he would participate in the forced relocation of Indians across the Mississippi River.

During the Revolutionary War era, St. Louis was still beyond the colonies' grasp. Americans traded with Indians along the Mississippi River, but with unease on all sides. Some of the Indians trading along the Mississippi were members of tribes engaged in warfare farther north. In 1790, Cherokees and Shawnees approached an American military trading ship, waving a white flag of truce; when they were invited onboard, they killed the officers.

"We perceive in them the cunning of the Rattle snake who caresses the Squirrel he intends to devour," said a Chickasaw chief. He was right. An explicit goal of American trading policy was to make Indians so dependent on a market economy that they would sell land to gain cash. Government trading posts were set up to further that goal and to ensure that the immediate profits of trade accrued to Americans, rather than European rivals. Lieutenant William Clark was sent to the Chickasaws on a trading mission in 1793 and came back with Chickasaw scouts, demonstrating for the first time his potential as a diplomat as well as a fighter.

In 1795, Spain and America were maneuvering against each other for control of the lower Mississippi River and access to New Orleans and the Gulf of Mexico. Spain stuck a toe across the river and built a fort at Chickasaw Bluffs (now Memphis, Tennessee) on the east side of the river, the American side. William Clark was sent to investigate. The Spanish commander said he had bought the land directly from the Chickasaws. As the 18th century approached the 19th, New Orleans was opened to American trade, but was then closed, prompting American interest in acquiring that vital link to world commerce.

Lieutenant Clark resigned from the army in 1796 and returned to Kentucky. His brother George was now deep in alcoholism and debt. Traveling on horse-back, William arranged for the sale of much of George's land to pay his debts.

These journeys saw the young Indian fighter camping among the Delaware Indians and visiting St. Louis, where he met the Choteau family.

The tobacco plantation owned by the Clarks' father remained intact for several more years, as did the slave workforce that made it profitable. William took a flatboat full of tobacco down the Mississippi to New Orleans in 1798. In 1799, Kentucky held a constitutional convention and considered outlawing slavery; the idea was voted down by the landed slave owners who dominated the convention.

In 1801, Clark traveled east through the Cumberland Gap on family business, stopping in Fincastle, Virginia, where he met the Hancock family, his future in-laws. His future wife was 9 years old. In Washington, President Thomas Jefferson and his secretary, Meriwether Lewis, were settling into the White House.

In 1800, Spain agreed to hand Louisiana back to France, effective in 1802. To protect American commerce on the Mississippi River, President Jefferson instructed his envoy in France to offer to buy New Orleans. French diplomats surprised the American negotiator by offering to sell not just New Orleans but all of Louisiana. On May 2, 1803, the United States bought Louisiana from France for $15 million. The nation nearly doubled in size, adding all the land between the Mississippi and the Rocky Mountains, comprising all or part of sixteen states.

Both free blacks and slaves were living in St. Louis at that time, side by side with Spaniards, French, Indians, and *metis* (mixed French-Indians). Now Americans came in large numbers from Virginia and Kentucky, seeking land not worn out by tobacco, bringing their human property. Missouri would be admitted to the union as a slave state, although it would not secede during the Civil War.

Meriwether Lewis and William Clark were soon sent to explore the Louisiana Purchase. They were in St. Louis preparing for their expedition on March 9, 1804, when the Spanish flag was lowered and the French flag was raised. The next day, the American flag took its place. The frontier had moved from the Mother of Presidents to the Father of Waters. The land and people to the west awaited conquest. It started with a journey that envisioned empire but shunned murder.

Chapter 6

A Voyage of Discovery

"In all your intercourse with the natives, treat them in the most friendly and conciliatory manner which their own conduct will admit."

Thomas Jefferson to Meriwether Lewis

*S*acagawea and her baby peer at us from a dollar coin that never caught on – the one you get in change from the postage stamp vending machine. This poor woman from a poor tribe would have been amazed at her posthumous fame.

As with Pocahontas, some basic facts about Sacagawea remain open to challenge, starting with her name. William Clark's journals used variations of "Sah-cah-gar-we-ah" but years later noted the death of "Se car ja we au." Sacagawea with a hard g is close to Sakakawea, which means Bird Woman among the Hidatsa people that kidnapped and adopted her and now remember her as their own. Her native people, the Lemhi Shoshone, pronounce it with a soft g as Sacajawea, meaning Boat Pusher or Boat Launcher, or Saka tza we yaa, meaning Burden. As with Pocahontas, Sacagawea's legacy belongs to more than one people.

Sacagawea probably died young, like Pocahontas, but we will explore the mystery of an old woman who claimed to have accompanied the explorers to the western sea. Unlike Pocahontas, Sacagawea was little known in her lifetime. We know her story because of the papers of William Clark and the journals of the Lewis and Clark expedition.

How the journals came to be is a story in itself. The "writingest" of explorers included eight men who kept journals during the two-year journey. "Your observations are to be taken with great pains & accuracy," instructed President Jefferson, and were to include climate, geography, Indians, minerals, animals and plants – "especially those not known in the U.S." Clark's journal entries used a favorite phrase, "We proceeded on," capturing the spirit of perseverance in the face of hardship.

When the expedition returned to St. Louis in 1806, Lewis kept the original journals, planning to publish an official account; they were with him when he died, apparently by his own hand, in 1809. "[W]hat will become of his paprs?" was one of Clark's first reactions to the death of his genuinely cherished friend. Only months earlier, Clark had named his first child Meriwether Lewis Clark.

Fortunately, Clark was able to retrieve the journals, and arranged for a young lawyer named Nicholas Biddle to edit them. As well as working from the journals,

Biddle interviewed Clark, and was assisted by a young expedition member, Private George Shannon. The result was a *History of the Expedition,* published in 1814. The original journals were published much later, in multiple volumes and one-volume summaries. None of these editions paid much attention to the young woman with the baby on her back.

Then Sacagawea was rediscovered by historians interested in the voices of native people and women. Her role was exaggerated. Sacagawea was "the principal guide of the expedition and back again," according to a 1969 children's encyclopedia. In fact, she was an interpreter, not a guide, although she occasionally helped identify a landmark, and helped the expedition in many other ways. The true story is impressive enough.

Why the expedition? Partly to explore the Louisiana Purchase. But it was in the works earlier. Colonizing inward from the Atlantic and Pacific, the European powers looked for routes across the continent, starting with Balboa's crossing of the Isthmus of Panama. Alexander Mackenzie crossed the Canadian Rockies to the Pacific in 1792. Always, they looked for a water route – a Northwest Passage. There isn't one, not below the Arctic. Lewis and Clark would prove that once and for all.

Thomas Jefferson had broached an expedition to the Pacific with George Rogers Clark while William Clark was still a boy. The Spanish, Russians, and English had explored the Pacific Northwest and its rich potential in furs while the new republic was getting on its feet. The United States soon joined that quest. In 1790, the American Captain Robert Gray sailed from Boston "round the horn" – Cape Horn, the tip of South America – and up the Pacific coast. He met up with the English Captain Vancouver, arriving at the island that now bears Vancouver's name. In 1792, Captain Gray saw the mouth of a great river and named it for his ship, the *Columbia Rediviva.* Gray's first meeting with the Indians of the Pacific Northwest was peaceful. These were apparently the first white people the Indians had seen, but fear quickly gave way to trade: salmon and furs for cloth and metal. Once again, the whites were few in number at the start, and it looked to the prosperous Chinook tribes like a profitable arrangement.

In January, 1803, a few months before France agreed to the Louisiana Purchase, President Jefferson secretly asked Congress to appropriate $2,500 for a voyage to explore a route of commerce across the whole continent. Funds secured, Jefferson appointed his secretary Meriwether Lewis to organize the expedition. Thus, the Lewis and Clark expedition began taking shape before the

Louisiana Purchase was completed. With Louisiana in American hands, the expedition took on new importance. The western borders of the new territory were hazy. Lewis and Clark's trip would map the vast region.

President Jefferson was also thinking ahead about bolstering America's claim in the places we now call Oregon and Washington. Under the prevailing view that some "civilized" nation would claim the Pacific Northwest, the question was whether it would be England or the United States. The expedition would add "right of exploration" of the Pacific Northwest to the "right of discovery" of Captain Gray's visit to the Columbia River.

A commercial passage to the Pacific, the beaver trade, mapping and securing the Louisiana Territory, building claims to the Pacific Northwest – the expedition had political and economic goals well beyond simple exploration. But it was also a voyage of natural science and anthropology. Thomas Jefferson's interest in knowledge for its own sake was genuine.

It was also to be a voyage of diplomacy with Indian tribes. Lewis and Clark carried medals to distribute to Indian chiefs. On one side was a picture of Jefferson; on the other, the words "peace and friendship," a picture of a handshake, and a peace pipe crossing a tomahawk. They carried gifts: blue beads (used as money), red paint, brass kettles, bronze buttons, knives, scissors, fishhooks, needles, mirrors, textiles. And whiskey. These gifts had two purposes: creating goodwill and advertising the benefits of trading with Americans. "In all your intercourse with the natives, treat them in the most friendly and conciliatory manner which their own conduct will admit," the president instructed Lewis.

We have heard this before. Of course, this was the same Jefferson who had suggested extermination or removal during the American Revolution, noting that "The same world would scarcely do for them and us." Somehow Americans could convince themselves that things would be different: the Ohio was for farming but the Missouri was for trade.

When President Jefferson appointed Lewis to lead the expedition, Lewis in turn sought out another Virginian as co-captain. This was his friend from the army: William Clark. Lewis had served briefly under Clark's command. If Clark would join the expedition, with "it's fatiegues, it's dangers and it's honors," Lewis wrote to Clark, "believe me there is no man on earth with whom I should feel equal pleasure in sharing them as with yourself." Thus deepened a friendship and began a legendary partnership. Technically, Lewis was a captain and Clark a lieutenant, but Lewis held Clark out as a captain, his equal in all respects, for two years.

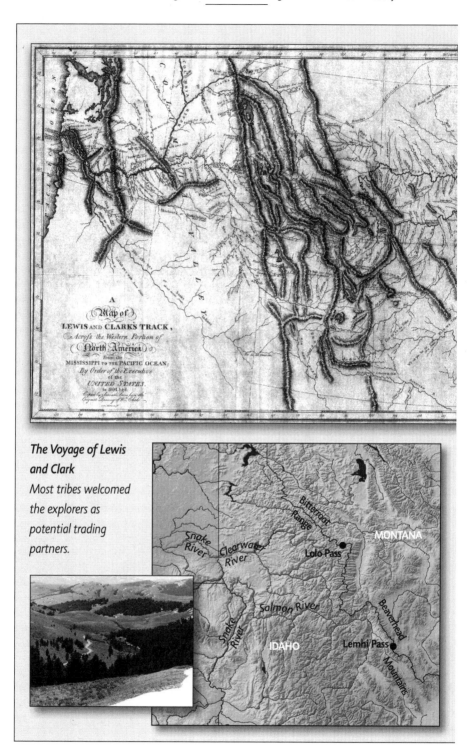

The Voyage of Lewis and Clark

Most tribes welcomed the explorers as potential trading partners.

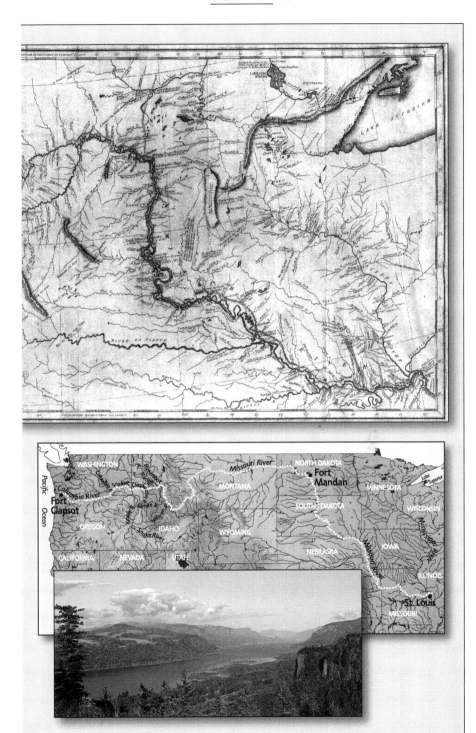

Meriwether Lewis stopped at the foundry in Harper's Ferry (in today's West Virginia) in the summer of 1803 to collect knives, rifles, bullet molds, spare parts, and metal trade goods as gifts for the Indians he would meet. Then he proceeded to Pittsburgh to get the keelboat to transport goods down the Ohio River. Clark, meanwhile, started recruiting men in Louisville, Kentucky and at army posts in the lower part of the Northwest Territory. The captains met in Louisville and continued to where the Ohio River met the Mississippi, then on to St. Louis. Throughout the spring of 1804, Lewis and Clark were in St. Louis, assembling supplies, boats, and men into the Corps of Discovery.

Lewis and Clark had available a few maps of the Missouri River, including the location of Mandan villages, Sioux hunting grounds, and the Shoshones, who lived in the Rocky Mountain ranges and the Great Basin to the west of the Rockies. While in St. Louis, Clark cultivated friendships with the Choteau brothers, who knew the fur trade and the tribes on the two great rivers that had made them rich. "A good portion of the trip," wrote an Indian historian, "merely followed paths already well established." Both Plains and Pacific Northwest tribes had dealt with Europeans; Lewis and Clark would encounter people of second and perhaps third generation French-Indian heritage. A French explorer had met the Mandans of North Dakota in 1738 and explored as far west as the Shoshone country of the eastern Rocky Mountains.

The Shoshone country marked the start of the true unknown: the Rockies and the Great Basin to the west. That is where Sacagawea would help. But she was not yet with the corps when it set out from St. Louis.

One thing the explorers didn't bring was an appreciation of the importance of the river in the hearts of its original inhabitants. White Americans were a people on the move. Their institutions were portable. Indian cultures were, and are, grounded in the land.

The Corps of Discovery started with about forty men and one dog, a water-loving Newfoundland belonging to Lewis. One man died early in the journey, probably of appendicitis. A few were sent back with specimens and messages during the first year. Part of the Corps was under U.S. Army discipline; young men in St. Louis eagerly volunteered for the adventure. Others were civilian employees, including Frenchmen and metis valued for their knowledge of river travel, Indian languages, and wilderness survival.

One member of the Corps was neither an employee nor a volunteer. Clark brought York, his "servant," as southerners called the slave assigned to personally attend to his master. York had been Clark's slave since they were children playing together. After the expedition, York would ask for his freedom and Clark would respond with extremely harsh treatment. At the moment, however, York must have felt the same sense of adventure as the rest of the Corps.

The Corps of Discovery started out in May 1804, in a keelboat and two pirogues (boats with sails and oars). They traveled north on the Missouri River. That's the upstream direction. They rowed, poled, and walked on shore or in the shallows, pulling the boats by rope.

Now the American invasion reached the Plains, a land that had been fundamentally changed by the Spanish invasion. When Columbus made his second voyage in 1493, he brought horses. There were no horses in the Americas before European contact. Previously, the peoples of the Plains had lived by a combination of farming and hunting. The horse changed everything. The mounted hunters and warriors of Hollywood westerns – the nomadic Sioux, Cheyenne, and Crow with their moveable *tipis* – were the descendants of settled farmers. Their ancestors were raising corn in the American heartland hundreds of years before white men in John Deere caps took over the role.

The tribes along the Missouri River had been devastated by a series of smallpox epidemics between 1780 and 1802, and would be again. Whole villages disappeared. Political relationships were in a state of upheaval. Still, the tribes were open to new ideas and the people who brought them. They had adapted to Spanish horses, French trappers, and English manufactured goods. With a few exceptions, Lewis and Clark were received with hospitality. The meetings were aided by a metis interpreter named George Drouillard. This able frontiersman, who was half-French Canadian and half-Shawnee, knew the sign language that tribes used to communicate across their own language barriers.

From the midwestern heartland along the Platte River to winter camp in North Dakota, Lewis and Clark exchanged hospitality and diplomacy with one tribe after another. The Corps offered gifts of food and trade goods, and a little whiskey. Smallpox had done its work; now alcoholism was working its way upriver. Peace medals, military coats, and American flags were presented to chiefs. The explorers fired their guns in a "traveling medicine show" – remember firing guns to awe the Powhatans?

The diplomatic message to the chiefs, starting with the Oto tribe of Nebraska, was presented through the interpreters. The Spanish and French fathers were gone, replaced by a new father presiding over seventeen council fires. "[T]he great chief of the Seventeen nations, impelled by his parental regard for his newly adopted children on the troubled waters, has sent us to clear the road, remove every obstruction, and make it the road of peace between himself and his red children residing there." The tribes were invited to send delegations to Washington. They were promised the benefits of trade, if only they would make peace among themselves, and not listen to the counsel of "bad birds."

Maybe Clark understood the Indian usage of "father and children." Maybe he was as condescending as he sounded. At any rate, the two captains were ill-informed about the political and economic complexities that stood in the way of peace among the red children.

The speech would be repeated many times, possibly with less confidence when the Corps was hungry, the rich central plains were behind them, and winter food supplies were scarce for everyone. The medals and other gifts were supposed to perform the same function as the Powhatans intended with John Smith's adoption, and as the English intended with Powhatan's coronation: to establish a relationship of sovereign and vassal, a relationship based on mutual interest rather than conquest. In the words of a future great chief and his Red Bolling wife, the tribes would retain self-determination, in all but overarching sovereignty.

In late summer, the Corps of Discovery came to the land of the Sioux, now South Dakota. The Sioux, comprising several related tribes, were well-known for their military strength, and were sought after as allies and trading partners. Sioux was the name given by outsiders to tribes that called themselves Lakota, Dakota, and Nakota. They were among the tribes that had left agriculture behind. Before the century was over, white farmers would take their hunting lands to grow corn again. But the plow wasn't yet on its way.

The Yankton Sioux had longstanding interactions with British, French, and Spaniards, and were eager to talk trade with the newcomers. The Yankton hosted the explorers with a feast of roast dog. Music, dancing, and archery contests welcomed the strangers. Then the hosts got down to business. The women and children were hungry, and what the tribe really needed was guns and ammunition. Lewis promised that they were opening the way for trade boats

Negotiations with the Teton Sioux, in particular the Brule band, were much more tense, and almost led to bloodshed. "A band of the Teton Sioux..., also familiar with white traders but more aggressive in exacting tribute and exerting control over the river, attempted to block passage...," according to Indian historians. "[T]he pirates of the Missouri," Clark called them. Sacagawea wasn't yet with the expedition, to reassure tribes by her very presence with a baby that the expedition's purpose was peaceful. And the Teton Sioux were never known for pacifism.

The Teton Sioux were middlemen in the river trade. They bought manufactured goods that originated in St. Louis from downriver tribes, and then exchanged these goods for food with the Arikara, an upriver farming tribe. That arrangement worked only if they controlled the Upper Missouri.

It was late September 1804 when the expedition set up camp on the Bad River in South Dakota. Unfortunately, the expedition had left a key interpreter with the Yankton Sioux to promote peace with the Omahas. The captains and the Brule chiefs exchanged gifts of meat, and the "traveling medicine show" was performed. Gifts were given to the chiefs, in particular to Black Buffalo. This was in keeping with the Anglo-American belief that there must be one man in charge, and mired the explorers in tribal politics involving chiefs competing to show their strength. The chiefs began demanding more gifts – tribute, in their minds. The captains demonstrated their air guns. They broke out the whiskey – just a little. One of Black Buffalo's rivals, called the Partisan, staggered against Clark in feigned drunkenness and told him the expedition could not pass. Three young warriors seized the pirogue.

"[T]he 2d Chief was verry insolent," wrote Clark of the Partisan. "Stateing he had not receved presents sufficent from us, his justures were of Such a personal nature I felt My self Compeled to Draw my Sword ....Most of the Warriers appeared to have ther Bows strung and took out their arrows from the quiver...."

Lewis readied guns. Black Buffalo ordered the warriors away from the boat. "[T]he pirogue Soon returned with about 12 of our determined men ready for any event," continued Clark. "This movement caused a [number] of the Indians to withdraw at a distance...."

With the chest-pounding on all sides over, the Brule hosted the explorers at a council fire, with a feast of buffalo and dog, ceremonial smoking, music and dancing, and a speech by Black Buffalo, most of which the explorers couldn't understand. The captains rejected the offer of young women as bed partners, although Clark understood that this "curious custom with the Souix" was meant "to Show some acknowledgements...." White men had been encountering this type of hospitality ever since young Powhatan women had entreated John Smith with "love you not me?"

Omaha prisoners held by the Sioux warned the expedition that the Sioux planned to stop the Americans. After three days of uneasy diplomacy, as the expedition prepared to continue upriver, the Brule renewed their demands for tribute, and the Partisan's warriors seized a mooring cable. Clark readied a gun and warriors readied their bows. Once again, Black Buffalo restored calm.

"[W]ith the help of diplomacy, a few gifts, and a very small amount of alcohol, the captains were able to persuade the Sioux to back off," concludes an Indian version. Whether the Brule backed down in response to American firmness or decided there was no harm in letting the small group pass still depends on whom you ask.

Although the Americans did not accomplish their immediate goal of negotiating a trading relationship with the Teton Sioux, "the way was open and stayed that way." A series of events set in motion in Jamestown, which would eventually starve the Sioux and break their power, proceeded on. If those proud warriors had seen what was coming.... But that wasn't the Virginians' intention, not yet, so how could the Sioux foresee that a tug-of-war over river trade was the first skirmish in a battle for survival?

In October 1804, the explorers reached the land of the Arikaras. They noted abandoned villages and fields; smallpox had claimed perhaps three-fourths of their population. Arikara women raised corn, beans and squash for both subsistence and trade; Clark called them "gardners for the Soues." Arikara men hunted buffalo and dealt in horses raised by the Cheyenne, another Plains tribe that had given up farming. The Arikara were descended from Pawnee bands that had migrated north from Nebraska to the Dakotas, putting them in conflict with earlier arrivals, the Mandan and Hidatsa.

The Arikara were hospitable. The explorers distributed the usual gifts, minus whiskey. The Arikaras had long made it clear that alcohol was not welcome. Although many of them were familiar with whites, a black man was something new. York, who was a large man, kept the children in a state of happy fright, chasing them and pretending to be a bear; he "made himself more turribal" than the captains wished. Sexual invitations were plentiful, often with the encouragement of male relations eager to be good hosts. This time the captains did not object. Reflecting the fascination with York as a source of new spiritual powers – or hybrid vigor – the Arikara called him "the Big Medison." One Arikara husband invited York to his lodge, offered his wife, and stood guard outside; he told a member of the expedition who was looking for York that he would have to wait.

However, these hospitable people would not give up their alliance with those "bad birds," the Teton Sioux, and would not make peace with the Mandan and

Hidatsa on American terms. Clark thought the Sioux poisoned the minds of the "Rickeres." A few years later, Arikara warriors would attack white traders, including one who had traveled with the Corps of Discovery.

Six months and 1,600 miles past St. Louis, the Corps stopped for the winter in the region of the Mandan and Hidatsa tribes. The Mandan and Hidatsa lived in separate villages, not without some conflict. They were located near each other for defense against common enemies: the Arikara and the Teton Sioux. Despite population losses caused by smallpox, the Mandan and Hidatsa villages were a hub of trade for both neighboring tribes and French and British fur traders.

In response to the captains' diplomacy, the Mandan chiefs Black Cat and Big White (Sheheke) stated their support for regional peace – as Black Cat said, so that "they now could hunt without fear, and their womin could work in the fields without looking every moment for the enemy." This was hard to achieve in practice. An Arikara-Sioux raiding party attacked Mandan hunters a few weeks later. The captains offered to defend their new hosts, "our Dutifull Chieldren," and were ready to go after their previous hosts. The Mandan chief Big Man explained that the snow was too deep and revenge would have to wait. This gave Clark a chance to remember his diplomatic mission. "Do not get mad with the recares [Arikaras]," he said, "until we [know] if those bad men are countenanced by their nation...."

In anticipation of a North Dakota winter that would fall 40 degrees below zero, the explorers built a winter camp they named Fort Mandan. During the Corps' five-month stay, the Mandan shared the tribe's food stores – sometimes as a gift, sometimes in trade. There was a blacksmith in the Corps, and Indians traded corn for repairs of hoes, guns, and hatchets. When the need for corn became more urgent than the diplomatic mission, the Corps went into the business of manufacturing battle axes.

The explorers and Mandans hunted for buffalo together in the bitter cold. The Indians were fascinated with devices such as the thermometer and the spyglass, and paid careful attention to the methods used in building Fort Mandan. The white men danced reels for the Indians; the Indian told them stories. On New Year's Day, 1805, the explorers celebrated in one of the villages with tambourine, fiddle, and horn, and the Indians gave them gifts of buffalo robes. Lewis had trained as the Corps' medic, and both captains provided medical care for the Indians.

There was sexual hospitality, although Clark once had to intervene to protect a woman who was beaten and stabbed by her husband, who believed that she had slept with a Corps member without his consent. By the end of the winter, Clark recorded that the men were "generally healthy except Venerials complaints...." "Louis Veneri" was a frequent complaint throughout the journey. Lewis treated this ailment with mercury; mercury deposits in the latrines would help an archeologist find one of the expedition's camp sites almost two centuries later.

Living among the Hidatsa was a French Canadian named Toussaint Charbonneau. His ancestor, Olivier Charbonneau, came from France to Montreal in 1659. The patriarch left many descendants, one of whom has written a biography of Sacagawea's son.

Toussaint was born in Quebec province in 1767. The British military victory in Quebec a few years before Toussaint's birth had secured Canada for the British Empire, but the British subject Toussaint Charbonneau spoke French. He became a *voyageur*, a trapper and trader, and worked for the Northwest Fur Company in Canada before settling with the Hidatsa. This move placed him in the Louisiana Territory, held by Spain but as French as ever.

All over North America, voyageurs married Indian women. Toussaint had two Shoshone wives – "Squars" (squaws) in Clark's words. One of them was named Sacagawea.

Chapter 7

A Baby on Her Back

"*Your woman who accompanied you*
[on] that long dangerous
and fatigueing route...diserved
a greater reward for her...services...
than we had in our power to give her..."

William Clark to Toussaint Charbonneau, August 20, 1806

*S*acagawea's people were Shoshone, a group of tribes also known as the Snakes, whose lands include the Snake River. Her tribe is now called the Lemhi Shoshone; in the early 1800s, they were a group of bands that called themselves the *Agaideka* or Salmon Eaters. By the Salmon River, in the place we now call Idaho, the Lemhi fished, hunted, and gathered plant foods, mixing older practices with the new horse culture of the Plains.

In the century before Sacagawea's birth, several factors combined to impoverish the Shoshone. Sacagawea's people embraced the horse, but they had less access to guns and buffalo than did the Plains tribes, which crowded against the Shoshone as one tribe pushed another west. They also had "suffered much by the small pox," if not directly, then by the devastation the disease wrought on their trading networks. The combined effect of these dislocations left Sacagawea's people without a reliable supply of food.

A girl on the cusp of womanhood – an encounter with foreigners – kidnapping – adoption – marriage to an older man – young motherhood – long journeys. But the foreigners who kidnapped Sacagawea were Indians. Like Pocahontas, she was about 12 years old when her life changed. Around 1800, Hidatsa or Blackfeet raiders attacked a Lemhi foraging party. The men were killed. Several women and children, including Sacagawea, were captured.

A Hidatsa oral tradition suggests that "Sakakawea" was actually born among them. That's inconsistent with the fact that Sacagawea spoke the Shoshone language and with her joy when she returned to her native land and people. However, the existence of this oral tradition is a hint that she was adopted rather than enslaved. In fact, the Hidatsa did not practice chattel slavery. Adoption was rebirth. Sacagawea apparently became one of their own.

It's not clear how she came to be Charbonneau's wife, when she was about 16 and he was 37. There is an oral tradition that Charbonneau either bought her or won her in a gambling game. If so, we may draw a comparison to modern sex trafficking. We may also ponder the role of chance in the faces presented to history, remembering that John Smith was selected by lot to explore the river that led him to Pocahontas. However, there is no solid evidence for the gambling story.

If Sacagawea was an adopted member of her new tribe – as suggested by the Hidatsa tradition that sees Sacagawea as one of their own – she would have enjoyed the respected status of Hidatsa women. Indian women, as a rule, could choose their own mates, with advice from older and wiser relations, who probably saw a trader as a good provider. If Charbonneau "bought" her, this could have been a bride price. It might even have been a marriage of love. That seems a little doubtful, in light of that other Shoshone wife, but polygamy was widespread. As for the age difference, that was common among both whites and Indians. Sex slave to a man twice her age, adopted daughter in a good match, or young woman in love? The least dramatic story – a pragmatic but unforced marriage – makes the most sense.

With one of his wives six months pregnant, Toussaint Charbonneau approached Lewis and Clark in November and offered a package deal: his services as an interpreter, aided by one of his Shoshone wives. The captains had already hired one interpreter who was living among the Mandan that winter: the metis trader Rene Jessaume. Jessaume, with the help of a dead rattlesnake, would soon help Sacagawea's pregnancy reach a successful conclusion.

Sacagawea give birth to a "fine boy" on February 11, 1805 at Fort Mandan. As Lewis recorded, "this was the first child which this woman had borne, and, as is common in such cases her labor was tedious and the pain violent." Lewis, whose medical training probably didn't include obstetrics, tried to help. On Jessaume's advice, Lewis crumbled two snake rattles into water and gave the potion to the

Sacagawea imagined
Unlike Pocahontas, Sacagawea lived and died in obscurity, and no image was made during her lifetime.

suffering woman. "Whether this medicine was truly the cause or not, I shall not undertake to determine, but I was informed that she had not taken it more than ten minutes before she brought forth." The baby was named Jean-Baptiste Charbonneau.

As the winter drew to an end, Toussaint signed on as an interpreter. The travelers had built canoes to replace the keelboat as the river narrowed. On April 7, 1805, thirty-three people proceeded up the Missouri – now including a young woman carrying an 8-week-old baby on her back.

At the same time, the keelboat was sent back with notes, specimens, and a party of chiefs and warriors representing several tribes. The Indians were escorted all the way to the nation's capitol, where Thomas Jefferson hosted them on New Year's Day, 1806. We are "united in one family with our red brethren here," the president told them. Then he reinforced the message of sovereignty: the Spanish, French, and English were gone. "We are strong, we are numerous as the stars in the heavens, & we are all gun-men." Like the Powhatan delegation in London, these Indians saw it all plainly: they were outmatched. And, like the Powhatan delegation, they fell prey to illness; an Arikara chief died.

But strength and numbers were not the case on the Upper Missouri; the explorers needed help. Charbonneau spoke the Siouan languages of the northern plains; Sacagawea, her native Shoshonean. The captains already knew why they would need her skills: her people lived near the headwaters of the Missouri. With a language bridge, they could negotiate to buy horses, in order to cross the mountains when the mighty river became a trickle; they could also learn about trails and perhaps the secret to the long-sought water route. Imagine the translation process: English to French, French to Siouan, Siouan to Shoshonean, and all the way back again.

Charbonneau was hired – not Sacagawea. It wouldn't have been her money, anyway. A man controlled his wife's wages in 19th century America. Under the common law, husband and wife were one, and that one was the man. In this respect, the westward sweep of Anglo-American civilization was not at its best.

As well as translating, Sacagawea could recognize edible plants, such as the difference in flowers that separates the camas with the edible root from its cousin, the "death camas." The preferred foods were venison and buffalo – including Charbonneau's specialty, cooked intestines – but plants were an essential supplement to uncertain luck in hunting. As soon as the party stopped for the night after leaving Fort Mandan, "the squaw busied herself in searching for the wild artichokes," reported Lewis. Later she showed Clark "a bush something like the Current, which she said bore a delicious froot."

Little Baptiste made a difference too. No Indian tribe would send a mother and baby into danger, so Sacagawea and her son were living proof that this was not a war party. During the coming months of fatigue, fear, cold, and hunger, there would be some comforts of home: Pierre Cruzatte's fiddle, Lewis' dog, and a "fine boy."

North and then west they traveled, through today's Montana, the land of beaver, buffalo, and grizzly bear – "the white bear," Lewis and Clark called it. Game was plentiful. They struggled upstream against the spring current through "seens of visionary inchantment," the beautiful White Rocks region and the dangerous white water.

Sacagawea showed her calm courage when the boat she was riding in almost capsized, and essential supplies floated into the river. "[T]he Indian woman to whom I ascribe equal fortitude and resolution, with any person onboard at the time of the accident, caught and preserved most of the light articles which were washed overboard," wrote Lewis. This, of course, with a baby on her back.

May was ending. Finding the Shoshone and their horses was much on the explorers' minds. They came to an abandoned Indian camp near a river Clark named Judith, possibly for his future wife. Clark had last seen Julia Hancock, nicknamed Judy, when she was only 9 years old; he probably named the river after he returned. At this camp, "The Indian woman with us ex[a]mined the mockersons," wrote Lewis, "and informed us that they were not of her nation the Snake Indians, but she believed they were some of the Indians who inhabit the country on this side of Rocky Mountains and North of the Missoury...."

They saw the remains of a buffalo jump, a hundred or more rotting carcasses of buffalo that had been driven over a cliff by Indian hunters. "[I]n this manner the Indians of the Missouri destroy vast herds of buffaloe at a stroke," wrote Lewis in disgust, unable to foresee the near-extinction for which he was paving the way.

There's no evidence that Sacagawea helped decide which way to go when they encountered a major junction of the Missouri. Which was the great river? The Corps scouted ahead on both rivers, analyzed currents and sediment, studied the incomplete map of a fur company surveyor, and finally made the correct choice. Lewis named the other river for Maria, a "lovely fair one" of his acquaintance.

Approaching the Great Falls of the Missouri River in June, they got ready to portage, carrying the canoes and essential supplies, and caching what was too big to carry. Sacagawea became seriously ill and Lewis took care of her. "[T]his gave me some concern as well as for the poor object herself, then with a young child in her arms," wrote Lewis, "as from the consideration of her being our only dependence for a friendly negociation with the Snake Indians on whom we depend for horses to assist us in our portage from the Missouri to the columbia river." Soon, she was "much better" and ate "as heartily as I am willing to permit her of broiled buffaloe well seasoned with pepper and salt and rich soope of the same meat."

At the end of June, the Charbonneau family and Clark were nearly caught in a flash flood. On this occasion, the young mother was paralyzed with fear, and Clark and Toussaint had to pull her and the baby to safety. All survived, although they lost the rawhide cradle in which Baptiste had been traveling, and other valuable belongings.

In July, with the portage over the Great Falls completed, the Corps continued through Montana. The short high country spring was crowding into summer. The river narrowed, and the banks were full of sharp rocks and prickly pear, which cut through the moccasins that had long since replaced worn-out shoes. Lewis called the area "the gates of the Rocky Mountains," adding that "the prickly pear is now in full blume and forms one of the beauties as well as the greatest pests of the plains." They saw elk, bighorn sheep, geese, red choke cherries, purple currants, and plenty of "musquetose and knats."

They were entering Sacagawea's country. "The Indian woman recognizes the country and assures us that this is the river on which her relations live, and that the three forks are at no great distance. this peice of information has cheered the sperits of the party," wrote Lewis. They soon arrived at the Three Forks of the Missouri River, and none too soon: "the men complain of being much fortiegued. their labour is excessively great."

The Three Forks was the spot where Sacagawea had been kidnapped. "Our present camp is precisely on the spot that the Snake Indians were encamped at the time the Minnetares [Hidatsa] ...first came in sight of them five years since. from hence they retreated..and concealed themselves..., the Minnetares pursued, attacked them, killed 4 men 4 women a number of boys, and mad[e] prisoners of all the females and four boys, Sah-cah-gar-we-ah o[u]r Indian woman was one of the female prisoners taken at that time...." Sergeant John Ordway's journal added, "She tells us that she was taken in the middle of the River as she was crossing at a Shole place to make hir ascape."

The captains decided to proceed up the middle fork, which they named the Jefferson River. The men struggled with the boats as they gained elevation and approached the source of the Missouri through ever-narrowing rivers. This was the second great spine of North America, the set of mountain ranges collectively called the Rockies. The explorers were now beyond the Louisiana Purchase, but colonial claims on the other side were ill-defined outside of Spanish California and New Mexico.

This was the sparse homeland of a tribe on the margin of the rich Plains. There were "no buffalow in the Mountains." There were old buffalo bones and droppings, "but we have long since lost all hope of meeting with that animal in those mountains." This was an ominous sign of depleted resources: "if any Indians can subsist in the form of a nation in these mountains with the means they have of acquiring food we can also subsist." In fact, the Lemhi were preparing to descend to the Three Forks for the buffalo hunting season, but at the moment they were close to starvation.

It was now crucial to find the Shoshone and their horses. "If we do not find them or some other nation who have horses I fear the successful issue of our voyage will be very doubtful or at all events much more difficult...." The explorers saw signs of recently abandoned Shoshone camps, but the Shoshone were deliberately elusive, fearing raids from the Hidatsa, Blackfeet, and Atsina (Gros Ventre). The captains hoisted small flags in the boats to show that "we were not Indians, nor their enemies."

Injuries accumulated among the exhausted group, "a lame crew." On August 8, Sacagawea identified a high point called the Beaver's Head and told the explorers they were near her people's summer grounds. The Beaver's Head, she explained, was near the place where the Shoshone were accustomed to cross the Continental Divide, now called Lemhi Pass in Montana. As the narrowing waters forked again, the Corps proceeded up the Beaverhead River.

Scouting with a small group, Lewis encountered an Indian mounted on an "eligant" horse. The captain made a sign of friendship, and called out "tab-ba-bone," which he thought meant "white man," to explain that he was not a member of a hostile tribe. However, the word meant "stranger" or "foreigner" – probably the best the interpreters could come up with. The Indian fled at the sight of the other men; had Sacagawea and little Baptiste been with Lewis at that moment, that would have shown the group's peaceful intentions. Lewis even tried tying small gifts around the necks of the Indians' inquisitive dogs, but the dogs wouldn't cooperate.

Despite this frustration, the Corps was about to reach one of its most important goals: "the most distant fountain of the waters of the Mighty Missouri in surch of which we have spent so many toilsome days and wristless nights," wrote Lewis on August 12. "thus far I had accomplished one of those great objects on which my mind has been unalterably fixed for many years, judge then of the pleasure I felt in allying my thirst with this pure and ice-cold water...." The party had reached the Continental Divide, where the water flows east on one side and west on the other. Two miles below, "McNeal had exultingly stood with a foot on each side of this little rivulet and thanked his god that he had lived to bestride the mighty & heretofore deemed endless Missouri." Descending west, Lewis "first tasted the water of the great Columbia river." The Corps' accomplishment was monumental, but their discovery was of land that was intimately familiar to the Shoshone.

The next day, again without Sacagawea's reassuring presence, Lewis and three men met "three female savages." One ran away. An elderly woman and a girl about 12 years old remained while Lewis advanced. "they appeared much allarmed but saw that we were to near for them to escape by flight. they therefore seated themselves on the ground, holding down their heads as if reconciled to die...." Lewis took the old woman by the hand, raised her up, repeated "tab-ba-bone," and rolled up his sleeve to show his light skin, "for my face and hands which have been constantly exposed to the sun were quite as dark as their own." This reassured the women, and Lewis gave them some small gifts. The old woman called back the young one who had fled, and Lewis "painted their tawny cheeks with some vermillion which with this nation is emblematic of peace." Probably it was Sacagawea who told him that red meant peace.

The women conducted Lewis and his men toward their camp. On the way, "we met a party of about 60 warriors mounted on excellent horses who came in nearly full speed, when they arrived I advanced towards them with the flag leaving my gun with the party about 50 paces behind me." The women confirmed the group's peaceful intentions, and the warriors greeted the explorers warmly. Among them was the "principal chief" Cameahwait. Lewis didn't know it yet, but Cameahwait was Sacagawea's brother. The captain was conducted to the camp, smoked with Cameahwait, and explained the purpose of the journey.

Sacagawea was not there, but she was not the only channel of communication. "The means I had of communicating with these people was by way of Drewyer [Drouillard] who understood perfectly the common language of jestication or signs which seems to be universally understood by all the Nations we have yet seen. it is true that this language is imperfect and liable to error but...the strong parts of the ideas are seldom mistaken." In fact, Lewis was able to broach the all-important question of trading for horses without Sacagawea.

However, "I had mentioned to the chief several times that we had with us a woman of his nation who had been taken prisoner by the Minnetares, and that by means of her I hoped to explain myself more fully than I could do with signs." Sacagawea's presence as a goodwill ambassador was as important as her translation services.

The women and children gathered for their first look at whites. The explorers were hungry, with only flour with them. So were the hosts, with only berries and a little dried salmon. Cameahwait explained the difficulty of passing the mountains "to the great lake where the white men lived as he had been informed." Lewis hoped this "unwelcome" news was "exagerated." The next day, the whites and Indians hunted together, without success.

On the third day, a party of warriors accompanied the explorers back to their camp on the Jefferson River, along with women whom the Corps hoped to employ as porters to carry their gear over Lemhi Pass. Drouillard finally killed a deer, and the famished Indians ate their share raw, guts and all. Clark's group was not where it was supposed to be. The Indians suspected a trap, fearing that the newcomers were allied with their enemies. They were also reluctant to waste a day of the buffalo hunting season. All passed an uneasy night, Lewis reassuring himself that he had told Cameahwait that he and his "brother Chief" were traveling with a "woman of his nation," Cameahwait as yet unaware that this woman was his own sister.

The boats were on their way, delayed as they struggled upstream. That morning, Clark, Charbonneau, and Sacagawea had walked ahead, while Drouillard and an Indian walked downstream looking for them. Then they met. Sacagawea was reunited with her people. She "began to dance and show every mark of the most extravagant joy" as she recognized them, "sucking her fingers at the same time to indicate that they were of her native tribe." There were warm greetings all around, but none warmer than Sacagawea's. One of the women present had been captured in the Hidatsa raid that took Sacagawea, but had escaped. And then Sacagawea recognized the chief, her brother. "she jumped up, ran & embraced him, & threw her blanket over him and cried profusely: The chief was himself moved, though not in the same degree. After some conversation between them she resumed her seat, and attempted to interpret for us, but her new situation seemed to overpower her, and she was frequently interrupted by her tears. After the council was finished the unfortunate woman learnt that all her family were dead except two brothers, one of whom was absent, and a son of her eldest sister, a small boy, who was immediately adopted by her." Lewis also noted that she had been betrothed to an older man, but "as she had had a child by another man....he did not want her."

Now Sacagawea's job as translator began. The captains spoke English to Private Francois Labiche; Labiche spoke French to Charbonneau; Charbonneau spoke Hidatsa to Sacagawea; and Sacagawea spoke Shoshone to Cameahwait. And back again. They talked geography and horses and trade.

Cameahwait wanted guns so that the Lemhi could compete with their enemies on the Plains. The explorers counted only three guns among all the warriors, probably obtained in trade with tribes that traded with Spanish colonies or English fur traders in the Pacific Northwest. They had little or no ammunition. With firearms, "We could then live in the country of the buffalo and eat as our enemies do and not be compelled to hide ourselves in these mountains and live on roots and berries as the bear do," said Cameahwait. The explorers agreed to trade guns for horses. Once again, immediate needs trumped the peacemaking mission.

Cameahwait shared all he knew about the mountains and rivers to the west. Hopes of a navigable water route across the continent were dashed once and for all. The chief explained that the Nez Perce to the west crossed the mountains every year in search of game on the Plains, but that it was a very difficult path, with little game along the way. That was enough for the explorers; they hired a Shoshone guide named Old Toby and prepared to move west. There was a hard frost on August 21. Summer was ending.

Sacagawea, too, proceeded on, without the adopted nephew. We don't know the boy's fate.

As promised, the trails into the Bitterroot Valley of western Montana and through the Bitterroot Mountains to Idaho were almost impassable. On "Some of the worst roads that ever horses passed, our horses frequently fell," wrote Clark. They met the Salish (or Flathead), friends of the Lemhi, but part of a different language group, a hint of the expedition's progress toward the Pacific Northwest. Living with the Salish was a Shoshone boy, captured by raiders and later freed; he joined the Labiche-Charbonneau-Sacagawea translation chain. The Salish were cautious but hospitable. They too needed guns and ammunition. Clark apparently accepted all forms of hospitality: a Salish family named Clarke claimed descent from a Peter Clarke, who was born after this visit.

The Corps stopped at a creek that Clark named Travelers' Rest, where an archeologist has found evidence of the explorers' journey at latrine sites and fire pits. The mercury administered for "Louis Veneri" was one of the clues.

Then came a desperate struggle across Lolo Pass in the Bitterroot Mountains, "the most terrible mountains I ever beheld," wrote Sergeant Patrick Gass. Old Toby took a wrong turn. There was tangled growth and fallen timber. Food was scarce. Snow fell on September 16. "I have been wet and as cold in every part as I ever was in my life," wrote Clark.

The expedition proceeded on and reached a Nez Perce (Choppunnish) camp. Living among the Nez Perce was an old woman who had once been captured by Blackfeet or Atsina and then sold to a trader in Canada. She recalled that she had been treated well by whites and urged the Nez Perce to do the same for the explorers.

The Nez Perce were near enough to the Pacific Northwest and Canadian trading networks to own copper kettles. However, like the other mountain tribes, they were short on guns and ammunition. Communication had to rely on sign language, because the Nez Perce spoke a Sahaptian language of the Pacific Northwest. The Indians drew a map of the rivers of Idaho, and two chiefs agreed to accompany the expedition as translators. With water travel possible again, the Corps built canoes, left their horses in the care of the Nez Perce, and proceeded down the Clearwater River toward the Snake River and finally the Columbia.

Next came the land of salmon. The two Nez Perce chiefs smoothed the way for the Corps to meet the tribes of Idaho and Washington, where some tribes were frightened of the unfamiliar white people. All this changed as they approached the Pacific. The Pacific Coast tribes were used to trading with British, Spanish, Yankee, and Russian ships. The Pacific Northwest trading system extended as far west as the Shoshone, although manufactured goods were scarce in the Shoshone lands far from the coast.

With Indian help, the explorers portaged around falls and navigated through whitewater. The tribes they passed were friendly. Clark attributed this to Sacagawea: "a woman with a party of men is a token of peace." Trading for dried fish, horse meat, and live dogs (for food), the captains gave out peace medals. The river tribes feared "the Snake Indians," probably the Bannocks.

They explorers passed through the Sahaptian region and said goodbye to their Nez Perce guides, who were anxious to avoid trouble with the Chinookan peoples closer to the coast. Now the language barrier was great. Indian theft, with its completely different cultural meaning, put the explorers on guard. Eventually, the captains ordered the men to fire on any Indians who were suspected of stealing guns. It never happened.

"Ocian in view O! The joy." This was Clark's famous journal entry on November 7, although he soon realized that the broad expanse of water was still the Columbia.

Joy turned to misery. "Wet and disagreeable ... rained verry hard ... horriable...." wrote Clark. "Tremendious gusts of wind ..." Late fall and winter are not good times for camping in the Pacific Northwest. Firewood was scarce. Fleas were plentiful. Navigation at the mouth of the Columbia was daunting during the stormy weather. "Those Indians are certainly the best Canoe navigeters I ever Saw," wrote Clark as he watched them handle the swells. The Corps sometimes huddled on the shore for days at a time, wet and miserable, waiting for safer travel conditions. One riverside site is known to this day as "Dismal Niche."

The captains beheld the Pacific Ocean itself in late November. Clark carved on a tree, "William Clark December 3rd 1805. By land from the U. States in 1804 & 1805." For a winter camp, they built wooden structures south of the Columbia River, in today's Oregon. They called the place Fort Clatsop, as they pronounced the name of the nearest Chinookan village; *clatsop* meant "dried salmon." In choosing this site, Lewis and Clark polled every man in the expedition, including York. Sacagawea's vote wasn't tallied but Clark noted "Janey in favour of a place where there is plenty of Potas." She apparently was thinking of *wappato* roots, which Clark called "equal to the Irish potato." This incident has been described as a first for equal participation in an American election. But it was only a brief illusion of equality, especially for York.

Janey was a nickname of affection (if not equality – Clark's brother owned two slaves by that name). The friendship between Sacagawea and Clark showed itself in other ways. On one occasion, Clark admired a robe of sea otter skins so much that Sacagawea let him trade her belt of blue beads for it. During the miserable autumn at Fort Clatsop, "The Squar, gave me a piece of Bread to day made of Some flower She had Cearfully kept for her child." On Christmas Day, when dinner was spoiled elk, spoiled fish, and a few roots, Sacagawea gave Clark "two Dozen white weazils tails." It is a touching parallel to the friendship between young Pocahontas and Captain John Smith.

The fort was not on the ocean, but men were sent to the shore to make salt. There, they reported kindness from the Clatsops. When Clatsops came to trade at the fort, they reported on a dead whale. This was something Sacagawea wanted to see; in fact, she had not yet laid eyes on the Pacific Ocean. When Clark went to visit the salt camp, "the Indian woman was very impo[r]tunate to be permitted to go, and was therefore indulged," wrote Lewis. "she observed that she had traveled a long way with us to see the great waters, and that now that monstrous fish was also to be seen, she thought it very hard she could not be permitted to see either." She got her wish. It was the first week of 1806.

For various reasons, this winter camp was lacking in the rapport that the Corps had shared with their Mandan hosts the previous winter. The Pacific Northwest Indians knew enough English to trade, and the explorers learned some of the Chinookan language. However, years of Indian-white commercial contacts had produced a hybrid culture that the Virginia gentlemen found ugly: cutthroat dealing, complete with English profanity, prostitution, and, of course, theft. The captains allowed Indians into Fort Clatsop to sell food but watched them closely. They did make some friends, such as the Clatsop chief Coboway, whom Lewis described as "friendly and decent," "kind and hospitable." Then they violated their own moral code and stole from him.

At the end of their stay near the coast, desperate for canoes, the Americans decided to steal one from Coboway. Lewis rationalized the canoe theft as pay-back for an earlier Indian theft from a cache of elk meat, for which the Clatsops had made restitution. Worse, Lewis went on about the "treachery" of "savages" in general. It was a stark contrast to the time that he gently painted the faces of frightened Shoshone women, and a dire reminder that the Americans were willing to rationalize stealing Indian resources of far greater value than a canoe.

Clark spent the wet winter drawing a map of their travels, from St. Louis to the Columbia River. All were eager to leave the cold and damp behind, but local Indians warned them that the snow inland would remain deep for months. When they prepared to leave in March, they gave a written report of their journey to Coboway, posting a copy in the fort as well: a written record to support American territorial claims. The Corps had met no European ships or traders. The captains considered and rejected the idea of leaving a party to wait for water passage home. On March 23, they departed by canoe on the rough waters of the Columbia: upstream again, against the spring flood.

Portaging back through the Cascade Mountains, they were harassed by the Watlala Indians, who controlled this key spot. After three Watlalas stole Lewis' dog, the captains ordered the men to shoot thieves. The dog was returned, with an apology from the chief. Deciding to switch from water to land, the captains bought horses, too few and at a high price, purchased after days of haggling and changing terms. This deepened their distrust of the Pacific Northwest peoples.

They found a Nez Perce guide to accompany them on the return. Arriving among the Walla Walla (Walula) Indians of Washington, they found hospitality and a Shoshone woman, "prisoner among those people by means of whome and Sah-cah-gah-weah, Shabono's wife we found the means of converceing with the Wallahwallars." Conversation flowed, horses were purchased, Western medical care was provided, the fiddle was played, and people danced.

Leaving the Walla Walla, "those honest friendly people," they continued east on Indian trails, re-entering the land of the Nez Perce. They received a mixed reception because of disputes within the tribe about its ongoing dealings with the explorers. The Indians had little food to share or sell in this still-freezing season. On May 10, with "the air keen and cold the snow 8 inches deep on the plain," the snow-covered Bitterroot Mountains loomed in the distance.

A meeting of Nez Perce chiefs was the occasion for the "traveling medicine show." Apparently the frozen and hungry explorers hadn't been in any condition to demonstrate American power on the westbound leg of the trip. Now a Shoshone captive of the Nez Perce joined the translation chain. There was talk of trade and peace, and an invitation to send a delegation to the Great Father. An elderly chief recounted feuds between his people and the Shoshone that could be put behind them, and the Walula, Nez Perce, and Shoshone soon declared a truce. But the chiefs still had to protect their people against the Blackfeet and Atsina. The goals were in tension: the Americans wanted inter-tribal peace to promote trade, while the Nez Perce wanted to trade for guns. The traveling medicine show was intended to display American firepower, and the chiefs wanted that power.

Snow held the Corps in place for four weeks. In this unanticipated "winter camp," the personal relationships between travelers and Indians were good, more like Fort Mandan than Fort Clatsop. The captains provided medical care as they had along the whole journey. In mid-June, with the horses that the Nez Perce had kept for them, and with food bought with the remaining trade goods – including buttons cut from the Americans' uniforms – they set out. This was against the advice of the Indians, who refused to provide guides while the snow remained so deep. For once, the Corps had to turn back and wait for better weather. They tried again, with Nez Perce guides who agreed to the task in exchange for guns and ammunition. With these guides, they arrived safely at Travelers' Rest on July 1.

To cover more ground in exploration, the captains now divided the party in two, with Lewis heading north to negotiate with the Blackfeet and Atsina. Sacagawea and Charbonneau went with Clark, the emblem of peace traveling with the calmer of the captains. Lewis and his party ended up in a fight with the Piegan Blackfeet, leaving two Indians dead. This incident at Two Medicine River in Montana was the only killing during the expedition. Four years later, Drouillard would die at the hands of the Blackfeet, part of the ongoing struggle for control of the Upper Missouri and the Plains.

Clark's party, meanwhile, passed through the territory of the Crow Indians, on the Yellowstone River in Montana. These mounted Plains warriors kept out of sight, but managed to steal the expedition's horses in the night.

The captains met as planned on August 12 on the border of Montana and North Dakota, at the mouth of the Yellowstone River. At the Mandan-Hidatsa villages, they tried again to promote peace with the Arikaras in order to break the Arikara alliance with the Sioux. To their frustration, they learned that Hidatsa war parties had attacked not only the Arikara but the Lemhi. Clark pleaded for an end to raids against "the pore defenceless Snake Indians." The Americans persuaded the Mandan chief Sheheke to return with them to Washington. There was widespread reluctance to travel through the land of the Sioux enemies, and women wept as Sheheke departed.

At last, the Corps floated downstream toward St. Louis, noting with excitement the signs of civilization: honeybees and cows. They enjoyed biscuits, chocolate, sugar, and whiskey shared by a trader who had served in the army with Lewis. This host "informed us that we had been long Since given out by the people of the U S Generaly and almost forgotton" but that President Jefferson "had yet hopes of us." The United States had heard no word from the explorers since they had sent messages from Fort Mandan in the spring of 1804. The Corps reached St. Louis on September 22, 1806. Lewis immediately wrote to President Jefferson and Clark to his brother George.

The Corps had traveled over 7,000 miles, returned safely, and would never be "forgotton." They had laid the foundation for a great nation and for genocide. Their accomplishments and the terrible consequences, some intended, some not, hopelessly intertwined, are the story of America.

Chapter 8

My Little Dancing Boy

"[I]f you bring your son Baptiest to me ... I will educate him and treat him as my own child."

William Clark to Toussaint Charbonneau, 1806

*T*he Corps of Discovery completed its journey with Sheheke and his family, but without Sacagawea and hers. The Charbonneau family stayed with the Hidatsa. But only temporarily. During a year and a half, the bachelor Clark had grown to love little Jean-Baptiste. He nicknamed the child "Pomp," short for Pompey, and gave the name "Pompy's Tower" to a stone pillar on the Yellowstone River; it is now a national monument called Pompey's Pillar. There might have been a touch of racial condescension to mar the charm: slaves were sometimes given the names of classical heroes in ironic mockery of their lack of power. But there was affection too; Clark later used the nickname for one of his own sons.

When it came time to say goodbye to the interpreters, Clark "offered to take his little son a butifull promising child who is 19 months old." The parents "wer willing provided the child had been weened. they observed that in one year the boy would be sufficiently old to leave his mother & he would then take him to me if I would be so freindly as to raise the child for him in such a manner as I thought proper...."

Even before reaching St. Louis, Clark wrote a letter to Toussaint Charbonneau to confirm the offer. "You have been a long time with me and have conducted your Self in Such a manner as to gain my friendship, your woman who accompanied you [on] that long dangerous and fatigueing rout to the Pacific Ocean and back, diserved a greater reward for her attention and Services on that rout than we had in our power to give her at the Mandans. As to your little Son (my boy Pomp) you well know my fondness for him and my anxiety to take and raise him as my own child. I once more tell you if you will bring your son Baptiest to me I will educate him and treat him as my own child...." Clark offered Charbonneau land and other inducements if he would "leave your little Son Pomp" with me. He signed off "with anxious expectations of seeing my little dancing boy Baptiest...."

Listen for echoes in this earnest letter of John Rolfe's plea to be allowed to marry Pocahontas as an opening to Christianizing her people. The newcomer sincerely believed that personal bonds could transcend race, and that there was room enough for all in the great land, provided that the future proceeded on the stronger culture's terms. "Thomas Jefferson and his fellow Virginians, Lewis and Clark, were men of the Enlightenment," noted Baptiste's distant cousin and

William Clark
The Red-Headed Chief earned the respect of Indians for maintaining a degree of fairness during a harsh era of conquest.

biographer. "Jeffersonians... were devoted to the concept that all men should be given the opportunity to develop their talents to the fullest." Even Andrew Jackson, the architect of the Trail of Tears, would raise a Creek child who was orphaned on the battlefield. Lewis, too, brought a metis child to St. Louis: the 13-year-old son of the translator Jessaume.

By the late 19th century, the white man's offer to educate Indian children ceased to be a generous invitation. Indian children would be separated from their families, often by force, and sent to boarding schools with the declared intent to wipe away traces of "savage" culture and language. We can't know how Sacagawea and Charbonneau felt about being separated from their son, but they did eventually turn Baptiste over to Clark's care.

Probably one of their reasons was the same that caused future Indian parents to acquiesce: poverty. With Clark, the boy would enjoy far better prospects in life. Maybe this widely-traveled couple consented because they were, in their own way, people of the Enlightenment, open to new ideas. In addition, they may have seen St. Louis as safer than the Upper Missouri, where tensions were growing between Indians and whites. Separation from children was common in those days. Among Indians, there was kidnapping. Among whites, boys aged 10 to 12 were sent away to become apprentices, ship's boys, or drummer boys. As an alternative to the ultimate separation of death due to hunger and cold, the parents certainly had their child's best interests in mind when they accepted Clark's offer.

Accompanied by Sheheke and by members of the Osage tribe, the captains were welcomed by President Jefferson in Washington. In 1807, Lewis was appointed governor of the Louisiana territory, and Clark was promoted to brigadier general, assigned to lead the territorial militia and act as principal Indian agent in the territory. While visiting Virginia, Clark fell in love with Julia Hancock. She was now at the marriageable age of 15; he was 36. When Clark returned to St. Louis with his bride in 1808, he found a home waiting. Lewis had secured a house big enough to share with the newlyweds. Soon, however, the couple had their own house and Lewis, calling himself a "musty, fusty, rusty old bachelor," moved in with Pierre Choteau. Lewis and young Jessaume still shared meals with the newlyweds. Their first son, Meriwether Lewis Clark, was born in January 1809.

Another member of the Clark household fared very badly after the expedition. York remained a slave. For years, Clark refused York's requests to be freed in recognition of his service during the expedition. Back in St. Louis, confronted with a slave who had proven that he was equal to any man, Clark would exercise the southern master's right to beat his fellow explorer. It was a terrible blind spot in a man who told Sacagawea's husband "Your woman...diserved a greater reward...than we had in our power to give her...." Clark had it in his power to give York the reward he deserved, and he did the opposite.

York was denied the marital happiness that Clark enjoyed. He had a wife in Kentucky, whom he seldom saw after Clark settled in St. Louis. York became "insolent and Sulky," Clark complained. "I gave him a Severe trouncing the other day." Clark routinely whipped his slaves. As York's resentment grew, Clark threatened to sell him or hire him for a while to "Some Severe master." Eventually York was hired out near his wife, but to a master who left him "wretched." Then the wife's master moved away, taking his human property with him and apparently parting the couple forever. Too late, Clark freed York and set him up in a wagon business. Years later, Clark reported that York had failed in the business, sarcastically calling him "the hero of the Missouri expedition." That moment of equality when York's vote was tallied on the Columbia River was long over.

Clark showed more respect for the tribes whose lands he had explored than he showed his black fellow explorer. For the rest of Clark's life, he would exercise enormous power over the western tribes in his role as regional superintendent of Indian affairs. He was a conqueror in the mold of John Smith, a mix of ruthlessness and integrity. The tribes accorded him a grudging respect and called him "the Red Headed Chief." Like many Indian agents, he took both sides of the job, control and concern, equally seriously. For example, the Shawnee tribe, much dispersed, included a community of farmers who lived peacefully alongside whites in Missouri. Clark wrote to President James Madison, asking that these Indians be granted land "where the White people might not encroach on them...and where the white people will not be permitted to sell them spirituous Liquors." The request was not granted. Clark wrote that it was hard to protect the Indians under his charge when "nine out of ten of the Indian Traders have no respect for our Laws."

These traders were licensed by the U.S. government. The beaver trade, not farm land, was still seen as the main economic prize of the Louisiana Territory. Trade meant not just acquiring beaver pelts, but dominating the entire system of Indian commerce, so that tribes would come to depend on Americans as the source of manufactured goods. Part of Clark's job was to establish trading posts, or "factories," in the areas he had explored. Factories were secured by forts, enforcing American sovereignty and extending both control and protection to tribes which had accepted this arrangement by treaty. The factory system was resented by traders, particularly British traders who did not hold the coveted trading licenses. The paternalistic side of U.S. policy saw the system as protecting Indians from the most unscrupulous of the traders, and included half-hearted attempts to limit the sale of alcohol.

While Lewis and Clark were gone, the United States had been busy extracting more land from Indians. The Sauk and Fox gave up land in Illinois, Missouri, and Wisconsin in 1804. One of Clark's first duties as Indian agent was to respond to Sauk and Fox complaints that their negotiators had not been authorized to make the concessions; one negotiator said that he was drunk when the treaty was signed. At the same time, white settlers in Iowa were encroaching on land that had been reserved for the Shawnees and Delawares after the bitter wars of the Old Northwest.

Unlike the worst of the Indian fighters, Clark could distinguish friend from enemy, the friendly band called the "Little Osages" from the "vicious" Great Osages. In August, 1808, Clark led a militia to meet with both bands, demanding an end to "Theft Murder and Robory on the Citizens of the U.S." In negotiations over the next year, Clark extracted treaty concessions covering much of today's Missouri and Arkansas. Toward the end of his life, he said this "was the hardest treaty on the Indians he ever made and that if he was to be damned hereafter it would be for making that treaty."

The Osage bands made up the largest tribe in the vicinity of St. Louis, and the Choteau family had grown rich trading with them. The Choteaus faced competition from Manuel Lisa, who received a trading license during the days of Spanish control. As Clark settled into his new duties in April 1807, several men who had served with the Corps of Discovery joined Lisa on a trapping expedition.

Other veterans of the expedition set out to accompany Sheheke and his family homeward; they too were in the company of traders, these working for the Choteau family. This party was attacked by Arikaras, who killed and wounded several soldiers; George Shannon of the Corps ended up with his leg amputated. They were forced to turn back before reaching Sheheke's Mandan village, and Clark grimly anticipated the prospect of Americans fighting their way past the formerly friendly Arikaras as well as the belligerent Sioux.

The competing fur companies joined forces for a time. In 1808, Manuel Lisa and members of the Choteau family, together with William Clark and other partners, formed the St. Louis Missouri Fur Company. Once again, soldiers and traders escorted Sheheke upriver. Another group was sent to build trading posts and forts. Governor Lewis advanced his own money for this project. The cozy dealings were criticized, and the federal government refused to reimburse Lewis.

Lewis was already in debt. Clark tried to help, but the Lewis family had a history of "melancholia," and Lewis was drinking heavily and taking opiates. The two gunshots that ended the storied friendship in 1809 were most likely self-inflicted. Speculation persists that Lewis was murdered; it's hard to accept that a legend could take his own life. Modern medicine might have saved him: a course of Prozac or even the insights of the shaman named Freud.

Upon hearing the tragic news, Clark wrote to his brother: "I fear O! I fear the waight of his mind has over come him, what will become of his paprs?" Clark retrieved the journals and proceeded on. His family grew. Soon it included Sacagawea's children.

The Charbonneau family came to St. Louis in 1809. Toussaint, far less inclined to be a settled farmer than many Indians, tried that life in Missouri for less than a year. In early 1811, he signed on as an interpreter and trader with Manuel Lisa. Charbonneau and Sacagawea set out upriver once again in April 1811. "We have on board a Frenchman named Charbonet, with his wife, an Indian woman of the Snake nation, both of whom accompanied Lewis and Clark to the Pacific, and were of great service," wrote Henry Marie Brackenridge, a passenger on that journey. Baptiste probably remained in St. Louis with Clark. Sacagawea may have made the return trip to St. Louis and seen Baptiste one last time, early in 1812, or she may have remained among the Mandan-Hidatsa when Charbonneau returned to St. Louis.

Charbonneau signed on with Manuel Lisa again, and set out on a second trip with him in the spring of 1812. Sacagawea joined him at some point on the journey. The party wintered at the brand-new Fort Manuel, on the Missouri River in South Dakota. The river trade was growing more dangerous as Upper Missouri tribes resisted white encroachment.

That was Sacagawea's last journey. The clerk of Fort Manuel, John Luttig, made this sad entry dated December 20, 1812: "[T]his Evening the Wife of Charbonneau a Snake Squaw, died of a putrid fever she was a good and the best Women in the fort, aged about 25 years she left a fine infant girl."

The baby girl was named Lisette or Lizette. Luttig brought her to St. Louis and applied to become her guardian, but Clark took over this duty for both of

Sacagawea's children, becoming guardian of Baptiste and Lisette in December 1812. Nothing more is known of Lisette, except that a woman born Elizabeth Carboneau gave birth to a daughter in Missouri thirty years later.

Sacagawea, like Pocahontas, died young. Or did she?

Most likely, yes. Henry Brackenridge identified the wife of Charbonneau who traveled upriver with him as the woman who had accompanied Lewis and Clark. "The" wife of Charbonneau, not "a" wife, died upriver nineteen months later. Neither Brackenridge nor Luttig made any mention of a second wife. Luttig's death notice has the right age and the reference to an infant girl. "Se-car-ja-we-au dead," wrote Clark in the 1820s, in a list of the fate of the expedition's members. If she was alive, she probably would have maintained contact with her children's guardian.

Two entirely different stories are alive and well.

The first is that Sacagawea left Charbonneau, either because of his beatings or because she didn't get along with one of his other wives. Charbonneau did have multiple wives, and he did hit Sacagawea on at least one occasion during the journey to the Pacific. Clark came to her defense at that time, noting in his journal, "I checked our Interpreter for Strikeing his woman at their Dinner." If she wanted to be rid of Charbonneau, however, she could have stayed with her Lemhi people in 1805.

After leaving Charbonneau, the story continues, she lived for years among the Comanches, then returned to the Shoshone people on the Wind River Reservation in Wyoming and lived a long life under the name Porivo. Those who knew Porivo said that she spoke French, told stories of a great fish by the western sea, and kept a medal with the likeness of Thomas Jefferson. Porivo died in 1884. Her grave on the Wind River Reservation is marked as that of Sacagawea. This story was quite convincing to two different researchers in the early 20th century.

Porivo had sons named Bat-tez and Bazil (and, in some versions, one named Toussaint). A woman identified as "Bazil's mother" was listed as an enrolled member of the Northern Shoshone tribe at the Wind River Reservation in Wyoming. But Sacagawea's Lemhi Shoshone people lived in the Salmon River country in Idaho until 1907. By a treaty of 1868, the Wind River Reservation in Wyoming was assigned to the eastern bands of the related but distinct Northern Shoshone people. (When the Lemhi were forced onto the Fort Hall Reservation in 1907, they joined other Northern Shoshone bands).

Bazil became the ancestor of intermarried white and Indian families, who believe that his mother, Porivo, was Sacagawea. Bazil was a subordinate chief of Washakie, a chief among the Northern Shoshones. Because of a limp, Bazil has been called the "lame sub-chief of Washakie." The mark of "Bazeel" appears on the 1868 treaty, along with the mark of Washakie, signing for the "Shoshones."

Of course, a Lemhi woman could have lived on a Northern Shoshone reservation. And Bazil's name on the treaty might have been identified with the wrong tribe; a Lemhi who assented to the treaty was incorrectly listed as a "Bannack" (the Shoshonean Bannocks). However, most historians – including a modern Lemhi writer who can trace a clear line of descent to Sacagawea's brother Cameahwait – believe that Bazil and Porivo were not Lemhi, and hence that Porivo was not Sacagawea.

Porivo's other son, Bat-tez, has been remembered in oral tradition as Baptiste. Bat-tez has been described as semi-literate and taciturn. He died in 1885 and was buried in Wyoming. Jean-Baptiste Charbonneau could read and write in more than one language, and his biography paints a picture of a man who was gregarious, even charismatic. He died in 1866 and was buried in Oregon. Both were short and dark; that seems to be all these two men had in common. It is very unlikely that Bat-tez was the child who traveled with Lewis and Clark.

Still, a respected old woman is remembered for accompanying white explorers to the western sea. Perhaps she accompanied a different party. She seemed as earnest as the woman who insisted that she was Princess Anastasia. In both cases, a whisper of doubt remains.

The third version is based on Hidatsa oral tradition. In this version, Sacagawea was born Hidatsa, captured by Shoshones, and led home to the Hidatsa by four wolves who provided her with food along the way. In 1925, a Hidatsa man reported that "Sakakawea" was his grandmother, and that she died of a gunshot wound in middle age. There is even less support for this story, given its folkloric nature and the evidence that Sacagawea's original people were Lemhi. It does speak of the deep nature of the Hidatsa's adoption of the woman and her legacy.

So let's lay Sacagawea to rest, and turn to the world in which her son grew up.

A few years before Jean-Baptiste Charbonneau came to live in St. Louis, another child of mixed background was brought to the area. Sir Jennings Beckwith, a Revolutionary War veteran known by his grandfather's English title, was from a landed Virginia family. Beckwith had a son named Jim, born to a black mother. In the early 1800s, Beckwith left Virginia and headed west to a "howling wilderness," as his son remembered the homestead outside St. Louis, "taking with him all of his family and twenty-two negroes." Mother and son likely fit both categories. Usually the children of such encounters became the next generation of slaves. Sir Jennings, however, treated Jim as a son and executed the legal documents to set him free. If Jennings wished to live with Jim's mother as a common-law wife, as some believe, leaving racist Virginia behind was a good idea.

That Virginia-born child was the mountain man James Pierson Beckwourth, as he would spell his name. Beckwourth enjoyed a long friendship with Sacagawea's son. Jim was about five years older than Baptiste, but their first meeting could well have been in St. Louis, where Jim served an apprenticeship during Baptiste's schoolboy days.

One day, Jim's father asked "whether I thought myself man enough to carry a sack of corn to the mill." The corn was placed on the back of a gentle horse and "Young Jim" placed on top. The boy rode proudly by the home of a family with eight children, only to find all his playmates and their parents with their throats cut and their scalps torn off. Jim raced home and his father "gave the alarm throughout the settlement." A group of men set out for revenge. "In two days the band returned, bringing with them eighteen Indian scalps; for the backwoodsman fought the savage in Indian style, and it was scalp for scalp between them."

"The day when I beheld the harrowing spectacle of my little murdered playmates is still as fresh in my memory as at the time of its occurrence....," said Jim in his memoirs. "....I wondered how even savages could possess such relentless minds as to wish to bathe their hands in the blood of little innocents against whom they could have no cause of quarrel." As a grown man, Jim would live among the Crow Indians and come to understand their desperation.

James Beckwourth's recollections should be read even more skeptically than those of John Smith. Beckwourth was as much a self-promoter as Smith. The childhood stories were not at all fresh in his mind when he dictated them more than 40 years later. His dates are unreliable. There is no record of this massacre at the time and place he recalled. Spinning a wild tale was a favorite pastime of the mountain men. He dictated his autobiography to an author who obviously contributed some grandiose language. Still, the broad outlines of his life story fit well with known facts. Just as oral tradition contains its own truth, Beckwourth's stories paint a picture in time. Beckwourth and Baptiste walked similar paths, but it was Beckwourth who committed the tales to paper.

Even if Beckwourth remembered the wrong date for the massacre that haunted his memory, settler families near St. Louis would meet similar fates soon enough. Sacagawea and Charbonneau brought Baptiste to live with Clark during a period of growing tensions between Indians and whites along the Missouri and Mississippi. These tensions contributed to the War of 1812. This war was a continuation of the conflict for control of North America. Following the American Revolution, Britain had maintained Indian allies in order to limit American power near British Canada, once again bringing merciless Indian savages on the inhabitants of the frontiers. In addition, as part of its naval war against Napoleon, Britain interfered with American shipping and impressed American sailors into its own navy. The United States declared war on Great Britain on June 18, 1812. The war would end in a stalemate in late 1815, and Britain and the United States would never again fight each other.

In the years leading up to the War of 1812, whites and Indians were killing each other with regularity on the frontier, and tribes were still fighting other tribes. As a general in the territorial militia, Clark provided military assistance to the Osages, his treaty partners, against an alliance of Shawnees, Delawares, and the new community of western Cherokees. Members of those eastern tribes had migrated toward the heartland, Osage country, to escape white encroachment. This migration was part of a federal policy of voluntary removal across the Mississippi, which preceded the era of forced removal. Once the war with Britain began, Osage warriors offered to fight on the American side against their tribal enemies, but the idea of arming Indians on the frontier was rejected. Late in the war, Clark finally decided to arm the Osage and orchestrate tribal warfare, coming full circle from the peace policy of the expedition.

In the Old Northwest, Tecumseh and his brother, called the Shawnee Prophet, were championing unity among the tribes. "Let the white race perish!... Back whence they came, upon a trail of blood, they must be driven...into the great water whose accursed waves brought them to our shores....The red man owns the country and the palefaces must never enjoy it. War now, war forever!"

Clark, the diplomat, tried to counter Tecumseh's threat by organizing delegates from several tribes for a visit to Washington. In May 1812, a few weeks before war was declared, Clark accompanied this group east. This trip gave him a chance to escort Julia and their two children away from the growing tension on the frontier, to Julia's family in Virginia. Assuming Baptiste was already under Clark's care in St. Louis at that time, which is likely but not certain, there is no record that Clark took similar precautions for his foster son. Apparently, 7-year-old Baptiste was left in St. Louis as Julia's children were escorted to safety.

In fact, Baptiste never lived in the Clark household. Clark paid for Baptiste's room and board at a boarding house across the street from the Clark home. In other words, Clark did not entirely keep his promise to "treat him as my own child." Perhaps Julia or her family brought along Virginian prejudices. In any case, there was more to the relationship than simply paying bills. A lasting bond had been formed with the little dancing boy. Many years later, a traveler would describe Baptiste as "a son of Captain Clarke...."

Although Tecumseh never forgot the day "the gates were shut against us" by British allies in 1794, the War of 1812 provided another chance to join against their common foe. "The Americans we must fight, not the English," Tecumseh said. "The Americans are our eternal foes, the hungry devourers of the country of our fathers." Up and down the Mississippi River, from the Great Lakes to the Missouri Territory, Britain's Indian allies killed American settlers, before, during, and after the War of 1812. Clark worked to secure neutrality when he could. Two future presidents won their fame as Indian fighters during that war. William Henry Harrison's forces killed Tecumseh in 1813. Andrew Jackson defeated the militant Red Sticks band of Creeks in 1814, avenging a massacre of settlers in Alabama the year before. The Creeks, friend and foe, were then forced to cede two-thirds of their territory, opening more land for cotton planting and slave labor.

Clark was appointed governor of the Missouri Territory in 1813. In the tradition of his brother, with war in one hand and peace in the other, he placed gunboats on the Mississippi River, while offering land west of the Mississippi to neutral Sauk and Fox bands in order to split them from the hostile bands led by Black Hawk. This was Osage land, and it was already getting crowded with Cherokees. From the Osage point of view, Clark observed, "the Cherokees...were no better than the Virginians." In 1817, Cherokees attacked an Osage village in Missouri, killing or capturing many women and children. The Cherokee migration, combined with wasteful slaughter of buffalo by white settlers, eventually pushed the Osage – American allies – out of most of present-day Missouri.

In the summer of 1814, Clark led a force up the Mississippi in search of a British commander who was a notorious "hair-buyer," paying Indians for American scalps. Soon after, the British burned Washington, D.C. As 80-year-old Daniel Boone joined the Missouri militia, and Andrew Jackson defeated the

British at the Battle of New Orleans, negotiators in Europe were winding down the war. Although the British and their Indian allies had taken control of the Great Lakes and Upper Mississippi, the diplomats agreed to return to the pre-war boundaries. Betrayed again by their British allies, Indians kept scalping Americans. Wartime atrocities soon provided an excuse for Americans to dispossess any tribe, friendly or hostile, that stood in the way of westward expansion.

Throughout this turmoil, Clark was making good on his promise to educate Baptiste. Tuition at St. Louis Academy (now St. Louis University), a slate and quill pens, a dictionary, and a book of Roman history appear in Clark's records of expenditures for his ward. The academy taught classical and European languages, mathematics, and geography.

John Rolfe the Christian, if not John Rolfe the Protestant, would have been pleased: Sacagawea's child was baptized at least once, maybe twice. Jean-Baptiste Charbonneau's record of baptism in the Catholic tradition of his father is dated December 28, 1809. His godparents were Auguste Choteau and Choteau's daughter. William Clark, who had taken nephews into his home, had all the children in his household baptized on August 8, 1814, possibly including Baptiste.

In 1815, Clark convened a treaty conference near the confluence of the two great rivers, bringing together thirty-seven tribes, including American allies, British allies, and neutrals. Clark's old acquaintances Black Buffalo and the Partisan of the Brule (Teton) Sioux were there. Clark cultivated the enemies of the Sauk and Fox: the Sioux, Shawnees, Delawares, and Omahas. The Sauk chiefs who had allied with Britain came later, and Clark literally placed a sword and pipe in front of them. For the moment, it was a peace conference, not a land grab. However, the long-term policy never changed. The governor of Indiana wrote the Secretary of War that the local tribes should "be kept in a good humor for two or three years" while the white population increased. Increase it did, all along the Mississippi River, from the Great Lakes to Missouri. A few years later, Clark negotiated for fifty-one million acres of land concessions, to be used for white settlement and relocation of eastern tribes.

Despite this successful diplomacy, citizens of Missouri Territory never forgave their governor for smoking the peace pipe with tribes that had only recently tomahawked and scalped settler families. Worse, Clark announced late in 1815 that he would use the militia to remove whites from Indian land. "Our government, founded in justice will effectually extend its protection to the Native inhabitants within its limits," he insisted. When Missouri prepared for statehood in 1820, Clark ran for governor and lost, in good part because of his "undue partiality to Indians."

Baptiste was 15 when the vote went against Clark. There is no record of the boy's reaction. Although he was literate in more than one language, Baptiste left little in writing, and his biography is based on the recollections of others. Almost thirty years later, Baptiste would find himself in a similar situation, in a position of responsibility for Indians, pressured out of office for "partiality" toward them.

Julia Clark died in 1820, at the age of 28, having borne five children. A year and a half later, the widower Clark married Julia's first cousin, Harriet, a widow herself. The Clark household grew to include stepchildren, but apparently not Baptiste.

The competition between the English and Americans continued after the shooting war was over, with an eye to securing territory as well as profit. In 1818, the two countries agreed on the Canadian border as far west as the Rocky Mountains. The northern boundary of the Oregon Territory, however, remained in dispute until 1846. Chief Coboway, the friendly Clatsop whose canoe Lewis and Clark had stolen, and whom they had entrusted with a written record of their journey, had kept the document. In 1814, he showed it to a British trader, who callously threw this valued souvenir into the fire and presented him with a British replacement.

While British companies dominated the fur trade in the Pacific Northwest, Americans continued to use their base in St. Louis to trap and trade up the Missouri and into the Rocky Mountains. Toussaint Charbonneau continued to work in this trade. His son joined him. With his formal education completed, Baptiste spent a year or two working for the Missouri Fur Company.

Around 1822, a man of the Enlightenment traveled from Germany to St. Louis to learn about the New World. Duke Paul of Wurttemberg was a 25-year-old German of a royal house. He used his wealth to satisfy his curiosity. Duke Paul hired Toussaint Charbonneau as a guide and interpreter. Either through his father, foster father, or godfather Auguste Choteau, 18-year-old Baptiste was introduced to Paul. The French and Indian youth embodied the west that fascinated the nobleman. Duke Paul returned to Europe with Baptiste Charbonneau as a companion. The two traveled from St. Louis down the Mississippi River by steamboat to New Orleans, then on to France. For six years, Sacagawea's son traveled in France, England, Spain, and Germany. At Duke Paul's estate, Baptiste rode and hunted in the Black Forest. He added German to his knowledge of Spanish, French, English, and Indian languages.

Baptiste became a father and buried a child in Germany. A boy named Anton Fries was born to an unmarried woman named Anastasia Fries, daughter of a soldier. The father was described as "Johann Baptist Charbonnau of St Louis, 'called the American'...."

The baby survived for only three months. Baptiste returned home about 1829. A long life on the frontier was ahead for "the American."

Chapter 9

The Sons of the Red-Headed Chief

"While strong and hostile it was our policy and duty to weaken them; now that they are weak and harmless, and most of their lands fallen into our hands, justice and humanity require us to cherish and befriend them."

William Clark, 1826

A mountain man turned *alcalde*. An avenging Indian fighter. A light-haired Nez Perce warrior who called himself Clark. These were some of the sons of William Clark. The first was Baptiste Charbonneau. The second was Meriwether Lewis Clark. The third hints at William Clark's warm relations with at least one Indian woman. For good and ill, Clark and his sons played their parts in the disaster sweeping over the tribes. William Clark continued to be responsible for Indian affairs after his defeat as governor, and it fell to him to implement the federal policy of relocating Indians across the Mississippi. The Cherokee Nation challenged this crime in the Supreme Court, receiving a sympathetic but unavailing hearing from Chief Justice John Marshall, the Virginian whose Randolph family was intermarried with the Red Bollings. The interwoven legacies of Pocahontas and Sacagawea were continuing to shape the west.

After losing the election for governor, Clark held on to his position as regional superintendent of Indian Affairs, reporting to a new agency, the Bureau of Indian Affairs. The legislation creating this agency, in 1821, also eliminated the factory system of government-controlled trading posts. This policy change violated treaties with the Osage and other tribes who had come to depend on this arrangement for both a supply of trade goods and a modicum of protective regulation of trade. The elimination of the government monopoly on trade, the invention of the steel beaver trap, and the discovery of the South Pass through the Rocky Mountains in 1824 together stimulated a free-for-all of trapping and gave rise to the famously colorful annual trappers' *rendezvous*. There was more and more illegal trapping on Indian lands where Indians had been eking out a living by trapping beavers and selling them to traders. The South Pass, a relatively easy route through the Rockies in today's Wyoming, gave a boost to American fur traders, and eventually American claims of sovereignty, in competition with the British in the Pacific Northwest.

As the fur trade accelerated in the 1820s, the detailed maps Clark had drawn during the voyage of discovery guided the construction of a string of forts, consolidating American power against both British and Indian challenges. Comanches

A son of William Clark?

This photo of Tzi-kal-tza of the Nez Perce was taken in 1866. The original photo collection did not mention the relationship with Clark, but this claim was recorded when the photo was reproduced in the 1890s. Courtesy of the Wisconsin Historical Society.

and Blackfeet took aim at the invaders. Nez Perce, Shoshone, and other tribes continued as American trading partners. Rival fur companies fought among themselves until they made peace through merger.

As Indian superintendent, Clark issued a "trading" license in 1822 that would benefit his own business interests, well aware that "trading" with Indians was becoming "trapping" that cut them out. Much of the hostility from the Blackfeet and Arikara was due to American trapping, not American trading. These tribes needed manufactured goods but could not purchase them without pelts as currency.

In 1823, a trader in an Arikara village got into a dispute, possibly over a woman. The Arikaras gouged out his eyes, decapitated him, and then shot two dozen of the traders, including a free black man. American forces and Sioux warriors set out to avenge the conduct of "those inhuman monsters," to quote Clark's nephew, serving as Indian agent at one of the new forts. Under Colonel Henry Leavenworth, these forces attacked the Arikaras. Then, hoping to avert "a confirmed state of hostility to every white man," Leavenworth talked peace, with Toussaint Charbonneau serving as interpreter. After agreeing that the traders would be permitted safe travel up the Missouri, the Arikara withdrew in the night. Vengeful traders promptly burned the empty Arikara village, undermining Leavenworth's diplomatic efforts.

Leavenworth pinned the blame on the traders, pointing out that the "trapping business is carried on under a license to trade" and was thus a violation of law and "a violation of the rights of a poor miserable set of savages whose only means of support is thus destroyed contrary to the benign policy of our government." There was a brief period of calm after a treaty council in 1824, where Toussaint Charbonneau again served as interpreter.

Meanwhile, the federal government was accelerating plans to encourage eastern tribes to move across the Mississippi River. Forced deportations were yet to come. "To remove them from [their present territory] by force, even with a view to their own security or happiness, would be revolting to humanity and utterly unjustifiable," President James Monroe told Congress in 1824. "…[T]here is a vast territory to which they might be invited with inducements…." The "inducements," however, included federal acquiescence as settlers encroached on Indian land in the east.

The removal policy gradually replaced the civilization policy because most Indians refused to go along with the underlying purpose of the civilization policy: to replace hunting and farming on tribal land with dependence on a market economy and sale of land to white Americans. Even the most "civilized" tribe, the Cherokee, adopted a policy of maintaining tribal ownership.

Long before the Trail of Tears, the Cherokee Council's National Committee ruled that those who sold tribal lands and moved west to Arkansas were no longer part of the Cherokee nation because they were "committing treason against the motherland." Some chiefs ceded tribal land in exchange for personal rewards. In 1807, one of those chiefs, a notorious murderer named Doublehead, was killed as a warning to others. Ironically, the assassins included Major Ridge, who, nearly three decades later, would reluctantly sign the removal treaty and then die at the hand of Cherokee assassins.

Some Cherokees took advantage of a 1817 treaty clause that let Cherokees become individual landholders. They were called "citizen Cherokees," although they were not allowed to become U.S. citizens. Others fled west as poverty, encroachment, and discrimination made life intolerable. Sequoyah moved west in 1818.

There was many a trail of tears during removal. The Cherokees' is best known, partly because that literate tribe and its allies left a damning record for posterity. Yet the removal policy remained "voluntary" up to and including the Cherokee removal treaty because the federal government considered tribes sovereign nations that could only be dispossessed through negotiated treaties. Even during Jackson's presidency, when the notion of sovereignty was weakened, removal was voluntary in the sense that one tribe after another signed oppressive treaties under overwhelming coercion.

In 1825, Clark negotiated land cessions with Sauk bands (not Black Hawk's militant band, which still had ties with the British through the Canadian fur trade). The following year, Clark persuaded peaceful farming communities of Shawnees and Delawares to move farther west; pressured Osage bands to do the same, before they had a chance to start their own farms on land they had recently been promised; and pushed the Kansas tribe out of eastern Kansas. These treaties secured parts of the future states of Missouri, Kansas, and Arkansas for white farmers. The western land, Clark insisted, was "wonderfully adapted to an Indian population in the first stages of civilization." The Choctaws, Chickasaws, and Creeks sent delegations in 1826 to inspect the land intended for them.

On both expansionist and paternalist grounds, Clark accepted the removal policy, while calling for "humain feeling." American leaders were never comfortable with naked territorial expansion and sought to rationalize it with a civilizing mission. Anglo-American agricultural technology has never been rivaled, and its expansion over the continent has justified land grabs from the days of Jamestown. "The hunter state...yields to the more dense and compact form and great force of civilized population," argued President James Monroe in 1817. "[A]nd of right it ought to yield, for the earth was given to mankind to support the greatest number of which it is capable...."

The paternalist rationale was that Indians were "debased" by contact with whites – indeed, impoverishment, disease, and whiskey were taking their toll – and that they would be better off living separately while they learned the ways of whites. They could give up their tribal identities, sell their lands, and live among whites – or they could maintain their tribal identities far from their original homes.

"[I]t would afford me pleasure to be enabled to meliorate the condition of those unfortunate people placed under my charge," Clark wrote in 1825, "knowing as I do their [w]retchedness and their rapid decline." The Indian fighter was generous in victory: "While strong and hostile it was our policy and duty to weaken them; now that they are weak and harmless, and most of their lands fallen into our hands, justice and humanity require us to cherish and befriend them." So wrote Clark in 1826, after personally negotiating treaties that extinguished Indian claims to more than 100 million acres of land. Clark was humane compared to his contemporaries. Indians had reason to trust "the Red-Headed Chief."

As Clark was busy implementing a "humain" removal policy, his foster son joined the fur trade that was so profitable to the extended family. Baptiste returned from Europe to St. Louis around 1829. Now a 24-year-old man of the world, Baptiste turned west to the life of the mountain man.

Imagine Baptiste, recently returned from an 11th century castle, with his shoulder-length black hair and buckskin clothes. For the rest of his life, he would make an impression on one frontier traveler after another, with his mix of classical education and wilderness skills. "His mind...was well stored with choice reading, and enriched by extensive travel and observation," wrote a traveler. "It is said that Charbenau was the best man on foot on the plains or in the Rocky Mountains," according to another journal.

Baptiste could dance an Indian war dance and comfort a friend whose wife was dying after childbirth. He once stabbed a man in the shoulder with a butcher knife after the fellow threatened to flog him and another time used a bullwhip to prevent onlookers from breaking up a fight.

The younger Charbonneau followed his father into a business that would be an abomination under modern standards of animal welfare, environmental protection, and worker safety. Beaver felt hats were a fashion must for gentlemen. Early trappers shot and clubbed the playful mammals. Underwater steel traps came along in 1823. The beaver drowned, unless it escaped by chewing off the trapped limb. French Canadian *voyageurs* risked drowning to transport the pelts; when waterways ran out, they bent double carrying huge loads on their backs. Mercury used in the felting process poisoned the central nervous systems of the hat makers, who became "mad as hatters." Beavers would be saved from extinction only when their scarcity made trapping unprofitable at the same time that Chinese silk provided an alternative material. But the fur trade permitted coexistence between Indians and whites.

Baptiste spent the 1830s in the fur trade, returning to the Rocky Mountains and Snake River of his mother's people, and attending some of the annual rendezvous, where French, English and Indian trappers brought their harvest of furs. There they escaped the solitude of the wilderness for male camaraderie: drinking, fighting, gambling, and competing at horse racing, marksmanship, and boasting. There was the camaraderie of Indian women as well, in marriage and otherwise. The party ended in 1840 with the collapse of beaver populations and the substitution of silk hats.

What a shame that Sacagawea's son, one of the most literate of the mountain men, didn't write about these adventures. But his friend Jim Beckwourth's memoirs trace a similar story, as the two crossed paths, from the Rockies to the Sierra, as trappers, traders, interpreters, scouts, and hunters.

Jim Beckwourth lived for years among the Crow Indians and became a war chief in that tribe. The Crows had split from the Hidatsa after European contact, leaving settled farming behind in favor of the Plains horse and buffalo culture. Had Beckwourth crossed paths with the fair-haired Nez Perce named Clark, his courtship of a legendary Crow woman warrior might have moved faster. Pine Leaf (or Woman Chief) had pledged not to marry until she took a hundred Blackfeet scalps to avenge the death of her twin brother. She put Beckwourth off with a promise to marry him when the pine leaves turned yellow and when he found a red-haired Indian. Pine Leaf finally relented and became one of his Crow wives. So Beckwourth told the tale.

The mountain men – with their Indian wives, some with Indian mothers – acted as guides and interpreters for the migrants from the east. The farmers, ranchers, miners, missionaries, and entrepreneurs would soon transform the west, dispossessing one tribe after another with growing numbers and brutal certainty about their civilizing mission. But for one last time, there seemed to be room enough for everyone.

In the east, there was no longer room for everyone. During the Black Hawk War of 1832, Sauks killed encroaching white farmers, and their wives and children, in Illinois and Wisconsin. "A war of Extermination should be waged against them," William Clark wrote. "[T]he pease & quiet of the frontier – the lives and safety of its inhabitants demand it." Meriwether Lewis Clark served as a militia officer in that war, as did Abraham Lincoln. The younger Clark wrote his father "well it will only make me add one to the few scalps I am going to take from Black Hawk, Napope &c." Avenging whites massacred Sauk women and children, and the defeated tribe ceded a portion of today's Iowa. Thus was more of the heartland secured.

Black Hawk himself survived the war and the massacre. In 1835, the old warrior met with Clark to complain about white incursions on treaty lands, and then went on to meet with Andrew Jackson in Washington. Black Hawk was imprisoned briefly in Virginia. Clark was one of those who successfully appealed for his release.

The parallel policies of coexistence and displacement, bloodshed and paternal care, continued. The same year he was urging extermination of Black Hawk's band, William Clark oversaw the inoculation of Plains Indians against smallpox. The terrible disease had destroyed the younger generation of Pawnees the year before. Their heartbroken elders, the survivors of an earlier epidemic, were immune. Congress appropriated $12,000 for vaccinations in 1832, but the Commissioner of Indian Affairs, Clark's superior, declined to extend the program to the North Dakota tribes. The tribes that had hosted the explorers – the friendly Mandans and Hidatsa, as well as the intermittently hostile Arikaras – were left to a fate that would soon decimate them.

For eastern tribes, time was running out also, for different reasons. In 1827, the Cherokee Nation adopted a constitution that delineated the tribal boundaries secured by treaty with the United States. The constitution stated its purpose: "to establish justice, promote our common welfare, and secure to ourselves and our posterity the blessings of liberty." They had reached the culmination of civilization but, in doing so, had refused to give up their sovereignty and their land.

The Cherokee Constitution of 1827 set the stage for a political drama that pitted states' rights against federal power. Indians within the borders of a state, argued Georgia, could not exist as a nation. A state could not undermine federal treaties with Indian nations, replied the Cherokees. In reality, over and over, states or territorial settlers defied federal restrictions on white settlement. Squatters seized Indian land and then called for protection against warriors. The federal government, instead of removing the squatters, pressed the tribes to concede more land.

As the federal union had taken shape a generation earlier, Georgia and other southern states had surrendered to the federal government their claims to western territory. In return, the United States in 1802 promised Georgia that federal negotiators would work to extinguish Indian land titles inside state boundaries. But the Cherokees wouldn't leave, and Georgia wanted that land for cotton. Responding to the Cherokee Constitution, the State Assembly announced its intention to take possession of Cherokee lands, declared that the civil and criminal laws of Georgia extended into those lands (while forbidding Indians from testifying in court), and renounced all laws adopted by the Cherokee Council.

Andrew Jackson agreed with Georgia. Indian tribes were not sovereign nations, he believed, contrary to longstanding federal policy. In his message to Congress in 1829, President Jackson said that no tribe had the right to enact laws without the consent of the state where it resided. Indians could submit to the laws of the states – which left them as non-citizens, subject to discrimination at every turn – or they could retain their tribal identity west of the Mississippi River. Those who held individual title to land could keep it, but not those who claimed "tracts of country on which they have neither dwelt nor made improvements, merely because they have seen them from the mountain or passed them in the chase."

This was Jackson's removal policy. It was for their own good, as "this much-injured race" could not otherwise survive. "It has long been the policy of the Government to introduce among [the Indian tribes] the arts of civilization, in the hope of gradually reclaiming them from a wandering life. This policy has, however, been coupled with another wholly incompatible with its success. Professing a desire to civilize and settle them, we have at the same time lost no opportunity to purchase their lands and thrust them farther into the wilderness.... A portion, however, of the Southern tribes, [have]... made some progress in the arts of civilized life...."

Some progress? Those wandering Cherokees must have had a hard time carrying their printing press and log cabins as they passed "in the chase."

That the Five Civilized Tribes had adopted the farming methods of whites did not save them. The competition for land in the southeast was complex: subsistence farmers against cotton planters, Indians against whites, and Indians against Indians. Back in his Indian-fighting days, when Andrew Jackson had Indian allies, it was because one southeastern tribe was fighting another. Those warriors had fatally miscalculated who their real enemy was. The Creeks lost their land in 1827, the Choctaws in 1830.

The Cherokees' days on the Warriors' Path were in the past, and they fought removal with every weapon of literate people. Elias Boudinot, whose young bride had been humiliated for marrying an Indian, published the *Cherokee Phoenix,* a newspaper written in both English and Sequoyah's syllabary. The very existence of an Indian newspaper belied the distinction between civilized whites and savage Indians, and Boudinot used the *Phoenix* to rally public opinion. Cherokee delegations and petitions to Washington were supported by sympathetic whites, particularly church leaders from the northeast. When Congress passed Jackson's Indian Removal Bill in 1830, the vote was especially close in the House of Representatives: 102 to 97.

The Indian Removal Act provided for the exchange of existing tribal lands for land west of today's Missouri and Arkansas. One problem was that other Indian tribes were already living in these lands. In 1830, Sauk and Fox bands were squeezed between white squatters in Illinois and tribes already living on the western land now promised to these eastern tribes. White squatters took over Sauk and Fox cornfields in Illinois while the Indians were away hunting. Tribes competed for diminishing buffalo. There was another treaty council in 1830, and another successful negotiation by Clark, acquiring a chunk of today's Iowa under the pretext of creating a buffer between tribes. Chickasaws and Cherokees, coerced onto the plains, were fighting with the tribes that were there first.

Removal, Jackson insisted, was still voluntary. As he spoke, hungry Indians were moving west as game disappeared in the Old Northwest and settlers encroached on farmland. In St. Louis, Clark provided the refugees with food and lodging, blankets and clothing, rifles and farm equipment. "Although there is no obligation to clothe them," one Indian agent wrote to Clark, "it is impossible to refuse clothing to many women and children, suffering in cold weather."

With these minimal provisions, the refugees were led west by Indian agents. The peaceful Osage pleaded for the farming implements they had been promised.

Whites stole migrants' horses with impunity. Indians on the move died in the bitter winter of 1830-31. Measles and cholera struck many down. This was the voluntary phase of Indian removal.

Cash annuities paid to the refugees often disappeared into whiskey. Clark urged the prohibition of liquor in the region now called "the Indian country" but continued to issue permits for its transport. The permits were supposed to be for the personal use of the boatmen, but twelve gallons per person was a suspicious amount. Liquor was finally banned in 1832.

John Ridge and Elias Boudinot
The cousins fought Cherokee removal until they judged it hopeless, then signed a removal treaty, and paid with their lives.

In 1832, Clark negotiated the extinguishment of remaining Indian land titles in Illinois and Missouri. He had long objected to dispossessing the Kickapoos, whom he called "the most orderly and sober Indians within the State of Illinois," but they had taken in refugees from Black Hawk's band, and they were removed to Kansas. Peaceful Shawnees and Delawares who had been left alone in earlier treaties now had to leave Missouri.

The Cherokees petitioned the U.S. Supreme Court to uphold previous treaties guaranteeing their holdings in Georgia. The first of the "Cherokee cases" involved a murder; the second, a missionary.

In the first case, a Cherokee was accused of murdering another Cherokee on Cherokee land. His arrest by Georgia law enforcement and trial in state court raised the question of which law governed: Cherokee tribal law, underpinned by federal treaty, or Georgia law. The accused, George Corn Tassel, was convicted and sentenced to hang. The Cherokee Nation's lawyers argued to the U.S. Supreme Court that imposing state law within tribal boundaries was unconstitutional because, under the federal supremacy clause of the U.S. Constitution, a federal treaty trumps state law.

First, the Supreme Court had to decide whether the Cherokee Nation had legal standing to sue Georgia, which turned on whether the Cherokees were a "foreign nation." Chief Justice Marshall directed Georgia to halt the execution while these issues were resolved, and subpoenaed the governor. The governor ignored the subpoena, and Tassel was hanged on December 24, 1830. With that act, Georgia "hoist[ed] the flag of rebellion against the United States," wrote Boudinot.

Boudinot was right. The union was on shaky ground in the 1830s, with South Carolina arguing that a state had the right to "nullify" federal legislation, in this case a tariff that favored northern industry at the expense of the southern plantation economy. This threat inspired Jackson's famous toast: "Our federal union: it must be preserved." If the United States tolerated Georgia's defiance, warned Boudinot when Tassel was hanged, "the Union...will soon fall and crumble into atoms." Sacrificing the Cherokee postponed the collapse for thirty years.

Tassel was dead, but the Cherokee Nation proceeded with its petition for an injunction declaring the Georgia legislation unconstitutional. The case got only as far as a technical question. In 1831, a majority of the U.S. Supreme Court decided that the Cherokee Nation did not have standing to sue. Chief Justice John Marshall was part of that majority.

"John Marshall was a Virginian...." That's how one biographer introduces the Chief Justice. He was a son of the Virginia Enlightenment. As Chief Justice, he established the role of the Supreme Court as overseer of the constitutionality of

Chief Justice John Marshall
This distant relative of Pocahontas was sympathetic to the Cherokees, but could not overcome President Jackson's insistence on Indian removal.

legislation and gave meaning to the constitutional provision that federal law was supreme over state law. But the court's power depended on enforcement by the executive branch, and that would be denied by President Jackson.

Although the Cherokees lost in their first appeal to the Supreme Court, the Chief Justice was sympathetic to their cause. Indian tribes were not nations, wrote Marshall in *Cherokee Nation v. Georgia,* but the Cherokee Nation "was a distinct political society...capable of managing its own affairs and governing itself." "The acts of our government plainly recognize the Cherokee nation as a state," the opinion continued. However, because it was within American boundaries, it was not a foreign state, but a "domestic dependent nation." His reasoning was paternalistic: a tribe's relationship with the United States "resembles that of a ward to his guardian."

Georgia made plans to give away Cherokee land by lottery and passed a law requiring whites on Cherokee land to take an oath of obedience to state law, on pain of imprisonment at hard labor. The law targeted missionaries who had supported the Cherokees in their fight against removal. As the Supreme Court was hearing arguments in the first Cherokee case in March 1831, several missionaries who refused to take the oath were arrested. They were convicted and given the choice of taking the oath or leaving the state. Reverend Samuel Worcester and Doctor Elizur Butler refused, and their appeal became the second Cherokee case, *Worcester v. Georgia.*

This time, the court ruled 6-1 for the Cherokees. On March 3, 1832, the convictions were reversed on the grounds that the law the men had broken was unconstitutional. Marshall repeated his belief that the Cherokee Nation had sovereign powers, except as it had given them up by treaty, with first England and then the United States. Only the federal government, not a state, could make treaties with an Indian tribe, sovereign to sovereign.

The Cherokees had won, but they still lost. President Jackson was not willing to risk a federal-state showdown, especially when he had never believed that tribes were sovereign. The famous quote, "John Marshall has made his decision; now let him enforce it," was a newspaper editor's accurate description of the president's position. The events following the Cherokee cases were a low point, not just for the Cherokees, but for the union, checks and balances, and the rule of law.

President Jackson personally told John Ridge that the United States would not enforce the *Worcester* decision. In despair, the Cherokee delegates in Washington began to negotiate the terms of removal, over the objections of

Chief John Ross. Ross continued to mobilize sympathetic voices across the United States, hoping that voters would remove their unjust president in the election of 1832. But Jackson was re-elected.

The "treaty party" included Major Ridge, John Ridge, Elias Boudinot, and Boudinot's brother Stand Watie. "I know we love the graves of our fathers, but an unbending necessity tells us we must leave them," wrote Major Ridge. "[W]e can't be a Nation here," John Ridge wrote to Chief Ross in 1833. "I hope we shall attempt to establish it somewhere else!" Ridge rejected proposals for individual land ownership and citizenship because the Cherokee Nation would cease to exist, leaving the assimilated people at the mercy of racist America. We "will never consent to be citizens of the United States," said the man whose New England bride had been ridiculed as a squaw.

As the Cherokee leadership split into factions, Georgia handed out title to Cherokee lands by lottery. The process was supposed to protect occupied homes and farms, but settlers simply drove the Cherokees out. An estimated two-thirds lost their homes. In 1834, Georgia's governor threatened to remove all Cherokees from the state, "forcibly if we must." Early in 1835, Chief Ross came home from Washington to find a strange family sitting at his dinner table. Later that year, the Georgia legislature abandoned all pretense of protecting occupied homes and set a date for lottery winners to claim their prizes. For the Cherokees of Georgia – about half of the Cherokee Nation – removal was already a reality.

As the Treaty of Sycamore Shoals had divided the Cherokees in 1775, the 1835 Treaty of New Echota divided them again. The final "treaty council" was attended by less than a hundred families. Because New Echota was in Georgia, these were the people who had lost all hope. The removal treaty was approved by a large majority of this small minority, and signed on December 29, 1835. Boudinot, John Ridge, Major Ridge and Stand Watie signed. John Ridge said that he was signing his death warrant.

He was right. In 1839, Cherokee assassins stabbed him to death in front of his family. Major Ridge and Boudinot were executed at about the same time. Only Stand Watie survived, to fight on the confederate side during the Civil War, against the federal government that had betrayed his people.

As Dragging Canoe had predicted in 1775, the people were now "compelled to seek a retreat in some far distant wilderness." Chief Ross and thousands of his followers signed a petition rejecting the treaty. They saw hope of fighting on for their land in states other than Georgia. But the U.S. Senate approved the treaty in 1836, setting May 23, 1838 as the date of removing the entire Cherokee Nation. Hundreds of Cherokees departed "voluntarily" between 1836 and 1838, including members of the "treaty party." Eight babies died along the way in the cold autumn of 1837.

Elias Boudinot's faithful New England bride did not live to see either the final expulsion or the assassination of her husband. Harriet Gold Boudinot died of illness in 1836. She had spent her married life among "the sons of the Forest," wrote the *New York Observer*, joining her husband in opposing the policies that the newspaper described as wrong and oppressive. Boudinot was left with six young children. Harriet Boudinot's death was not directly related to the expulsion, except that stress and heartbreak must have taken their toll.

Now the lives of conqueror and conquered paralleled each other in facing one of the common enemies of humankind. Clark's second wife, also named Harriet, had died of illness, in 1831, and William Clark was also left with young children.

While eastern Indians were being removed across the Mississippi, western Indians were still trading with whites, and that was how smallpox traveled up the Missouri in 1837. Thousands of Mandans, Arikaras, Hidatsas, Blackfeet, and others died. "[U]nless it be checked in its mad career I would not be surprised if it wiped the Mandans and Rickaree Tribes of Indians clean from the face of the earth," an Indian agent reported to Clark. "The Mandans, consisting of 1600 souls, had been reduced by the 1st of October last to thirty-one persons," came another report. In some areas, with "not more than one out of fifty recovering from it," grieving survivors threw themselves over cliffs into the Missouri. It was too late to immunize the stricken tribes, but Clark arranged for an Indian agent and a doctor to take a steamboat and locate the nomadic Lakota Sioux before they came in contact with the epidemic. With heroic effort and personal sacrifice, this doctor saved the lives of about 3,000 Sioux. This was one year before at least 4,000 Cherokee died on the Trail of Tears.

When the final deadline for Cherokee removal arrived in 1838, the U.S. Army rounded up the remaining 13,000 members of that nation. Parents were separated from children. Disease spread in miserable internment conditions. Next came forced marches in extremes of heat and cold. Soldiers killed a man who ignored orders because he was deaf and a woman who collapsed while in labor. One of the thousands who died was the wife of Chief John Ross, who died of pneumonia after giving her only blanket to a child.

A man over 100 years old was left behind. An old man with a human face, he was taken care of by white children who brought him food.

As for black slaves and free blacks living among the Cherokees, some went west. A 90-year-old former slave of a Cherokee planter died on the Trail of Tears. This old woman's children, Nanny and Peter, had recently purchased her freedom, but remained enslaved themselves. One of the planter's last acts before he was forced west was to sell Peter and his wife to slave traders.

The stories of endless walking, hunger, thirst, heat, cold, and the tiny graves of children are similar to the stories that would emerge during the next decade on the Oregon Trail. Coercion, brutality, and gross indifference to the fate of the migrants mark the difference between two of the most famous migrations in American history.

The Trail of Tears was in progress when William Clark died. He lived his last years as a widower but in the company of family and friends. In their care, he died in his home at age 68, on September 1, 1838. He was not personally responsible for the Cherokee removal, but he contributed to many a trail of tears. It would be many years before the inexorable logic of removal forced Clark's Nez Perce and Lemhi friends from their homelands, but their turns would come.

Not all Cherokees were forced west. The Oconaluftee held onto individual plots of land in North Carolina, and today are known as the Eastern or Qualla Band. Others escaped removal by fleeing into the Appalachian Mountains. One of those fugitives was named Tsali. His family was captured by soldiers. They escaped, killing two soldiers. They were captured again, this time by other fugitives who secured their families' right to remain by executing Tsali, his brother, and his two sons as punishment for the deaths of the soldiers. The capture of Tsali was arranged by William Holland Thomas, adopted son of the Cherokee chief Drowning Bear. Thomas spent his life advocating for the rights of the Eastern Cherokees. The Eastern Band now honors Tsali with a street that bears his name, in a bilingual street sign using English and Cherokee characters.

The Appalachian ranges didn't stop the American advance, but they did shelter some of its victims. Cherokee fugitives in the mountains froze and starved at first, but they eventually became Thomas Jefferson's independent farmers. Their blood mingled with that of other Americans. It still does.

Between 1834 and 1842, all of the five Civilized Tribes were removed to Indian Territory in Oklahoma. The east was conquered. The sons of the Red-Headed Chief would now play their parts in the conquest of the west.

Chapter 10

Baptiste and Beckwourth

"Where then shall the Indian betake himself? There are no more Mississippis to drive him beyond."

James P. Beckwourth

*I*n 1840, beaver populations were approaching collapse. The era of the French trapper and his Indian bride was coming to an end. Missionaries would soon head west, then wagon trains. The U.S. army marched west in 1846 and took the Southwest and California from Mexico. Then came the 49ers, the homesteaders, and the railroad. The western tribes were doomed. So were the great buffalo herds. Jean-Baptiste Charbonneau and James Beckwourth were in the middle of it all.

Jim Beckwourth's adopted Crow tribe was one of those that had given up raising corn when the horse came along. Horses made it possible for the buffalo herds to sustain entire societies. In the old days, hunters had to sneak up on buffalo with bows and arrows, or surround them, or stampede them into a narrow place – all very dangerous. Another method was the buffalo jump.

The buffalo jump, or *pishkun,* involved chasing a herd off a cliff. Pishkun is a Blackfeet word meaning deep kettle of blood. This was the wasteful slaughter that had appalled Meriwether Lewis. The mounted hunt did not completely replace the pishkun. Stories were told of the bloody mess, horrible stench, and moans of dying animals. The carnage and waste troubled Indians. Some worried that the Great Spirit, who had given the buffalo to the People, would be offended by the slaughter and take the buffalo away. These seers were right. The buffalo did come close to extinction, the People starved, and the Ghost Dance later in the century was an attempt to make amends. Ultimately, however, it was not the pishkun that destroyed the herds and the people who depended on them.

As the beaver trade ended, buffalo robes came into fashion in the United States. In addition, buffalo tongues took their turn as a delicacy. Sportsmen came west to enjoy the hunt. This new round of slaughter would have very different implications than the mutually profitable beaver trade of the past. A vital food source had become a profitable commodity on an industrial scale.

The U.S. government actively encouraged the destruction of the buffalo in order to break the power of the Plains Indians. "They are destroying the Indians' commissary," said the Civil War hero General Philip Sheridan. "Let them kill, skin, and sell until the buffalo is exterminated, as it is the only way to bring

JAMES P. BECKWOURTH IN HUNTER'S COSTUME.

James P. Beckwourth

The famous mountain man, son of a black mother and an English nobleman turned American patriot, was a friend of Sacagawea's son. Engraving courtesy of the Bancroft Library, University of California, Berkeley.

lasting peace and allow civilization to advance." Millions of buffalo were slaughtered for their hides, the meat left to rot on the plains. The carnage went far beyond the pishkun.

To make it worse, buffalo hides were accepted as currency to buy whiskey. Jim Beckwourth was part of this business. Under the name Medicine Calf, he had fought against the Crows' enemies, the Cheyenne and Blackfeet, and achieved the status of a war chief. He went on to become a trader, a friend to any tribe that would sell buffalo pelts. Beckwourth spent time at Fort Clarke in the Mandan area around 1833, with one of his Crow wives – not Pine Leaf, but his beloved "little wife" – and their son, called Black Panther or Little Jim. "My boy could now speak quite plain," the proud father recorded. "The men at the fort had taught him to swear quite fluently both in French and English, much more to their satisfaction than to mine. But I trusted he would soon forget his schooling, as the Crows never drink whisky, nor use profane language."

The Crow people were one of the few who remained safe from the white man's liquid currency. "This trading whisky for Indian property is one of the most infernal practices ever entered into by man.... In two hundred gallons [of water] there are sixteen hundred pints [of alcohol], for each one of which the trader gets a buffalo robe worth five dollars! The Indian women toil many long weeks to dress these sixteen hundred robes.... [T]he poor Indian mother hides herself and her children in the forests until the effects of the poison passes away from the husband, fathers, and brothers, who love them when they have no whiskey, and abuse and kill them when they have. Six thousand dollars for sixty gallons of alcohol! Is it a wonder that, with such profits in prospect,...the poor buffalo are becoming gradually exterminated, being killed with so little remorse that their very hides, among the Indians themselves, are known by the appellation of a pint of whisky?"

The profit motive overcame Beckwourth's scruples. When a Cheyenne named Bobtailed Horse demanded that Beckwourth open a keg, his brother-in-law Porcupine Bear tried in poignant terms to stop the damage: "I am now about to fight my brother.... In doing this, I do not fight my brother, but I fight the greatest enemy of my people. Once we were a great and powerful nation.... Once we could beat the Crows.... [N]ow...we cannot defend ourselves from the assaults of the enemy. How is this, Cheyennes? The Crows drink no whisky. The earnings of their hunters and the toils of their women are bartered to the white man for weapons and ammunition. This keeps them powerful and dreaded by their enemies. We kill buffalo by the thousand; our women's hands are sore with dressing the robes; and what do we part with them to the white trader for? We pay them for the white man's fire-water, which turns our brains upside down, which makes our hearts black, and renders our arms weak.... We are only fearful to our women, who take up their children and conceal themselves...." That day, Chief Old Bark arranged a compromise: his men would drink "a little whisky... but... we will not quarrel and fight, and frighten our women and children." To make sure, he demanded their weapons.

The pressure on buffalo intensified as more Indians sought to survive on the land west of the Mississippi. To the Plains came the displaced eastern tribes, where they competed, sometimes violently, for land and game. The last of the Cherokees arrived in Indian Country in 1839, joining the treaty party and those who had migrated earlier, including Sequoyah. As usual, the promised government support was barely adequate to avoid starvation. Despair led to drinking. Bitter divisions remained among the Cherokees, despite the efforts of Sequoyah and others to reunite the nation. Eventually, the Cherokees rebuilt their society and economy in Oklahoma. The factions formally resolved their differences in 1846. Once again, there were farms, schools, a constitution, and a newspaper. Some call it a Golden Age. It ended with the American Civil War, when the Cherokee Nation was again divided about how to face the crisis. The confederacy held out a promise of sovereignty. Also, throughout all their suffering, the Cherokee had held onto their human property. Stand Watie, the surviving leader of the treaty party, took up arms for the confederacy. So did many other Cherokees, including William Holland Thomas, the adopted son of Chief Drowning Bear. The union victory provided an excuse to reduce the size of Cherokee holdings in Indian Country.

The buffalo herds were already shrinking early in the century, but there were still enough to sustain the Plains tribes as late as the 1850s. "The incessant demand for robes has slain thousands of those noble beasts of the prairie," reported Beckwourth. When the buffalo are gone, "what shall they resort to? Doubtless, when that time arrives, much of the land which they now roam over will be under the white man's cultivation.... Where then shall the Indian betake himself? There are no more Mississippis to drive him beyond."

That was written in 1856. In 1831, there were still very few Anglo-Americans between the Missouri River and the Pacific Ocean. Only the hardiest of men traveled across the Plains and Rockies. That year, four adventurers undertook the journey, but they traveled from west to east. They were Indians, and they were in search of knowledge.

In 1831, three Nez Perce and one Salish accompanied a group of trappers on their return trip from the Rocky Mountains to St. Louis. They were curious about the ways of the whites, including religion. Their visit started missionaries on their way. Marcus and Narcissa Whitman and Henry and Eliza Spalding went west in 1836. They were not the first missionaries, but Mrs. Whitman and Mrs. Spalding gained fame as the first white women to make the overland trip.

The Whitmans provided medical care, food, and shelter to the Cayuse Indians of today's Washington State from 1836 until they were murdered in 1847. Reverend Spalding turned his attention to the Nez Perce. The Nez Perce welcomed him at first, as they had welcomed Lewis and Clark. "At first he did not say anything about white men wanting to settle on our lands...," recalled a Nez Perce. "At first our people....thought there was room enough for all to live in peace, and they were learning many things from the white men that seemed to be good. But we soon found that the white men...were greedy to possess everything the Indian had."

Baptiste Charbonneau went to work along the Santa Fe Trail in the late 1830s, using river routes to take buffalo pelts to St. Louis. This trail linked the Mexican settlements of the southwest to American trade networks. In 1842, delayed by low water in the South Platte River, Baptiste made camp on an island he named "St. Helena." There he hosted his friend Jim Beckwourth and the explorers John C. Fremont and Kit Carson. Perhaps Baptiste's choice of refreshments for his guests reflected his connection to the Virginia aristocracy. Somehow, he served them mint juleps.

John C. Fremont was married to Jessie Benton, daughter of Senator Thomas Hart Benton. The family championed the idea of westward expansion. Fremont's political connections and Carson's wilderness skills brought attention to the South Pass. Like the Cumberland Gap, the South Pass became a gateway for mass migration. It was suitable for wagons. First in small numbers, then in long caravans, wagons started on the Oregon Trail toward the South Pass and the Pacific Northwest beyond.

The first great wagon train rolled across the Oregon Trail in 1843. For the first few years, most travelers headed to Oregon Country, as the Pacific Northwest was called. The lush Willamette Valley beckoned farming families. But emigration to California was on the rise even before gold was discovered.

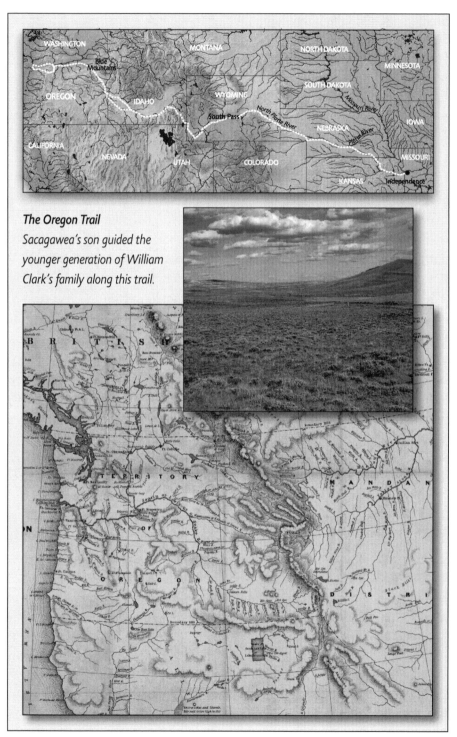

The Oregon Trail

Sacagawea's son guided the younger generation of William Clark's family along this trail.

One of the largest migrations in history was underway. Even displaced Indians headed west: a group of Cherokees traveled the Oregon Trail in 1843. Wealthy adventurers as well as settlers traveled the trail. In 1843, Baptiste served as a hunter and cart driver for a party that included members of his foster family: William Clark's son Jefferson Clark (twenty years younger than Baptiste), stepson, and two nephews. "By a singular coincidence he was now again to make the same journey and guide the son of William Clark through the same region," wrote one of the nephews. Old chiefs recognized Jefferson Clark's red hair and invited the young man to a feast. A Sioux showed his Jefferson Peace Medal to the explorer's son.

The gentlemen adventurers brought servants to make the trip more comfortable. For most, the trip was anything but. Wagons carried goods and frail people. Everyone else walked. They walked 2,000 miles with the aim of doing back-breaking work to feed their families. They buried their children in lonely graves. The wagon ruts are still visible, in silent testimony to their determination. Because of them, America would have bread and meat when the rest of the world went hungry.

Not just bread and meat. In 1847, a nurseryman named Henderson Luelling brought an extra wagon full of fruit trees and grape and raspberry vines. "That load of living trees and shrubs brought more wealth to Oregon than any ship that ever entered the Columbia River," wrote a later emigrant. The Luelling nursery is credited with introducing the Gravenstein apple to Oregon. It's also said that the Bing cherry was named for one of Luelling's Chinese workers. But the original inhabitants of the rich land would not share in the bounty.

The towns of St. Joseph and Independence, on the Missouri River, were jumping off points for wagon trains. The trip started in the spring, when the grass was green enough to feed horses and oxen. The route followed the Platte River through modern Nebraska, with most travelers crossing the Rocky Mountains through the South Pass. Then the emigrants struggled to cross the Blue Mountains to Oregon or the Sierra Nevada to California before the winter snow. The emigrants of 1843 constituted themselves the provisional government of Oregon Territory on July 5, 1843, with the intent of becoming part of the United States.

Oregon or California? One place to make the choice is now called Fort Hall, on the Snake River in today's Idaho. Modern Fort Hall is the reservation of several Shoshonean-speaking tribes forced together by shared misfortune. They include Sacagawea's Lemhi, some bands of the Northern Shoshone, and the once-formidable Bannocks.

In Fort Hall, our story of emigrant farmers intersects with the Truckee-Winnemucca family of the Northern Paiutes, a Shoshonean tribe of the Great Basin and Sierra Nevada. The Paiute Chief Truckee, or Captain Truckee, guided a group of wagons from near Fort Hall to California in 1844. Once again, Shoshonean Indians assisted white travelers. Truckee and Winnemucca are landmarks familiar to anyone traveling the Union Pacific Railroad or Interstate Highway 80 in Northern California and Nevada. We will soon turn to the story of Truckee's granddaughter, the remarkable Sarah Winnemucca.

At first, Plains bands and wagon trains passed each other with little conflict, other than livestock theft. Settlers and Indians traded. Emigrants prepared a feast for the Sioux at Fort Laramie, Wyoming in 1845. The early emigrants circled the wagons to keep their cows and horses from wandering off. It was a dangerous journey, but mostly due to disease and accidents. Many pioneers maimed themselves with their own guns.

In 1845, Colonel Stephen Watts Kearney traveled the Oregon Trail and met with the Sioux. Stephen Kearney was married to a stepdaughter of William Clark. After competing with Meriwether Lewis Clark for the hand of Harriet Clark's beautiful daughter Mary Radford – Meriwether was in love with his own stepsister, but she married Kearney – Kearney became Meriwether's close friend. Kearney would die in the St. Louis home of his former rival, an untimely death from disease contracted during the Mexican War.

On that trip in 1845, Kearney showed off the power of his guns and proclaimed the goodwill of the Great White Father in Washington, as his wife's stepfather had done forty years earlier. Kearney had extensive experience negotiating among the Plains tribes, learning about their traditional conflicts and the new ones brought about as eastern tribes were forced onto their land. He made a point of warning all the tribes that "firewater" was their greatest enemy. On this mission, he warned the tribes not to molest peaceful emigrants. For the most part, they complied. To make sure, Kearney was sent out again in 1846 to establish the first of a string of forts to protect settlers.

As thousands of settlers rolled toward Oregon, the exact border between Oregon Country and British Canada was still in dispute. James Polk was elected president in 1844 on the campaign slogan "54 40 or fight." That would have been latitude 54 degrees, 40 minutes: straight through present-day Canada. Polk did not make any pretenses about his expansionist dreams, and his views were popular. It was America's "manifest destiny" to spread from ocean to ocean, proclaimed a New York editorial writer in 1845, and the phrase stuck.

British negotiators proposed setting the Canadian border at the Columbia River, which today separates Washington from Oregon. In the end, Washington became one of the United States instead of a Canadian province in part because one multiracial family refused to retrace its 2,000 mile walk.

George Washington Bush and his wife and children traveled the Oregon Trail in 1844. Of black and Irish parentage, Bush had fought with Andrew Jackson in the Battle of New Orleans and later worked for a French fur trader in St. Louis. Arriving in Oregon Country, Bush learned that the provisional government had voted to exclude not only slavery, but free blacks as well. (A few years later, he might also have been told "no Irish need apply.") The Bush family settled in the disputed territory north of the Columbia, accompanied by white friends who had traveled with them. Their presence helped the U.S. argue successfully in negotiations with Britain that the American "right of occupation" extended north of the Columbia.

In 1846, the U.S. and Britain compromised on the present border. Congress enacted the Donation Land Act of 1850, allowing settlers to claim land in Oregon Territory. The right was limited to whites or those half white, half Indian. When Washington Territory was carved out in 1853, the territorial legislature persuaded Congress to make an exception for George Washington Bush, but turned down his request for full citizenship and the right to vote.

With the Canadian border in place, President Polk had to settle for an expansionist war against Mexico instead of Britain. Mexico had declared its independence from Spain in 1821, but the struggling new republic could not effectively govern Texas, California, and New Mexico at a distance. American planters were attracted by the possibilities of raising cotton in Texas, and gradually won permission to bring in their slave-based economy. Many of the planters were Virginians; some were Cherokees. Mexico proceeded to abolish slavery. The prospect of losing their human property, coupled with the authoritarian excesses of the faraway Mexican government, led Texans to declare independence from Mexico in 1838. Spanish-speaking *Tejanos* fought side by side with English-speaking Texans to achieve independence. But Anglo-Americans soon dispossessed *Tejanos* and pushed for admission to the union. Texas was admitted as a slave state in December 1845.

American soldiers died in a clash with Mexican troops in April 1846 on the unsettled border between Texas and Mexico. That was the excuse President Polk needed. He announced that American blood had been shed on American soil, even though there was no agreement where American soil began. Polk asked for and got a declaration of war from the Senate. Congress approved funding. One of the congressmen who later had second thoughts was Abraham Lincoln.

As U.S. forces marched west to conquer Mexico, Meriwether Lewis Clark served as an artillery officer in the Missouri battalion. Another son of the Red-Headed Chief marched west as well: Baptiste served as a guide for the Mormon Battalion with Stephen Kearney's Army of the West along the Santa Fe Trail. Mountain men were in demand in this war; Beckwourth was a messenger, guide and interpreter in New Mexico. Accompanying Kearney to California, Baptiste reached the Pacific Ocean again, probably for the first time since his young mother insisted on seeing the dead whale.

If the struggling settlers of Jamestown could refer to the complex Powhatan society as "savage," the pioneers found it even easier to look down on the hunting and gathering tribes of California and the Great Basin. The relative ease of food gathering in coastal California and the harsh environment of the Sierra Nevada resulted in similar economies: hunters and gatherers who tended to live in small bands without settled agriculture or complex political organization. The whites called them diggers, an insult referring to the sticks used to dig for roots. They forgot the role played by Janey's potatoes in the opening of the west. Settlers expressed disgust that the diggers ate roasted grasshoppers. The Indians, for their part, knew that the Donners had eaten their dead comrades during the winter of 1846-47. There was disgust and terror at the prospect that people capable of eating their own friends might eat the Indians' children. Cannibalism was about the only atrocity that white Americans didn't inflict on California Indians. "Indian hunts" were popular during the second half of the 19th century. Men, women, and children were slaughtered for sport.

The colonization of California began in the 16th century with Spain. Under the *encomienda* system, Spanish explorers were paid with land grants, complete with the forced labor of Indians living on the land. Then came the missions. Some priests cared about the earthly welfare of their charges, but on the whole the mission system functioned as another way to enslave Indians. The Republic of Mexico adopted a policy of secularizing missions, turning them into *pueblos,* and declared equality of citizenship for Indians. However, the reality of exploitation and poverty remained when the United States took control in 1847, and Americans did little to change that. One who tried was Baptiste Charbonneau.

The United States army was briefly responsible for the governance of California and its people. Now Baptiste, like his foster father, was to hold office governing Indians. In 1847, he was named alcalde (magistrate) of Mission San Luis Rey de Francia, which was converted into an Indian sub-agency. Captain Jesse Hunter, the friend whom Baptist comforted as his wife lay dying, was appointed sub-agent.

Mission San Luis Rey was founded in 1798 and abandoned in 1834, but the local Christian Indian population remained in 1847. If agricultural labor was to be imposed from the outside, the southern California coast was at least the ideal region, with rivers, fertile soil, and the famously temperate climate. Corn and beans came to California; the Spanish used the mission Indians as laborers to raise these staples, as well as grapes and cattle. Tallow, hides, wine, brandy, leather, and blacksmith products were made at San Luis Rey. The old mission is gone, but it has been rebuilt in a place now called Oceanside, north of San Diego, California.

By a twist of fate, the Indians living at San Luis Rey were Western Shoshonean, speaking a dialect that Sacagawea might have understood. Thus, the alcalde might have been able to communicate in their traditional language as well as in Spanish. The *Payomkawichum* (People of the West) are also known as *Luisenos,* or the San Luis Rey Band of Mission Indians. They too have survived.

The friar responsible for San Luis Rey, Father Antonio Peyri, was said to care sincerely about the welfare of the mission Indians. That was the view of one of his most enthusiastic young converts, or neophytes, named Pablo Tac. Pablo Tac walked in the steps of Pocahontas. Because of his piety and intelligence, he was escorted to Rome to study. He died there of disease just before age 20.

This is how Pablo Tac described mission life. "[M]erciful God freed us" from the old religion through Father Antonio Peyri." The father oversaw Indian labor in building a church. Father Peyri appointed Indians who knew some Spanish as alcaldes to direct the Indians' daily labor. "In the afternoon, the alcaldes gather at the house of the missionary.... Returning to the villages, each one of the alcaldes wherever he goes cries out what the missionary has told them, in his language.... 'Tomorrow the sowing begins and so the laborers go to the chicken yard and assemble there....' With the laborers goes a Spanish majordomo and others, neo-phyte alcaldes to see how the work is done, to hurry them if they are lazy...and to punish the guilty or lazy one who leaves his plow...."

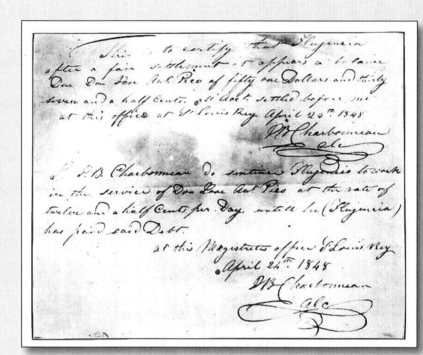

A sentencing order written by Jean-Baptiste Charbonneau.
This is one of the few documents written by Sacagawea's son. Reproduced with the
permission of the Santa Bárbara Mission Archive-Library.

For the "lazy" ones who resisted forced conversion or forced labor, punishment could be vicious in the absence of a humane missionary. A Kamia Indian named Janitin was on the beach south of San Diego collecting clams one day in the 1820s. Two Spaniards on horseback lassoed him and dragged to Mission San Miguel. He was locked up and told that "I was not going to be set free, and it would go very bad with me if I did not consent" to the instructions of the Dominican friars. "One day they threw water on my head and gave me salt to eat, and with this the interpreter told me that now I was a Christian...." He did a poor job of working with unfamiliar tools, was whipped every day, escaped, and was again caught by lasso and then whipped until he fell unconscious. Janitin lived to old age, to show the scars and tell the story.

Together with Captain Hunter, Baptiste was charged with the "care and protection" of Indians still living at the abandoned mission. Serving without pay, the new alcalde took the job seriously, too seriously for either the Spanish speakers who had long exploited California Indians or the Americans who were waiting their turn. During his brief tenure, he founded a school for the mission Indians, perhaps thinking of the education made available to him.

At San Luis Rey, Baptiste may have fathered a second child, this time with a Luiseno woman named Margarita Sobin. Maria Cantarina Charguana was born on May 4, 1848. The baptismal certificate identifies the father as "Juan Charguana, Americano" – possibly "John Charbonneau," again the "American." Maria Cantarina's fate is undiscovered.

The system Baptiste was expected to enforce was hopelessly unfair. He sentenced an Indian named Fulgencio to work off a debt to Don Jose Pico at 12 ½ cents a day. Don Jose operated a store, and the ledger of Fulgencio's purchases tells a sad story: an occasional purchase of shirts, meat, or cheese, but mostly wine and whiskey, possibly the brandy distilled at the mission. A copy of the sentencing order survives, written in the flowing penmanship Baptiste had learned in that other St. Louis of his youth. It is one of the few documents left to history by Sacagawea's literate son.

In April 1848, Baptiste was accused of joining with Indians in planning an insurrection. The official record of these events makes no mention of the alcalde's relationship with Sacagawea, who had not yet entered popular imagination, but we hear from Baptiste in his own defense. "Your Judgeship-sir," he wrote in a letter quoted verbatim in this record, "I have as I told Don Sandiego Arguello at parting from our visit ner [probably "near," indistinct handwriting] San Marcos rancho, got the individuals who had the impudence to use my name, or even to hint it, to Capt. Tomas of San Ysabel, the two [probably "two," indistinct] letterbearers, the writer, or Geronimo's clerk, and the letter, which I have the honor to enclose to you, you will peruse & judge how much I am implicated, or what part I taken [sic] in it....If it is necessary that I should go down, I am ready to appear, or I think will go to see the Indians safe." Apparently he had to "go down" (to San Diego) and present a further formal statement: "I, John B. Charbonneau of St. Louis, State of Missouri, came to California, in service of the U.S. as guide for the Mormon Battalion, under command of Col. Cook....I am prepared to prove that the Indian Paulino is guilty of what he has sworn to my charge."

Baptiste's explanation apparently satisfied the army, as he remained at his post for another three months, but he resigned in July 1848. Captain Hunter forwarded Baptiste's resignation to the governor, reporting that the alcalde "says that he has done his duty to the best of his ability but being 'a half-breed Indian of the U.S. is regarded by the people as favoring the Indians more than he should do, and hence there is much complaint against him.'" The district military commander, Colonel Stevenson, authorized payment of Baptiste's expenses, noting that the alcalde had served without pay. Like his mother, he had served beyond the military's ability to reward him.

A priest who wrote a history of the mission gave an additional reason for Baptiste's resignation. "It was distasteful for a decent man to sentence helpless Indians to slavery in order that they might pay for the liquor received in excess of 12 ½ cents, their day's wages for labor." The Red-Headed Chief would have been proud.

Jesse Hunter offered to resign when Baptiste did. He was granted a leave of absence instead, and the two set out for the next great adventure in the west: the gold fields of Sacramento.

Gold was discovered at Sutter's Fort in January 1848, the year after Mexico surrendered. Rumors of the discovery trickled east as Mexico was in the process of ceding the southwestern states and California. Emigrants loading their wagons for the spring departure on the Oregon Trail wondered whether it was a hoax. Communication was slow; that's why we ended up with 49ers instead of 48ers. As in Texas, Americans dispossessed Spanish-speaking *Californios*. California was admitted as a free state in 1850.

In the gold country, Beckwourth found Baptiste "house-keeping" on Murderer's Bar on the American River, near Auburn, California, and joined his friend in the inn-keeping business. In 1849, a friend from Baptiste's St. Louis school days reported staying with them on the trip from Sacramento to Placerville. Baptiste was in the area when his old friend, Duke Paul, visited the gold country, met some farm workers who happened to be Shoshone, and remarked, "One of these Snake Indians was a very bright fellow and reminded me of the B Charboneau who followed me to Europe...." There is no evidence that Paul and Baptiste crossed paths this time.

In 1848, Congress created the Oregon Territory, which would become Oregon, Washington, and parts of Wyoming and Montana. The heightened interest in Oregon Country came in response to the 1847 massacre of Marcus and Narcissa Whitman and several other innocent people in today's Washington. The immediate provocation for the murders was not land. The Indians had been persuaded by a notorious troublemaker that Dr. Whitman's treatment of Indian children who had measles was actually poisoning them. It was the Cayuse custom to kill a medicine man who did not heal.

In response to the massacre, the provisional government of Oregon Country declared war on the Cayuse, and killed a chief in battle. To the credit of that government, there was no mass retribution against innocent Cayuse. The settlers focused on bringing the killers to justice. The Cayuse turned over five men. They were tried by jury – not of their peers, of course – and were defended by an American official who took his job seriously enough to argue that the court had no jurisdiction because American law was not in force at the time of the murders. This was pretty good due process for that time and place – more than Indians usually got, and more than the Whitmans got when they were falsely accused of poisoning children. The five men were convicted and hanged.

Before the Gold Rush, travelers on the Oregon Trail numbered in the thousands. Beginning in 1849, there were tens of thousands. Oregon or California? Nowadays Oregonians like to joke that there was a sign at the junction, directing those who could read to Oregon, while a picture of a miner's pick pointed the illiterates to California. But when word of gold reached Oregon, farmers left their plows and headed south in droves. No comment from this California girl. When gold was found in Oregon in 1851, Indians were forced from their villages and killed by drunken whites, just as in California.

The Indians of the Plains and Great Basin began responding more aggressively to the westward intrusion. Pawnees captured some whites on the Platte River in 1848, but thought better of the military response they could expect, and set them free. The same group of whites was threatened by Sioux warriors, but the chief let them go when he recognized his son-in-law; white men were still marrying Indian women on the frontier. Family connections ran out on the Idaho-Nevada border, however, where the son-in-law was killed.

Indians starved on the Plains in the bitter winter of 1848-49. When the gold seekers came through in the spring, there was some trade and mutual cooperation, but also theft and murder. One emigrant company rescued a Pawnee child captured by the Sioux after the Sioux had massacred the boy's band. An American doctor treated Pawnee and emigrant alike.

Cholera was killing emigrants in 1850, so the Sioux and Cheyenne kept away. In what is now Kansas, smallpox killed one in five of the Sauk and Fox in 1851, but their Indian agent hired a doctor to vaccinate the others.

A great treaty council was called in 1851. It was planned for Fort Laramie, Wyoming, then moved to Horse Creek to provide forage. The Pawnees refused to attend. The Apaches, Arikaras, Assiniboins, Crows, and Atsina were there. The Sioux, Cheyenne, and Arapaho mingled freely. The army had to prevent hostilities between these Plains tribes and the "Snakes" at first. Later, the Oglala Sioux gave dog feasts for the Snakes and others. The formal council began with a procession of the tribes together, "not armed or painted for war," reported a newspaper, "but decked out...for peace." Agreements were reached that settlers and forts would be unmolested. In return, Indians could hunt in designated areas, and the U.S. government promised an annuity of goods.

This peace treaty soon fell apart for a number of reasons, in addition to American land lust. For one thing, the U.S. saw the assigned hunting grounds as strictly designated areas of control, while the Indians thought of broadly defined territories. For another, white Americans persisted in thinking that "the chief" could control breakaway bands or young warriors out to prove themselves. When settlers were killed, "the United States troops are often turned indiscriminately upon [the Indian] race," Beckwourth protested in 1855. "The officer having charge of an expedition ... should rightly understand which band of a tribe he is commissioned to punish...." Finally, tribe continued to fight tribe. In 1853, an emigrant remarked that the hostile Pawnee were held back by the Sioux.

The annuities promised by the government at the council of 1851 were part of a pattern in which Indians, deprived of hunting territory and game, became dependent on the federal government to supply their basic needs. The business of supplying these desperate people was ripe for corruption. Corruption took many forms. Indian agents and government-authorized traders sometimes siphoned off food and clothing and sold them for profit, substituting meager and inferior rations, or none at all. Or the annuities that had been promised in exchange for land weren't delivered on time, and traders refused to provide supplies until the Indians had cash on hand. When traders did issue supplies on credit, they more than repaid themselves when the annuities arrived at the agency. When the supplies or annuities didn't come through, Indians froze and starved, or took measures to keep their families alive and then faced the consequences.

In 1854, a hungry Brule Sioux killed a settler's cow. A Brule chief named Conquering Bear offered to make restitution. A lieutenant named Grattan demanded that Conquering Bear arrest the offender. When Conquering Bear explained that he had no authority to do that, Grattan opened fire. Conquering

Bear was killed but the army got the worst of it: Grattan and thirty of his men died. The military placed the blame on Lieutenant Grattan for escalating a minor conflict. Nevertheless, the army sent a punitive expedition in response. "The Indians showed signs of parley, but, as we had come for war and not for peace, we paid no attention to them...," wrote a reporter embedded with the troops. "The fun commenced in reality. I never saw a more beautiful thing in my life. We, of necessity, killed a great many women and children." This was the "battle" of Blue Water Creek.

In 1855, the Cheyenne chief Lame Bull signed a treaty to maintain peace with the U.S. and with other tribes in Montana. The parties included the Nez Perce and some Blackfeet bands. The agreement allowed roads, telegraph lines, and military outposts across 26 million acres.

What of Sacagawea's people during this turmoil? In 1855, Mormon missionaries arrived in their country and built a settlement that they named Limhi, for a king in the Book of Mormon. The Lemhi, as they would soon be called, sought peaceful relations with the newcomers, under the leadership of Sacagawea's Cameahwait family. The missionaries made an effort to learn the Shoshonean language, and the Mormon leader Brigham Young took a humane if paternalistic view of Indians. Once again, the newcomers had walked into complex internal politics, in which Sacagawea's kinsman Snag (or Naw-ro-yawn) was gaining recognition as "the chief" of the bands that were coalescing to deal with the challenge of white immigration. Snag even converted to the new faith. To foster goodwill, Young announced that Mormon men could marry Lemhi women, and three marriages resulted.

The Mormons wore out their welcome when increasing population and economic activity – timbering, pasturing, and commercial salmon fishing – depleted the Indians' resources. In 1858, 200 Lemhis attacked the mission, made off with horses and cattle, and killed two people. Other Lemhis tried to make amends, but the mission was abandoned. The name Lemhi, the stronger cohesion of a number of bands, and the Cameahwait family's leadership remained. When the Mormons departed, they gave a thousand bushels of wheat to their friend Snag.

And what of Sacagawea's son? In 1852, "John Charbonneau" was working as a surveyor in the Auburn, California area. Baptiste's address in the 1860 census was "P.O. Secret Ravine." An 1861 Placer Country Directory listed him as a hotel clerk in Auburn. Now in middle age, he was living a quiet life. Not so the nation.

The question tearing it apart was whether slavery would be extended into new territories.

In 1856, the newly formed Republican Party fielded its first presidential candidate, John C. Fremont, under the banner "free soil, free labor, free men." There was no question that soil was to be liberated from Indians as well as from slavery. The first Republican president, Abraham Lincoln, was a son of Kentucky, whose father and grandfather had fought the Shawnees for the right to wrest a living from the soil.

Virginia was about to take center stage again: reluctant to secede from the union for both patriotic and economic reasons, but the heart of the confederacy once it did. The slave-based plantation economy had caused the south to fall behind the north in financial capital, food production, manufacturing capacity, and an industrial labor force. Richmond, however, was growing in industrial importance, and there was little slave ownership or plantation agriculture in impoverished, mountainous western Virginia. Seven states formed the confederacy in response to Lincoln's election, and South Carolina fired on the flag at Fort Sumter, but Virginia delegates voted twice against secession. Virginia seceded only after President Lincoln called on loyal states for soldiers to suppress the rebellion. Then Virginia split in two, with the western counties staying in the union, soon to become the new state of West Virginia. The line of division lay roughly along the Appalachian ranges. The Old Dominion claimed the ultimate loyalty of men like Robert E. Lee, although he opposed both slavery and secession.

The war in the west continued during the war in the south. President Lincoln signed the Homestead Act in 1862, allowing white settlers to claim 160-acre lots. That year, there was starvation among the Dakota Sioux when annuities didn't arrive and traders refused to release food rations. In Minnesota, a sympathetic army officer got some food to the starving people. The Dakota chiefs Little Crow and Big Eagle counseled restraint. One night, some hungry young warriors killed five men and women on farming homesteads. Little Crow knew that retaliation was coming, and reluctantly ordered his warriors to take the offensive against government and military posts. He issued the order to kill the traders at the agency.

"[W]hen the force started to attack the agency, I went along," said Big Eagle. "I did not lead my band, and I took no part in the killing. I went to save the lives of two particular friends if I could. I think others went for the same reason, for nearly every Indian had a friend he did not want killed; of course he did not care about anybody else's friend."

Breakaway warriors didn't confine themselves to government targets. Hundreds of settlers in Minnesota were massacred: farmers, their wives, and their children. Many of the victims were Scandinavian immigrants who had fled from hunger in the old country. They had heard of land waiting for hard-working farmers, although many Sioux were successfully adopting farming by the 1860s.

One victim who was not innocent was the trader Andrew Myrick. He had said, "If they are hungry, let them eat grass." Myrick's body was found with his mouth stuffed full of grass. Strangely enough, Myrick had an Indian wife.

Hundreds of Dakota were captured, tried, and sentenced to be hanged. Men, women, and children were imprisoned and many died of disease, hunger, and cold. President Lincoln ordered a review to distinguish murderers from warriors, then commuted 265 death sentences. Told of the political consequences of those pardons, he said, "I could not afford to hang men for votes." Thirty-eight men went to the gallows in a mass execution. Just before the trapdoors opened, they cried out their names and "I am here!" Two were hanged by mistake; one had saved the lives of whites.

To finance the Civil War, the union needed gold and silver. Gold was discovered in Lemhi country at Grasshopper Creek, Montana in 1862, and a mining camp called Bannack sprang up. Several months later, Snag was shot to death while bathing in the creek. The killer was Buck Stinson, a notorious "road agent" (highway robber) who boasted that his only reason for shooting Snag was "to add another notch to his gun." Snag's dying wish was to transfer leadership to the level-headed Tendoy, another member of the Sacagawea-Cameahwait clan. Tendoy led his people from 1863 to 1907. His first act was to tell the miners at Bannack that his people wanted peace but were not afraid of war. The miners disavowed Buck Stinson and apologized for his crime.

Shoshone bands were starving by 1862. Attacks on settlers by Northern Shoshone warriors were increasing. Bannocks ambushed a wagon train in 1862 in Idaho, killing ten settlers at a place that became known as Massacre Rock. In retaliation, hundreds of Northern Shoshone Indians, including 90 women and children, were killed in the Bear River Massacre of 1863 in Idaho.

Chief Washakie, however, directed his people to extend a hand of friendship. This was the leader of the eastern bands of Northern Shoshone, whose sub-chief was Bazil, the supposed son of Sacagawea. Washakie's people even helped settlers get their wagons across rivers. Washakie was of the generation of Baptiste and Beckwourth. He was esteemed as a warrior against the Blackfeet and Crows, and also worked with white trappers as a guide. Washakie cooled the hot heads of young warriors, discouraging them from joining the Bannock attacks. The young men called him an old woman. In response, the chief disappeared for several weeks and returned with seven Blackfeet and Crow scalps.

The days of taking scalps were in the past for the Crow warrior chief Jim Beckwourth, the Medicine Calf. Once he had fought the Cheyenne. Now they

Chief Washakie
The Shoshone
leader was a
friend of
American
settlers and
an ally of the
American
military.

were his trading partners. The Cheyenne trusted Beckwourth and sought out his counsel. In 1864, however, Beckwourth failed to prevent a massacre of his Cheyenne friends at the hands of a U.S. army colonel named John Chivington.

Chivington had fought to abolish slavery and save the union, and now was burning to avenge the murders, kidnapping, rape, and torture that desperate Indians were unleashing on settler families. He had no trouble collecting volunteers for a mission of punishment. Chivington, a Methodist preacher, explained why he didn't spare Indian children: "Nits breed lice."

Black Kettle and White Antelope were Cheyenne chiefs in Colorado; Left Hand led a band of Arapaho. All three took peace negotiations seriously. Black Kettle was given an American flag as a token of his good faith, and told that no harm would come to his people as long as that flag flew over them. So the chiefs brought their bands to Sand Creek, Colorado, to camp under the protection of the army at nearby Fort Lyon. It was early morning and many of the Indians were still asleep when Chivington ordered his troops to open fire. Black Kettle frantically waved his American flag and a white flag of truce. White Antelope cried "Stop! Stop!" in plain English, then stood with his arms folded until he was shot to death. Left Hand also folded his arms, saying he would not fight his friends, until he was shot and wounded.

The surviving warriors desperately fought back as Chivington's men killed old men, women, and children in cold blood. Little children were shot while on their knees or waving a white flag.

Some of the officers refused to order their men to fire. Captain Silas Soule even placed his men between the shooters and the Indian camp for a brief period.

Black Kettle managed to take cover. His wife was badly hurt, but he carried her to Fort Lyon, where army doctors saved her life. They both were killed four years later during a similar atrocity at Washita Creek.

Jim Beckwourth was one of Chivington's guides on that bloody day, under threat of death if he refused. Another guide was Robert Bent, son of the old mountain man, William Bent, who had built the trading post called Bent's Fort. Chivington ordered his men to haul Robert Bent out of bed to accompany them. William had two Cheyenne wives, and Robert's brothers were camped at Sand Creek.

The Sand Creek massacre was so inexcusable that Congress directed the army to launch an investigation. Both Beckwourth and Soule testified against Chivington. The victims were mostly women and children, said Beckwourth, and ranged in age from 1 week to 80 years. Beckwourth managed to hide one of the brothers, Charlie Bent.

The army's judge advocate called it "cowardly and cold blooded slaughter," but no charges were brought against the colonel. Plenty of settlers thought Chivington was a hero, many soldiers were loyal to the colonel, and one of them decided to take revenge on Soule. Two men of conscience were assassinated in April 1865, but only Abraham Lincoln is famous. The other was Silas Soule, gunned down a few weeks after his wedding.

The massacre set in motion a cycle of revenge that took the lives of countless innocents on all sides. "In a few hours of madness at Sand Creek, Chivington and his soldiers destroyed the lives or the power of every Cheyenne and Arapaho

Captain Silas Soule
He defied orders to fire on a peaceful Indian camp, testified against his commanding officer, and was assassinated, apparently in revenge for his testimony.

chief who had held out for peace with the white men." The survivors "turned to their war leaders to save them from extermination."

Open warfare was soon underway across the Plains. Stagecoach drivers and passengers, as well as workers on the transcontinental railroad, became the targets of Indian rage. One of the Bent brothers who survived Sand Creek turned to a career of torturing and killing any whites he could find.

Beckwourth visited a Cheyenne village a few months after the massacre. "I went into the lodge of Leg-in-the-water. ... [H]e said, 'Medicine Calf, what have you come here for; have you fetched the white man to finish killing our families again?'.... I told them I had come to presuade [sic] them to make peace with the whites, as there was not enough of them to fight the whites.... 'We know it,' was the general response of the council. But what do we want to live for? The white man has taken our country, killed all of our game; was not satisfied with that, but killed our wives and children. Now no peace. We want to go and meet our families in the spirit land. We loved the whites until we found out they lied to us, and robbed us of what we had....We have raised the battle-axe until death.'" So Beckwourth told the military commission investigating Sand Creek.

The Civil War came to an end, and so did the eventful careers of the old mountain men. For Baptiste Charbonneau, there was one last adventure before a death notice dated May 16, 1866 and an obituary published several weeks later in the *Placer Herald*. "The reported discoveries of gold in Montana, and the rapid peopling of the Territory, excited the imagination of the old trapper," reported the obituary, "and he determined to return to the scenes of his youth." He died on the journey, at age 61. The cause of death might have been pneumonia, or "mountain fever," according to the obituary. "Metaphorically speaking, he had a case of the latter all his life...," notes his distant cousin and biographer.

Jean-Baptiste Charbonneau was buried along the Owyhee River in Oregon. He died as he was born, in the company of traveling companions. The obituary notice said he was "of pleasant manners, intelligent, well read in the topics of the day, and was generally esteemed in the community in which he lived, as a good meaning and inoffensive man." An inoffensive old man – no mention of the knife, the bullwhip, or the wild rendezvous – a man capable of friendship and fairness.

James Beckwourth died the same year as his old friend. His autobiography, written ten years before his death, is an epitaph for the Plains. "My heart turns naturally to my adopted people. I think of my son, who is the chief." A chief, not the chief. Either Beckwourth embellished, or the writer who took down his dictation had the white man's tendency to cast about for a single chief.

"As an American citizen, a friend of my race, and sincere lover of my country.... I cannot properly conclude...without saying something for the Red Man....," continued Beckwourth. "[T]hey resent in their hearts the invasion of the immigrant just as much as any civilized people would, if another nation, without permission, should cross their territory.... [T]he Indians believe the buffalo to be theirs...given to them by Providence for their support and comfort, and...when an immigrant shoots a buffalo, the Indian looks upon it exactly as the destruction by a stranger of so much private property."

Then came the chilling realism, or perhaps resignation, and the belief in Manifest Destiny, from the man who identified most of all with his father's people – from the son of the English nobleman and American patriot, Sir Jennings Beckwith. "If it is the policy of government to utterly exterminate the Indian race... the most direct and speedy mode of clearing the land of them would be by the simple means of starvation – by depriving them of...the buffalo.... To effect this, send an army of hunters among them.... [T]he devoted animal... serves...to preserve the Indian, and thus impede the expanding development of civilization." And so it soon happened.

With the nation reunited, the Indian wars drew toward their inevitable close. Another treaty council at Fort Laramie in 1868 guaranteed tribal hunting rights; the Americans would soon break that treaty too. Washakie and Bazil signed for the Northern Shoshone. In 1869, the transcontinental railroad was completed. In the Rocky Mountains, Sacagawea's kin led the Lemhi in their struggle to hold on to some of their land. And, in the Great Basin, Sarah Winnemucca played the roles of Pocahontas and Sacagawea during the final chapter of the western conquest.

Chapter 11

The Paiute Princess

"If I could tell you but a tenth part of all she willingly did to help the white settlers and her own people to live peaceably together I am sure you would think, as I do, that the name of Toc-me-to-ne should have a place beside the name of Pocahontas in the history of our country."

General Oliver O. Howard

*H*er name was Thocmetony, Shell Flower. She is better known as Sarah Winnemucca, when she is known at all. She was born to the Northern Paiutes around 1844, in present-day Nevada. She was the daughter of a shaman known as Old Winnemucca. Her mother was Tuboitonie, daughter of Captain Truckee.

The Northern Paiutes called themselves the Numa – the People. They lived in small bands, hunting and gathering in the Great Basin and eastern Sierra Nevada. The Northern Paiutes spoke a Shoshonean language, and whites sometimes called them the Snakes, the generic term for Shoshonean Indians that was used for Sacagawea's people too.

The area where the Northern Paiutes lived felt the impact of American emigration in the mid-1840s. Like the Powhatan leadership, the Truckee-Winnemucca family was divided in its response.

Captain Truckee acted as a guide for white emigrants and for John Fremont during the conquest of California. "Captain Fremont, who is now General Fremont…gave my grandfather the name of Captain Truckee," wrote Sarah many years later, "and he also called the river after him. Truckee is an Indian word, it means *all right,* or *very well.*" Captain Truckee returned from California with tales of modern wonders and optimistic stories of the goodness of the newcomers.

Around 1848, a group of white emigrants arrived, very late in the fall. "They could not get over the mountains, so they had to live with us," Sarah recalled. "During the winter my people helped them. They gave them such as they had to eat." Some whites returned the favor when they could. Others repaid generosity with murder. Truckee took pains to distinguish friend from foe. When a Paiute was shot near a white encampment, the people cried out for revenge, but Truckee reminded them that these whites had given them sacks of flour. "'I know and you know that those men who live at [Humboldt] sink are not the ones that killed our men,'" she recalled him saying. When Paiutes died of the waterborne illnesses that had made their appearance along with the settlers, Truckee argued that the whites would not intentionally poison a water source that they used too.

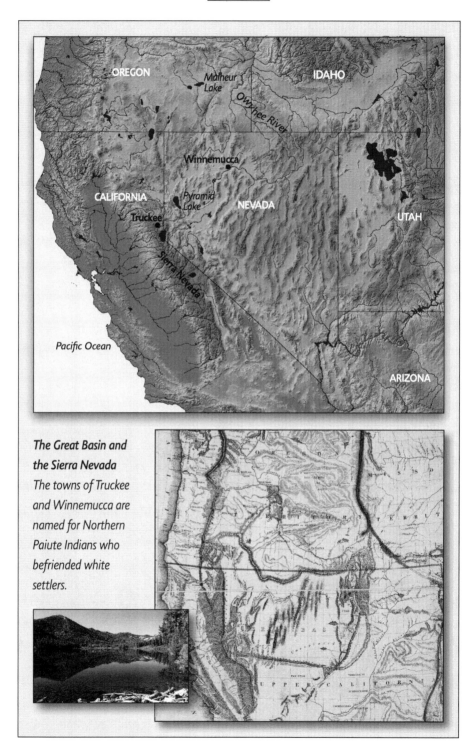

The Great Basin and the Sierra Nevada
The towns of Truckee and Winnemucca are named for Northern Paiute Indians who befriended white settlers.

From the first appearance of whites, Captain Truckee had spoken of the return of long-lost brothers and sisters. His reasons were practical as well. Whites had guns and horses – desired primarily for hunting. "[T]he Piutes, and other tribes west of the Rocky Mountains, are not fond of going to war," Sarah recalled. "I never saw a war-dance but once."

Whites offered new ways of making a living. They offered cures when the Numa became ill. They brought new kinds of food and other goods, which they often shared in friendly encounters. Captain Truckee made the most of these encounters by carrying and displaying a letter from John Fremont, attesting to his service in the Mexican War. He called the letter his "Rag Friend" and asked to be buried with it. He even taught his people to sing a version of "The Star-Spangled Banner," Sarah recalled.

Truckee's son-in-law, Old Winnemucca, lived in the old ways. Old Winnemucca was an antelope shaman who could lead his people to success in the hunt. His name means "one who looks after the Numa." Old Winnemucca learned quickly that white men looted and burned villages, killed Indians as sport, and treated Indian women as fair game. Whites cut down the trees that provided pine nuts. Whites, and later Chinese, invaded their fishing grounds. Old Winnemucca chose migratory paths as far as possible from whites. But the emigrants kept coming, settling on his band's hunting and gathering grounds.

The story of the Donner Party traveled quickly, and the warning "the whites are coming" sparked fears of cannibalism. Tuboitonie and her sister once hid little Thocmetony and her cousin by burying them in sand up to their necks, returning for them in the safety of darkness. "Oh, can any one imagine my feelings *buried alive,* thinking every minute that I was to be unburied and eaten up by the people that my grandfather loved so much?" So the memory of white brutality was seared in a child's mind, as a memory of Indian brutality haunted Jim Beckwourth. Irrationally, these settlers burned the winter supplies of these Indians who had been generous to other travelers. Then the common enemies of mankind turned on the invaders. "This whole band of white people perished in the mountains, for it was too late to cross them," Sarah recalled. "We could have saved them, only my people were afraid of them. So, poor things, they must have suffered fearfully, for they all starved there."

Still, Old Winnemucca shared his father-in-law's pragmatism and peaceful intentions, even after years of bitter experience. When gold and silver were discovered in Nevada, Old Winnemucca helped negotiate safe passage for miners through the country of the Bannocks. Silver from Nevada helped the union win the Civil War.

Despite her father's misgivings, Thocmetony and her siblings spent time with their mother and grandfather in white and Mexican communities in California. One of her first memories of California was white men threatening to rape her older sister. But, when little Thocmetony fell ill there, a white woman nursed her back to health. Sarah remembered this woman as a beautiful and kind "angel" who gave her good food and pretty clothing. She recalled several years of living in harmony with white neighbors.

As the Winnemucca brothers grew, they worked on ranches. Thocmetony learned English and Spanish. She worked in white households and was informally adopted in two of them. Like Matoaka, Thocmetony became a Christian and took a Biblical name: Sarah.

A girl on the cusp of womanhood – new ideas – adoption across peoples – but now the power was all on one side. Sarah was about 13 years old in 1857, living as an adopted daughter of Major Ormsby in Nevada, when two white traders were killed nearby. The traders were good men, friends of the Paiutes. By that time, Sarah's brother Natchez was a peace chief and their cousin Young Winnemucca was a war chief. Ormsby asked them to identify the fatal arrows. Washo, the young chiefs concluded. Major Ormsby and Young Winnemucca sent for Captain Jim of the Washo and demanded that the killers be turned over. Captain Jim insisted that all his people had been gathering pine nuts. Ormsby was insistent, and Young Winnemucca backed him: "'if you do not we shall have to fight you, for they [the murdered traders] have been so kind to us all. Who could have the heart to kill them? Now go and bring in the men,'" recalled Sarah.

So Captain Jim delivered up three men. Mothers, sisters, and a wife came along to plead their innocence with anguished tears. When an armed militia appeared to take the accused men to California for trial, they ran. All three were shot to death.

All three were innocent. Captain Jim later told Natchez, "It is true what the women say – it is I who have killed them." Two white men were found with the money stolen from the traders, and admitted they had shot them and planted Washo arrows in the wounds.

Washo Indians starved to death in the terrible winter of 1859. They blamed the settlers for the unusual weather and refused offers of food in fear that it was poisoned. They could not trust whites after the sacrifice of three innocent men.

Sarah Winnemucca

Teacher, author, scout, chief, and tireless advocate for her people, this Northern Paiute woman was the Pocahontas of the West. Courtesy of the National Portrait Gallery, Smithsonian Institution/Art Resource, New York.

Captain Truckee's good counsel against rushing to judgment was much needed during the Washo tragedy, but he was nearing the end of his days. He died around 1860, much mourned by Indians and whites alike, including a "dear beloved white brother" who held the old man's hand as he was entrusted with a dying wish: to send Sarah and her sister to a convent school. Sarah left inconsistent accounts about how long they stayed at the school, and recalled that white parents did not want the Indian sisters there.

Living with Major Ormsby, Sarah must have met the local Indian agent, Frederick Dodge. Dodge displayed the familiar mix of good intentions, condescension, and acquiescence in the inevitability of dispossession. He advanced his own funds to buy provisions for the people he called "my Indians" and argued that their reservations should be on familiar lands with adequate food resources. Over time, Agent Dodge would receive the criticism that is now a badge of honor: too easy on the Indians.

Although the Paiute bands did not have an overarching chief, whites began to see Sarah's father Old Winnemucca in that role, possibly with encouragement from Sarah. A traveler who met this "highly intelligent and educated" young woman in 1859 came away understanding that "Chief Winnemucca" was "the great chief of the Piute Nations."

In 1860, two young Paiute girls were kidnapped and raped by two white brothers. Members of their band killed the kidnappers plus a third man. Major Ormsby recruited a militia and came to demand the killers. The Pyramid Lake War was soon underway. The Paiutes won the first battle, and the Americans learned to take these peace-loving "diggers" seriously as fighters. Major Ormsby was killed, despite the efforts of Natchez to save this man who was simultaneously friend and foe. Young Winnemucca went on to impress American negotiators with his sincere desire for peace. A settlement confirmed the Paiutes' right to live at Pyramid Lake, Nevada, where they hold land today, despite rounds of relocation.

Old Winnemucca tried public relations. In 1864, he and his daughters gave theatrical performances in Virginia City, Nevada, and in San Francisco. In fluent English, Sarah told the audience that her father had refused to join a Plains tribe – possibly the Bannocks – in a war against whites. The entertainment included a re-enactment of Pocahontas' rescue of John Smith. This persona was one reason newspapers called Sarah "the Paiute princess." The show netted a little money and an impassioned letter to the editor from an anonymous white woman, who knew the family well and was appalled at the poverty that drove a respected shaman to perform on stage.

In the early spring of 1865, U.S. cavalry went to Winnemucca Lake (Mud Lake) on the Pyramid Lake Reservation, looking for Paiutes suspected of killing two miners. This time there was no pretext of justice. While the able-bodied men were off hunting, Captain Wells and his men simply massacred old men, women, and children. The camp was burned. Babies were thrown into the flames, including Sarah's baby brother. Newspapers wrote about "the slaughter of these women" and said "the killing was all on one side."

The Paiutes delivered up two men for the killing of the miners, but Captain Wells went on to "pacify" the region. Paiute, Bannock, and Shoshone warriors fought back. Settlers were terrified. A militia company ignored a white flag and killed Indians trying to hide or escape. Indians retaliated. Pacification became extermination. Paiute women fought alongside the men, knowing that the soldiers were likely to shoot them and their children, or simply leave them to freeze.

For a time, Sarah and her father recoiled from white society: Sarah went to Pyramid Lake, Old Winnemucca into the mountains. A younger sister, Elma, escaped these calamities by adoption and then marriage into white families. This Indian princess did marry a John Smith.

As the 1860s ended, Sarah seized on a rare chance to ask for justice from an Indian in a position of power. For the first time in American history, an Indian was appointed Commissioner of Indian Affairs. His name was Ely Samuel Parker. Ely Parker was a member of the Seneca tribe of New York. His Seneca name was Hasanoanda. As brilliant, ambitious, and dedicated to his people as Elias Boudinot, Parker studied law but was denied admittance to the bar because, as an Indian, he was not a U.S. citizen. He then changed his field to engineering. His accomplishments earned him the title of an Iroquois sachem. They called him Donehogawa, Keeper of the Western Door of the Long House of the Iroquois.

Parker and Ulysses Grant became friends before the Civil War. Parker's offer to raise an Iroquois unit to fight for the union was rebuffed, as was his offer to serve as an engineer, until Grant managed to get him a commission. Then Grant kept this talented officer close by his side. "I was the envy of many a pale-faced subordinate embryo-general...," Parker later remarked. It was Colonel Parker who wrote out the terms of the surrender at Appomattox. "'I am glad to see one real American here,'" Parker recalled Robert E. Lee saying that day. "I shook his hand and said, 'We are all Americans.'" Parker rose to the rank of Brigadier General. When he married in 1867, Ulysses Grant was his best man. Grant was elected president in 1868 and appointed Parker as Commissioner of Indian affairs.

Sarah Winnemucca wrote to Commissioner Parker in 1870, asking for protection against violence and encroachment by white ranchers. But Parker would soon resign. As Baptiste Charbonneau had learned, an Indian in a position to protect Indians did not last long. Parker was trying to reform corrupt Indian agencies, infuriating agents who felt cheated out of their share. He tried to enforce the promises made to the Plains tribes in the 1868 Treaty of Fort Laramie, making enemies out of the miners and ranchers who were waiting to steal the land remaining to the Sioux.

Parker and Grant initiated the so-called Quaker Policy, or peace policy, placing Christian agents instead of military men on reservations. The clerical collar, of course, was no guarantee of Christian mercy. The Paiutes would starve under a Methodist minister. "I sent professed Christian whites who waxed rich and fat from the plundering of the poor Indians," Parker recalled, "nor were there teacher-ships enough to give places to all the hungry and impecunious Christians. Then was the cry raised by all who believed themselves injured or unprovided for...." Parker's enemies accused him of corruption. He was cleared, but resigned in 1871: "it was no longer a pleasure to discharge patriotic duties in the face of foul slander and abuse." It was an echo of Jean-Baptiste Charbonneau's letter of resignation.

So the Indian wars continued. When Custer's force was destroyed in 1876, the *New York Herald* blamed the president. "Who slew Custer?" the newspaper asked. "The celebrated peace policy of General Grant, which feeds, clothes and takes care of their noncombatant force while the men are killing our troops... [and] the Indian Bureau, with its thieving agents and favorites as Indians traders, and its mock humanity and pretense at piety – that is what killed Custer."

Whether the People starved and froze depended on the integrity of individual agents, but the best intentions could not conjure up resources, and there was no political will to evict ranchers and miners who pressed on the western Indians' remaining land. Land promised to the Paiutes was taken to provide rights-of-way and lumber for the transcontinental railroad. Whenever an Indian stepped off a reservation in search of game, that was "unrest." If a hungry Indian stole a cow, the army was ordered to protect settlers' livestock. When a captain made sure the Paiute bands had adequate provisions and allowed them to hunt, some settlers grumbled that the army should have simply exterminated them. When an army doctor paid for vaccines out of his own pocket, there was no guarantee that the Indian agent would reimburse him. Young Winnemucca died in 1872 of tuberculosis, made worse by hunger and exposure, "for want of medicine and

Ely Parker

Educated as a lawyer and an engineer, this sachem of the Seneca nation achieved the rank of brigadier general in the U.S. army, and served as Commissioner of Indian Affairs under President Grant.

care," wrote a doctor who was assigned to the reservation but not given the resources to save lives. Then, in 1875, Sarah received an invitation from Sam Parrish, the agent at the Malheur Reservation in Oregon, to work as an interpreter. He was known as a fair man. Three bands of Paiutes gathered there.

Chief Oytes was the leader of one of these bands. Oytes held beliefs similar to the Paiute dreamers who gave rise to the Ghost Dance religion. The most famous of the Paiute shamans was Wovoka, or Jack Wilson. He was a prophet of the Ghost Dance revival that swept the Plains in the 1880s as the material prospects of the tribes became increasingly desperate. The Ghost Dancers had a millennial vision of resurrection and plenty. A flood would sweep the whites out of the land, Wovoka explained, while Indians stayed safely in the mountains. Then the game would be restored and the rightful inhabitants of the land would welcome the return of their beloved dead. Wovoka himself worked as a ranch hand, but Oytes was reluctant to break the soil of Mother Earth with a plow.

Sarah went to work at Malheur at a school run by the agent's sister-in-law, Annie R. Parrish. The Paiutes called Mrs. Parrish the "white lily" and "dear mother." Sam Parrish refused to let white settlers take all the good land, and the Paiute farming efforts thrived. He made sure the Indians received the supplies and pay they were promised. In this way, Sam Parrish joined the honor roll of Indian agents who lost their jobs. Settlers complained to Washington. In 1876, President Grant appointed a new agent who reneged on Parrish's assurances that the Paiutes would be able to keep the land they farmed. Having placed the Indians back in the position of pleading for subsistence, he sent out an order for rations, but it was delayed by bureaucracy and snow. Starvation and exposure to the elements loomed again. The school was closed.

Old Winnemucca refused to live at Malheur, but he proposed an alternative: let his band have land along the Owyhee River in eastern Oregon. There, on the river where Baptiste Charbonneau was buried, they could farm and raise stock. The new agent called the idea a hallucination.

Meanwhile, Chief Washakie continued his policy of allying with the Americans. This alliance meant that his bands received rations to avoid starvation and that they had a say in their assignment to the Wind River Reservation. He fought alongside U.S. troops against the Sioux in 1876, wearing a headdress of eagle feathers that swept behind his pony's tail. When he died at age 95, he was given an army funeral. His statue stands in a prominent place in the Montana State Capitol. He was no pacifist, but he saw the future and led his people there.

In June, 1877, there was speculation that Paiute bands in Oregon might rise up along with the Nez Perce. This was the tribe that had succored the Lewis and Clark expedition after the terrible crossing of the Bitterroot Mountains. "Thus began a long friendship between the Nez Perces and white Americans. For seventy years the tribe boasted that no Nez Perce had ever killed a white man."

A Nez Perce chief called Tuekakas had accepted baptism by Reverend Henry Spalding at the Lapwai Mission in 1838 and taken the Biblical name Joseph. But he refused to sign a treaty giving away the beautiful Wallowa Valley in the Oregon Territory. The chief eventually threw away his Bible in disgust.

When Old Joseph died, Young Joseph (Heinmot Tooyalaket, or Thunder Rolling down the Mountain) became Chief Joseph and continued his father's policy. The people lived well, raising cattle and horses that white settlers were glad to purchase. Then the chiefs of other bands signed away the rich land where Joseph's people lived. There was gold, and there was grazing land, and the whites wanted it all. Joseph's band was ordered to move to the Lapwai Reservation in Idaho.

General Oliver O. Howard was sent to carry out the order. Howard had lost an arm fighting for the union, but returned to the field and fought throughout the Civil War and Indian pacification campaigns. He was a pious man whose men called him "Old Prayer Book." Howard's sympathy for his adversaries was reflected in the title of a children's book he wrote late in life: *Famous Indian Chiefs I Have Known*. He was proud to call Washakie, Chief Joseph, and Sarah Winnemucca his friends. But he was a military man and he did his duty.

Chief Joseph resisted with every ounce of his famous charisma and eloquence. The Earth was his mother, and he could not trade it away. He finally bowed to the inevitable and agreed to move his people. His young warriors revolted and killed white settlers. The war no one wanted was underway.

Joseph's band decided to seek refuge in Canada. The warriors fought to cover their families' flight through Idaho and Montana. The Nez Perce made their eastward journey through the Bitterroot Mountains across Lolo Pass, along the same paths where Lewis and Clark had once staggered westward, cold and hungry, to their hospitality. The U.S. army responded by organizing a settler militia to stop them. However, once the Indians promised to pass through peacefully, the locals refused to fight, avoiding an escalation that might have endangered their own families. The entire band escaped, almost within sight of the makeshift fort, which was nicknamed Fort Fizzle.

It fell to General Howard to pursue the Nez Perce. The justice of the Indians' cause and their military skill earned considerable popular sympathy. General William Tecumseh Sherman said, "the Indians throughout displayed a courage and skill that elicited universal praise." Newspapers called Joseph "the Red Napoleon," although he was not a war chief; he guarded the camp while his brother Olikut led the warriors. They covered almost 1,400 miles, heading north into the bitterly cold autumn nights. The band was within forty miles of the Canadian border when army reinforcements surrounded them.

Joseph's surrender speech has never been forgotten: "The little children are freezing to death. My people, some of them, have run away to the hills, and have no blankets, no food. No one knows where they are – perhaps freezing to death. I want to have time to look for my children, and see how many of them I can find. Maybe I shall find them among the dead. Hear me, my chiefs! I am tired. My heart is sick and sad. From where the sun now stands I will fight no more forever."

One of the Nez Perce warriors captured at the end of Chief Joseph's War was Tzi-kal-tza, the light-haired man who also called himself Clark. He had a daughter named Mary Clark, who understood that she was the granddaughter of the explorer. This oral tradition, if true, was the legacy of the Red-Headed Chief: life and death, pride and shame.

The terms of the surrender provided that Joseph's band would be allowed to live at Lapwai, as Joseph had reluctantly agreed before the young warriors exploded in rage. But this promise was broken, like all the others, and they were sent to Indian Country in Oklahoma, where many died, including Tzi-kal-tza. General Howard pleaded their case. Eventually, some of the survivors were allowed to go to Lapwai, but Joseph and others were confined to a separate reservation in Washington.

The Northern Paiutes stayed out of the Nez Perce War. In 1878, the starving people scraped up money to send "our mother" to Washington, D.C. to argue for justice. Her journey was interrupted when Bannock warriors began fighting on Big Camas Prairie in Idaho. A group of whites had raped a Bannock girl and her brother had gotten drunk and killed a white man. Even though the tribe had complied with orders to bring the killer to justice, the colonel at Fort Hall confiscated the tribe's ponies and guns.

General George Crook spoke bluntly to a reporter in 1878: "I...found [the Bannocks] in a desperate condition.... Starvation is staring them in the face...."

The reporter suggested that it might be cheaper to treat the Indians fairly. "Of course it would be cheaper," said the general. "All the tribes tell the same story. They are surrounded on all sides, the game is destroyed or driven away, they are left to starve and there remains but one thing for them do to – fight while they can.... Our treatment of the Indians is an outrage."

Natchez and Old Winnemucca tried to persuade Chief Oytes to stay out of the Bannock uprising. In response, Oytes warriors' turned on the Winnemucca family. Learning that her father was captured, Sarah and her sister-in-law Mattie offered their services as scouts for General Howard. Sarah disguised herself, entered the Bannock camp, and organized a stealthy escape. When the Bannocks gave chase, she galloped for hours to get help. "[N]o white man can keep up with us," she once explained matter-of-factly when declining an army escort. "We can go alone quicker than with soldiers." The Bannocks and their allies in Chief Oytes' band surrendered before 1878 was over.

As the Paiute princess had confirmed her father's leadership years before, the old shaman now confirmed hers. "Her name is everywhere and everyone praises her. Oh! how thankful I feel that it is my own child who has saved so many lives, not only mine, but a great many, both whites and her own people. Now here-after we will look on her as our chieftain, for none of us are worthy of being chief but her."

The Lemhi Shoshone also stayed out of the Bannock and Nez Perce conflicts. Their chief Tendoy, the kinsman of Sacagawea, even offered to defend settlers if needed. But, as Natchez of the Northern Paiutes told the *Daily Silver State*, "No Indians can get anything from the government if they behave themselves." From 1880 on, the Lemhi were under relentless pressure to leave the Salmon River country.

Sarah's service to the United States was betrayed even sooner. Part of her mission during the Bannock War had been to bring neutral Paiutes a promise of food and safety: "Tell them I, their mother, say come back to their homes again [in Malheur Reservation]. I will stand by them and see that they are not sent away to the Indian Territory." But later the very same year, the order came that they must relocate to the Yakima Reservation north of the Columbia River. "My people will never believe me again," Sarah cried to the commanding officer. He was sympathetic and agreed to write to the president. As they awaited word from the Great Father, Mattie echoed Pocahontas' words to John Smith in London: "we cannot help it if the white people won't keep their word." The order stood. "In this cold winter and in all this snow?" Sarah protested in desperation. "They will die."

Old Winnemucca's band was excused from the order, but Sarah and Mattie went with the refugees. The forced march took place in December 1878, without blankets or adequate clothing. An old man froze to death, then three young children, two newborn babies, and a postpartum mother. The beloved teacher, Annie Parrish, met the miserable procession and cried with them, but could not help. When they arrived at Yakima, they found no food, shelter, or fuel. Fifteen months later, Sarah reported a death toll of thirty children and eighteen adults from disease, hunger and exposure. In the spring of 1879, the Paiutes were given plots to farm, as well as cloth so thin that Sarah claimed she could sift flour through it. The Yakima Indians had no love for the new arrivals. Still, "we had the finest wheat that ever was raised on the reservation," Sarah said proudly of the survivors.

Sarah visited San Francisco later in 1879 to continue her advocacy. Newspapers there called her "Princess Sarah." She wore a necklace engraved by settlers grateful to her for saving the lives of several whites during the Bannock War. At the same time, she lectured forcefully to sympathetic audiences, explaining why "the Indians go and harm some innocent white people in their vengeance. I do not excuse my people. But I say you cannot hold them from it unless you change your treatment of them."

In January 1880, Sarah resumed her interrupted mission to the nation's capitol. There, she secured a promise from the Secretary of the Interior to give the Paiutes reasonable options for farming, but this became a dead letter. The secretary also promised one hundred tents, and these did not arrive either. "I have lived many years with white people," said a Paiute as he waited for the tents. "I have never known one of them do what they promised. I think they mean it just at the time," he added charitably – or sarcastically, "but I tell you they are very forgetful." In the next few years, she tried again to get land in Oregon. Unfortunately, she had to make her case to General Phil Sheridan. "The only good Indians I ever saw were dead." That quote is generally attributed to Sheridan. The people were sent back to Pyramid Lake, where white squatters had long since taken the best land. The army cleared the squatters, but they soon came back.

Sarah took her case to Boston in 1883, where she moved in circles of New England reformers such as Elizabeth Peabody, Ralph Waldo Emerson, and Justice Oliver Wendell Holmes. The lecture circuit was the educational channel of yesteryear. From Vermont to Baltimore, Sarah was introduced as Princess Winnemucca. She wrote her story: *Life among the Piutes: Their Wrongs and Claims.* She made it clear that Indians knew a thing or two about democracy. "We have a republic as well as you. The council-tent is our Congress, and anybody can speak who has anything to say, women and all." She was blunt in her challenge to America. "For shame! You dare to cry out Liberty, when you hold us in places against our will, driving us from place to place as if we were beasts."

As Sarah was moving in the nation's highest circles, Old Winnemucca was dying. The old shaman, now a widower over 90, had married a widow with a young child. Shortly thereafter, he fell ill. When conscious, he said he had dreamed that his new wife had brought evil upon him. A council of Paiutes determined to kill the mother and her child. As the woman begged for mercy, a Paiute tore the child from her arms and dashed its head against the rocks. Then the Paiutes stoned the mother to death. None of this helped the dying chief.

News of the stoning hurt Sarah's efforts. Americans had left witchcraft trials in the past. Manifest Destiny would bring due process and modern knowledge. It was easy to use these worthy goals to justify theft and murder.

One of Sarah's lobbying efforts in Washington bore fruit that most Indians considered very bitter. She obtained almost five thousand signatures on a petition seeking land and citizenship for Indians; it was presented to Congress in 1884. The bitter side involved the breakup of tribal land through a process of "allotment" to individual households. A plague, most Indians would call the Dawes Act of 1887, a curse. But Senator Dawes introduced the act after he met the Paiute Princess and was moved by her ability to "stir hearts." She testified before a Senate subcommittee in support of his plan.

In 1887, Congress passed the Dawes Act, the allotment policy. In practice, it was another land grab. Each Indian head of household was allotted 160 acres. "Surplus" reservation land was auctioned off to white settlers. After twenty-five years, an Indian would receive U.S. citizenship and title to his land. Some tribes lost up to 90 perent of their land to this scheme, with Indian farmers receiving arid and marginal plots. "Gumbo with greasewood on it," said one Indian of his allotment. "There were cracks in it so big you could almost see China." Starting in 1890, Indians could lease their land to whites. Facing discrimination in everything from credit to water, many Indians leased and later sold on unfair terms, ending up with nothing.

As in the days of Washington and Jefferson, allotment started with surveying. The Dawes Commission was in charge. "Egypt had its locusts, Asiatic countries their cholera, France had its Jacobins, England its black plague...," said an Oklahoma Creek, "but it was left for unfortunate Indian Territory to be afflicted with the worst scourge of the nineteenth century, the Dawes Commission." The Yakima of Washington pulled out marking stakes; the Arapaho of Wyoming rode their horses through measuring tapes. "God damn a potatoe," cried Chief Washakie to a commissioner.

The allotment policy took deliberate aim at traditional social structures. "[T]he Indians as a body are deadly opposed to the scheme for they see too plainly the certain and speedy dissolution of their tribal and national organizations," said Ely Parker. That was what Senator Dawes had in mind: Indians should assimilate into the American mainstream and leave tribal identity behind.

Allotment was justified in terms of rugged individualism. "The common field is the seat of barbarism," said an Indian agent, "the separate farm the door to civilization." The Indian "must be imbued with the exalting egotism of American civilization," said a commissioner of Indian affairs in 1886, "so that he will say 'I' instead of 'We,' and 'This is mine' instead of 'This is ours.'" This rhetoric comes up every time Americans argue about social welfare policies, and ignores the communal reality of every endeavor that built America, from Jamestown to the wagon trains.

A Cherokee named DeWitt Clinton Duncan had survived the Trail of Tears as a boy. He graduated from Dartmouth College in 1861 and returned to Indian Territory after the Civil War. He taught English, Latin, and Greek, and he was a farmer. Age 76 in 1906, he told the Senate: "Under our old Cherokee regime I spent the early days of my life on the farm up here of 300 acres, and arranged to be comfortable in my old age; but the allotment scheme came along and struck me during the crop season, while my corn was ripening in full ear.... I had to relinquish every inch of my premises outside of that little 60 acres.... I have gone out there on that farm day after day. I have used the ax, the hoe, the spade, the plow, hour for hour, until fatigue would throw me exhausted upon the ground.... [L]et me tell you, Senators, I have exerted all my ability, all industry, all my intelligence, if I have any, my will, my ambition, the love of my wife – all these agencies I have employed to make my living out of that 60 acres, and, God be my judge, I have not been able to do it."

The Salish, another tribe that had been friendly to Lewis and Clark, were forced out of their prime farm land in the Bitterroot Valley in the 1890s. They started farming again on a reservation in Montana, and then lost their water to allotment. "In the Bitterroot when my grandfather, Victor, was chief, we Salish started farming. The government told us to do it and we did," said Martin Charlot. "Everything was going along fine. We were making a good living and learning the White man's way." Then whites wanted the good land. "'By the 1855 treaty, we don't have to move,'" said the next chief, Martin's father. "We tried to keep on farming, but Whites came in and homesteaded our land." After twenty years of encroachment, the chief agreed that the people would move. They were promised tools and livestock to replace what was left behind, but these supplies never came. They dug ditches for an irrigation system and after a time "made a good living" again. Then the surveyors came and "we were allotted." The government took over the irrigation system. "Pretty soon, most of them quit farming. The White man took over everything."

There was special irony in forcing Plains hunters onto homesteads, when their ancestors had raised corn along the Missouri River before the coming of the horse. "They had forgotten how," explained a Cheyenne named John Stands In Timber, "though they all used to garden in the old days before they hunted buffalo."

At least the Cheyenne found some enjoyment in learning new ways. The first time a man handled a plow correctly, "The women made war cries and everybody hollered just as if he had counted coup...." A government "farmer" (training agent) gave two Cheyenne men overalls and a wagon and told them how to drive. They went out to practice. It was hot work, so they cut their overalls away until their breech clouts showed. "They met the farmer on the way and he almost died laughing at them," wrote Stands In Timber. "'You have ruined the pants,' he said. 'No,' said Big Foot, 'not for us. We are mixed, half white and half Indian.'"

Another hated feature of the Dawes Act was the boarding school policy. Indian children were forcibly taken from their parents and sent to boarding schools, where they were harshly punished if they spoke a language other than English. The intent to erase the Indians' heritage was explicit.

The boarding school policy was a part of the Dawes Act that Sarah opposed. She had opened a school on her brother Natchez's farm a few years before the Dawes Act passed. It was named for her New England friend Elizabeth Peabody.

At the Peabody Indian School, Sarah taught in Shoshonean and English. After the passage of the act, she was asked to turn over her students for relocation to a boarding school in Colorado. She refused, but a number of Paiute children, including one of her nephews, were simply taken away by government officials. The *Daily Silver State* editorialized in her support that children should be educated "at home." Sarah's last, unsuccessful lobbying campaign was against this feature of the Dawes Act.

Sarah spent some of her few remaining years with her sister, Elma, Mrs. John Smith. This was in Bannock country, on the Idaho-Montana border, near the Lemhi homeland. John Smith had befriended the Bannocks. When he died in 1889, he left Elma with a home and savings. Elma worked as a midwife and took charge of two orphaned white boys, later helping one of them buy land of his own.

At Elma's house, on October 17, 1891, Sarah collapsed and died at age 47. General Howard later wrote: "If I could tell you but a tenth part of all she willingly did to help the white settlers and her own people to live peaceably together I am sure you would think, as I do, that the name of Toc-me-to-ne should have a place beside the name of Pocahontas in the history of our country."

Sarah died less than a year after the notorious massacre at Wounded Knee. The immediate antecedent to this atrocity was the Ghost Dance inspired by the Paiute shaman Wovoka. Not long before Wounded Knee, a student at the Pine Ridge boarding school remembered sneaking out of his dorm to see the Ghost Dance. "The rumor got about," he recalled. "' The dead are to return. The buffalo are to return. ... The white people will soon go away....'" The dancers saw visions of their dear ones who had gone and of a time of plenty. "Mother, hand me my sharp knife. Here come the buffalo returning," was one song. "Mother, do come back! My little brother is crying for you," was another. "Waking to the drab and wretched present...," this eyewitness remembered many years later, "they wailed as if their poor hearts would break.... But at least they had seen! The people went on and on and could not stop, day or night, hoping perhaps to get a vision of their own dead, or at least to hear of the visions of others." The authorities thought they were crazy, he concluded, "but they weren't. They were only terribly unhappy."

The authorities feared that the Ghost Dance could inspire an uprising. In the freezing South Dakota winter, a few days after Christmas in 1890, a starving group of Sioux Ghost Dancers were camped at Wounded Knee Creek. U.S. Cavalry found them, trained howitzers on their tipis, and searched for weapons.

A warrior spun around while holding his gun – one witness said he did not hear the order to disarm because he was deaf – and the army started shooting indiscriminately. Two hundred Indian men, women, and children were killed or wounded. The terrible milestone is remembered as the end of the Indian wars.

With its territorial conquest completed at the end of the 19th century, a mighty nation was ready to seek power and influence on a global scale, for good and ill.

"We're Still Here."

A century after the Lemhi welcomed the Corps of Discovery – three centuries after Pocahontas spared John Smith's life – our story ends. But, of course, it never really ends. This nation, created at such great cost, is an Indian nation as much as anything. The People live on – as Pamunkey and Lemhi, as Indians and Americans. "[L]ook for the 'indelible thread of red' in the tapestry of the American people," said a 20th century Virginia Indian activist. There are about 1.5 million people in the United States today who identify as Indians.

Resistance to discrimination, impoverishment, and forced assimilation has continued in legislative houses, in courts of law, and in the court of public opinion. Indians were finally granted American citizenship in 1924. The warriors honored at modern pow-wows wear the uniforms of the U.S. military. From Virginia to California, there are three refrains: "We're still here. Everyone is mixed together. We're all Americans."

On the Pamunkey Reservation in Virginia, corn and soy grow in neat rows, and deer leap in hardwood forests. A memorial to Pocahontas praises her kindness to the English. A museum is tended by a woman whose accent is pure Virginian. A man named Rolfe visited from England, she said, to see his "relatives."

Pocahontas' legacy in Virginia
A statue of Pocahontas at
Historic Jamestowne and the corn fields of the modern Pamunkey Reservation.

The Cherokee Nation of Oklahoma and the Eastern Band of North Carolina come together periodically for remembrance and reconciliation. "We are not a people of the past," said Principal Chief Chad Smith of the Cherokee Nation at a reunion in 2005. "We are a people of the present, and for many centuries, we will be a people of the future."

The Sioux continued their resistance in the American Indian Movement protests of the 1970s. Too many live in rural poverty and isolation, suffering alarming rates of alcoholism and diabetes, but their pride in their culture and struggles for their rights never diminish.

The Mandan-Hidatsa were nearly wiped out by smallpox. The survivors inter-married with their former enemies, the Arikara. Together on the Fort Berthold Reservation in North Dakota, they are now profiting from the fracking boom.

Sacagawea's people held on to their Salmon River homeland until 1907, when they were forced to join Northern Shoshone and Bannocks in Fort Hall, Idaho. Chief Tendoy died shortly before the final removal. The citizens of Salmon, Idaho built a monument to him. Then the Lemhi people went into exile. "The ranchers along the way could hear their crying," remembered a witness. "The ranchers were near tears and some did cry." To this day, the Lemhi struggle for federal recognition as a separate tribe and for the right to return to the land they have never forgotten. They continue to visit there, to fish and hunt and honor the graves of their ancestors. Cameahwait-Tendoy descendants continue to lead the tribe; they were present at the dedication of Yellowstone National Park, and they christened a U.S. navy ship named for Sacagawea. The Lemhi object to the Hidatsa spelling used for the ship and the dollar coin and in this book, as they remember a brave and resourceful woman by the name Sacajawea.

Luiseno Indians visit the California mission where Sacagawea's son once worked, when open houses and pow-wows are held there. A young Luiseno man who studies the cutting edge of biology in a quest to cure disease was featured in a recent article on promising Indian scholars.

The Northern Paiutes have engaged in long-running legal disputes over the little that is left to them, the water resources at Pyramid Lake. Everyone who travels through the Sierras and Nevada sees the towns of Truckee and Winnemucca, and few know who they are named for. The Paiute princess, unlike the Powhatan princess, never became a cultural icon. Perhaps it's because there is no way to make Sarah Winnemucca look like a paragon of virtue. The Paiute weroansqua was known for her hot temper. She drank and gambled and had three brief marriages – not so good for classroom plays. But, as a 19th century newspaper summarized her legacy, "In the history of the Indians she and Pocahontas will be the principal female characters...."

Chief Joseph and General Oliver Howard were photographed together in 1904 when they spoke at the commencement exercises at the Indian Industrial School in Carlisle, Pennsylvania. Their faces are deeply sad. When Joseph died in Washington, the reservation doctor reported the cause of death: "a broken heart." The Nez Perce still live in Idaho. Their graciousness to visitors is perhaps a legacy of the wise leader who was never allowed to return.

In the end, perhaps the simple stories we tell our children about Pocahontas and Sacagawea are their greatest legacy. They had open minds and open hearts. They tried to find ways to live with newcomers who were different. They helped their new friends. Against long odds, there are people today who do the same, in places where the violence of territorial conflict is still unresolved.

General Oliver Howard and Chief Joseph
The reluctant adversaries of 1877 were photographed together in 1904. Photograph courtesy of the Cumberland County Historical Society, Carlisle, Pennsylvania.

Bibliography

Akipa, Kathryn, "The Beginnings of Sorrows," pp. 7-17 in Howe, Craig and Kim TallBear (eds.), *This Stretch of the River: Lakota, Nakota, and Dakota Responses to the Lewis and Clark Expedition and Bicentennial.* Pine Hill Press, Sioux Falls, South Dakota, 2006.

Allen, Paula Gunn. *Pocahontas: Medicine Woman, Spy, Entrepreneur, Diplomat.* Harper Collins Publishers, San Francisco, 2003.

Ambrose, Stephen. *Undaunted Courage: Meriwether Lewis, Thomas Jefferson, and the Opening of the American West.* Simon & Schuster, New York, 1996.

Anderson, Fred. *The War that Made America: A Short History of the French and Indian War.* Viking Penguin, a member of Penguin Group (USA) Inc., New York, 2005.

Anderson, Irving W. "John Baptiste Charbonneau: Son of Sacajawea." *Oregon Historical Quarterly* 71: 246-64, 1971.

Anderson, Irving W. "A Charbonneau Family Portrait." *American West* 17(2): 4-13, 58-64, March-April 1980.

Auchincloss, Louis. *Woodrow Wilson.* Viking – Penguin Putnam Inc., New York, 2000.

Baker, Gerard A. "Mandan and Hidatsa of the Upper Missouri," pp.125-136 of Josephy, Alvin M., Jr. and Marc Jaffe (eds.). *Lewis and Clark through Indian Eyes,* 2006. Alfred A. Knopf, New York, 2006.

Bataille, Gretchen M. (ed.) *Native American Women: A Biographical Dictionary.* Garland Publishing, New York and London, 1993.

Beckwourth, James P., *The Life and Adventures of James P. Beckwourth,* as told to Thomas D. Bonner, introduced and with notes and an epilogue by Delmont R. Oswald (University of Nebraska Press, Lincoln, 1972), originally published as Beckwourth and Bonner, *The Life and Adventures of James P. Beckwourth, Mountaineer, Scout, and Pioneer, and Chief of the Crow Nation of Indians, written from his own dictation* (Harper & Brothers, Publishers, New York, 1856)

Biggers, Jeff. *The United States of Appalachia: How Southern Mountaineers Brought Independence, Culture and Enlightenment to America.* Shoemaker & Hoard, an imprint of Avalon Publishing Group, Inc., Emeryville, California, 2006.

Bolling, Alexander R., Jr. *The Bolling Family: Eight Centuries of Growth.* Gateway Press, Inc., Baltimore, 1990.

Brands, H.W. *Andrew Jackson: His Life and Times.* Doubleday, New York, 2005.

Brown, Dee. *Bury My Heart at Wounded Knee.* Holt, Rinehart, and Winston, Inc., New York, 1970.

Brown, Dee. *The American West.* Charles Scribner's Sons, New York, 1994.

California Archives, Unbound Documents, 364-65, Bancroft Library, U.C. Berkeley.

Canfield, Gae Whitney. *Sarah Winnemucca of the Northern Paiutes.* University of Oklahoma Press, Norman, 1983.

Colby, Susan M. *Sacagawea's Child: The Life and Times of Jean-Baptiste (Pomp) Charbonneau.* The Arthur H. Clark Company, Spokane, Washington, 2005.

Coleman, Arica L. *That the Blood Stay Pure: African Americans, Native Americans, and the Predicament of Race and Identity in Virginia.* Indiana University Press, Bloomington, 2013.

Confer, Clarissa W. *The Cherokee Nation in the Civil War.* University of Oklahoma, Norman, 2007.

Craven, Wesley Frank, *The Southern Colonies in the Seventeenth Century: 1607-1689.* Louisiana State University Press and the Littlefield Fund for Southern History of the University of Texas, 1949, 1970.

Cushman, Dan. *The Great North Trail.* McGraw-Hill, New York, 1966.

Custalow, Linwood "Little Bear" and Angela L. Daniel. *The True Story of Pocahontas: The Other Side of History.* Fulcrum Publishing, Golden Colorado, 2007.

Cutright, Paul Russell. *A History of the Lewis and Clark Journals.* University of Oklahoma Press, Norman, 1976.

Dary, David. *The Oregon Trail: An American Saga.* Alfred A. Knopf, New York, 2004.

Deloria, "Frenchmen, Sandbars, and Bears," in Josephy, Alvin M., Jr., and Marc Jaffe, *Lewis and Clark through Indian Eyes,* pp.5-23. Alfred A. Knopf, New York, 2006.

DeVoto, Bernard (ed.). *The Journals of Lewis and Clark.* Houghton-Mifflin Co., Boston and New York, 1953, 1981.

Diamond, Jared. *Guns, Germs and Steel: The Fates of Human Societies*. W.W. Norton & Co., New York and London, 1997, 1999.

Doran, Michael F. "Negro Slaves of the Five Civilized Tribes." 68(3) *Annals of the Association of American Geographers* pp.335-350, 1978.

Ehle, John. *Trail of Tears: The Rise and Fall of the Cherokee Nation*. Doubleday, New York, 1988.

Ellison, George. "Will Thomas, Tsali & Tsali's Rock." *Journal of Cherokee Studies*, Volume 24. The Museum of the Cherokee Indian, 2005.

Engelhardt, Father Zephyrin. *San Luis Rey: The King of the Missions*. The James H. Barry Co., San Francisco, 1921.

Faragher, John Mack. *Daniel Boone: The Life and Legend of an American Pioneer*. Henry Holt and Co., New York, 1993.

Finkelman, Paul. "'I Could Not Afford to Hang Men for Votes:' Lincoln the Lawyer, Humanitarian Concerns, and the Dakota Pardons." 39:2 *William Mitchell Law Review* 405-449, 2013.

Furtwangler, Albert. "Sacagawea's Son as a Symbol." *Oregon Historical Quarterly* 102(3): 290-315, Fall 2001.

George, Rozina http://www.trailtribes.org/lemhi/agaidika-perspective-on-sacajawea.htm.

Godbold, E. Stanley. "William Holland Thomas: A Man for All Seasons." *Journal of Cherokee Studies*, Volume 24. The Museum of the Cherokee Indian, 2005.

Hafen, Ann W. "Jean-Baptiste Charbonneau." In Le Roy R. Hafen (ed.) *The Mountain Men and the Fur Trade of the Far West*. Vol.1, p.205-24, Arthur C. Clark Co., Glendale, CA 1965.

Hine, Robert V. and John Mack Faragher. *The American West: A New Interpretive History*. Yale University, New Haven, 2000.

Hoig, Stanley. *The Cherokees and their Chiefs: In the Wake of Empire*. The University of Arkansas Press, Fayetteville, 1998.

Hopkins, Sarah Winnemucca. *Life among the Piutes: Their Wrongs and Claims*. Edited by Mrs. Horace Mann. Published by the author, Boston, 1883, and by G. P. Putnam's Sons, New York, 1883.

Howard, Harold P. *Sacajawea*. University of Oklahoma Press, Norman, 1971.

Howard, Oliver O. *Famous Indian Chiefs I Have Known*. The Century Company, New York, 1908.

Howe, Craig, and Kim TallBear (eds.). *This Stretch of the River: Lakota, Nakota, and Dakota Responses to the Lewis and Clark Expedition and Bicentennial*. Pine Hill Press, Sioux Falls, South Dakota, 2006.

Hoxie, Frederick, *This American Country: American Indian Political Activists and the Place They Made*. The Penguin Press, New York, 2012.

Hudson, Charles. *Knights of Spain, Warriors of the Sun: Hernando de Soto and the South's Ancient Chiefdoms*. University of Georgia Press, Athens, Georgia, 1997.

Johnson, Michael G. and Richard Hook (illustrator). *Encyclopedia of Native Tribes of North America*. Compendium Publishing Limited, London, 3rd ed., 2007.

Jones, Landon Y. *William Clark and the Shaping of the West*. Hill and Wang, a division of Farrar, Straus and Giroux, New York, 2004.

Josephy, Alvin M., Jr. *Chief Joseph's People and their War*. Yellowstone Library and Museum Association, 1964.

Josephy, Alvin M., Jr. *500 Nations: An Illustrated History of North American Indians*. Alfred A. Knopf, New York, 1994.

Josephy, Alvin M., Jr. and Marc Jaffe (eds.) *Lewis and Clark through Indian Eyes*. Alfred A. Knopf, New York, 2006.

Kelly, James C. *The Story of Virginia*. The Virginia Historical Society, Richmond, Virginia, and Publication Management Associates, Inc., Nashville, Tennessee, 2001.

King, Greg and Penny Wilson. *The Fate of the Romanovs*. John Wiley & Sons, Inc., Hoboken, New Jersey, 2003.

Knack, Martha C. and Omer C. Stewart. *As Long as the River Shall Run: An Ethnohistory of Pyramid Lake Indian Reservation*. University of California Press, Berkeley, Los Angeles, and London, 1984.

Langguth, A.J. *Patriots: The Men Who Started the American Revolution*. Simon & Schuster Paperbacks, New York, 1988.

Levin, Phyllis Lee. *Edith and Woodrow: The Wilson White House.* Scribner, New York, 2001.

Madsen, Brigham D. *The Northern Shoshoni.* The Caxton Printers, Ltd. Caldwell, Idaho, 1980.

Mann, Charles C. *1491: New Revelations of the Americas before Columbus.* Vintage Books, New York, 2005.

Mann, John W.W. *Sacagawea's People: The Lemhi Shoshone and the Salmon River Country.* University of Nebraska Press, Lincoln, 2004.

McMurtry, Larry. *Sacagawea's Nickname: Essays on the American West.* New York Review of Books, 2001.

McMurty, Larry. *Oh What a Slaughter: Massacres in the American West: 1846-1890.* New York: Simon & Schuster, 2005.

Meltzer, Milton. *Bound for the Rio Grande: The Mexican Struggle, 1845-1850.* Alfred A. Knopf, Inc., New York, 1974.

Mirsky, Jeanette. *The Westward Crossings: Balboa, Mackenzie, Lewis and Clark.* The University of Chicago Press, Chicago and London, 1946.

Morgan, Robert. *Boone: A Biography.* Algonquin Books of Chapel Hill, a division of Workman Publishing, New York, 2007.

Morris, Larry E. *The Fate of the Corps.* Yale University Press, New Haven and London, 2004.

Mossiker, Frances. *Pocahontas: The Life and the Legend.* Alfred A. Knopf, Inc., New York. 1976; republished by Da Capo Press, 1996.

Museum of the Cherokee Indian. *Journal of Cherokee Studies,* Special Issue, "History in the Making: Cherokee Events as Reported in Contemporary Newspapers," Spring 1979, Volume IV Number 2. Published by the Museum of the Cherokee Indian, Cherokee, North Carolina.

Nabokov, Peter (ed.) *Native American Testimony: A Chronicle of Indian-White Relations from Prophecy to the Present, 1492-1992.* Viking Penguin, New York, 1991.

Nies, Judith. *Native American History: A Chronology of a Culture's Vast Achievements and their Links to World Events.* Ballantine Books, New York, 1996.

Perdue, Theda and Michael D. Green. *The Cherokee Nation and the Trail of Tears.* Penguin Group (USA) Inc., New York, 2007.

Randall, Willard Sterne. *Thomas Jefferson: A Life.* Henry Holt and Company, Inc., New York, 1993.

Robertson, Wyndham. *Pocahontas, alias Matoaka, and Her Descendants through Her Marriage at Jamestown, Virginia, in April 1617, with John Rolfe, Gentleman.* J.W. Randolph and English, Richmond, Virginia, 1887.

Ronda, James P. *Lewis and Clark Among the Indians.* University of Nebraska, Lincoln and London, 1984.

Rountree, Helen C. *Pocahontas's People: The Powhatan Indians of Virginia through Four Centuries,* University of Oklahoma Press, Norman, 1990.

Rountree, Helen C. *Pocahontas, Powhatan, Opechancanough: Three Indian Lives Changed by Jamestown.* University of Virginia Press, Charlottesville, 2005.

Salmon, Emily J. and Edward D.C. Campbell, Jr. (eds.) *The Hornbook of Virginia History.* The Library of Virginia, Richmond, 4th edition, 1994.

San Diego Archives, Documents, vol. II, 328, the Bancroft Library, U.C. Berkeley.

Sandburg, Carl. *Abraham Lincoln: The Prairie Years, 1809-1861.* Dell Publishing Co., New York, 1954.

Sides, Hampton. *Blood and Thunder: An Epic of the American West.* Doubleday, New York, 2006.

Smith, Jean Edward. *John Marshall: Definer of a Nation.* Henry Holt and Co. Inc., New York, 1996.

Smith, John. *The Generall Historie of Virginia, New-England, and the Summer Isles, Fourth Booke.* Printed by I.D. and I.H. for Michael Sparkes, London, 1624

Stites, Francis N. *John Marshall: Defender of the Constitution.* Little, Brown and Company, Boston, 1981.

Thwaites, Reuben Gold. *Original Journals of the Lewis and Clark Expedition, 1804-06.* Dodd, Mead and Company, New York, 1905.

Trahant, Mark, "Who's Your Daddy?" pp. 51-68 in Josephy, Alvin M., Jr., and Marc Jaffe, *Lewis and Clark through Indian Eyes.* Alfred A. Knopf, New York, 2006.

Tyler, Lyon Gardiner. *Narratives of Early Virginia, 1606-1625.* Barnes & Noble, New York, 1907.

Udall, Stewart L. *The Forgotten Founders: Rethinking the History of the Old West.* Island Press, Washington, D.C., 2002.

Waugaman, Sandra F. and Danielle Moretti-Langholtz. *We're Still Here: Contemporary Virginia Indians Tell Their Stories.* Palari Publishing, Richmond, Virginia, 2000, revised 2006.

Wexler, Sanford. *Westward Expansion: An Eyewitness History.* Facts on File, Inc., New York, 1991.

Whitney, Ellen M. (ed.) *The Black Hawk War, 1831-32.* Springfield, Illinois State Historical Society, 1970. Accessed at www.wisconsinhistory.org/.

Wilson, Edith Bolling. *My Memoirs.* The Bobbs-Merrill Company, New York, 1938.

Wilson, Elinor. *Jim Beckwourth: Black Mountain Man, War Chief of the Crows, Trader, Trapper, Explorer, Frontiersman, Guide, Scout, Interpreter, Adventurer, and Gaudy Liar.* University of Oklahoma Press, Norman, 1972.

End Notes

The number before each note refers to the page in the text where the topic or quote first appears.

Introduction: Migration and Enlightenment

3: "complicated geographical diffusion" Johnson and Hook 10.

5: John Marshall's grandmother was Mary (maiden name Randolph). Mary's uncle, Richard Randolph, was married to Jane (maiden name Bolling). Jane was the great-granddaughter of Pocahontas. Smith 23; Stites 2.

Chapter 1: The Invasion of Virginia

9: "subdue the wilde Salvages." Mossiker 15, 19.

9: "Playful, sportive, frolicsome, mischievous, frisky." Mossiker 41. "Laughing and joyous:" Custalow 7. "Little wanton" comes from William Strachey, also with the meaning of playful or frolicsome: Mossiker 355.

9: Her age in January 1608 has been estimated at between 10 and 14 years, most likely 11 or 12, suggesting a birthdate of 1595 or 1596. When she sat for a portrait in January or February 1617, the artist recorded "the 21st year of her age." Rountree (*Three Indian Lives...*) 36.

9: John Smith wrote of both rescues in the "The Generall History of Virginia, New England, and the Summer Isles" (1624).

9: The biographer is Frances Mossiker. The anthropologist is Helen C. Rountree. The scholar of Native American studies is Paula Gunn Allen. The physician is Dr. Linwood Custalow of the Upper Mattaponi.

9: Fast destruction of population: Mann, Charles, *1491*, generally.

9: "Disease was the overwhelming cause ...." Nabokov 87.

9: Europeans claimed territory: DeVoto, *Journals,* introduction; Mossiker 3-5.

10: Activists claimed Alcatraz "by right of discovery." *San Francisco Chronicle,* June 11, 2011.

10: Walter Raleigh and the "Lost Colony." Mossiker 8-9, 24-25, 34-35, 54.

10: English scientist and artist among the Chesapeake Indians: Rountree (*Pocahontas' People*) 20.

10: John Smith counted under Powhatan's control 28 tribes, 36 tribal capitals, and 161 villages. Mossiker 32-33. The National Museum of the American Indian estimates at least 30.

10: Opechancanough, chief of the Pamunkey and leader of the militant faction: Mossiker 76.

10: Mattaponi oral tradition: Custalow, generally.

10: Tsenacommacah: Mossiker, Allen, and Rountree, generally.

10: Trading network: Salmon 7.

10: Foods: Mossiker 7-9, 23, 30-31, 77; Rountree (*Pocahontas's People*) 5; Rountree (*Three Indian Lives*) 43.

10: Population of 10,000: Johnson 33. Population of 15,000: Roundtree (*Three Indian Lives*) 13. Population of 8,500 to 9,000: Mossiker 31-33.

11: 3 million people today: Rountree (*Three Indian Lives*) 13.

11: Fallow: Rountree (*Three Indian Lives*) 13.

11: The James River was called the Powhatan. Werowocomoco was on or near the Pamunkey. Mossiker 27-32.

11: Patawomecks: Rountree (*Pocahontas's People*) 75; Mossiker 155.

11: "Appamattucks:" Rountree (*Pocahontas's People*) 3.

11: Wahunsenacawh was called mamanatowick, "great king." Rountree (*Three Indian Lives*) 17.

11: Powhatan meant spirit dreamer (Allen 21), leader (National Museum of the American Indian), or falling water: Rountree (*Three Indian Lives*) 33; Mossiker 20; Johnson 21.

11: Paramount chiefdom: Rountree, *Pocahontas's People* and *Three Indian Lives,* generally.

11: Matrilineal succession: Rountree (*Three Indian Lives*) 23; Rountree (*Pocahontas's People*) 101; Mossiker 120; Allen, 66, 72-73.

11: Powhatan increased his territory. Rountree (*Three Indian Lives*) 44.

13: Tribal enemies. Mossiker 32; Rountree (*Three Indian Lives*) 39, 42.

13: Haudenosaunee and federalism: Nies 56.

13: "[S]uch Majestie as he expresseth..." Mossiker 38, quoting Strachey.

13: "the Cheasapeak Bay .....he destroyed and put to sword...all the Inhabitants..." William Strachey recorded the prophecy and the killing of the Chesapeakes by Powhatan. Mossiker 35-36. However, Strachey did not arrived in Jamestown until 1610. Mossiker 98. Therefore, all his observations about Pocahontas and otherwise are based on the reports of other people.

14: John Smith's career: Mossiker 15-19, based on Smith's *The True Travels, Adventures, and Observations of Captaine John Smith, in Europe, Asia, Affrica, and America, from Anno Domini 1593 to 1629*, published in 1630.

14: "not to offend the Naturals, if you can eschew it." Mossiker 26.

14: "a man of his word, whether the word was a threat or a promise." Mossiker 69.

14: "the Salvages" shot arrows. Mossiker 11.

14: Don Luis: Rountree (*Three Indian Lives*) 38.

16: Jamestown was on Paspahegh land. Mossiker 20-26.

16: Voyage up the James River. Mossiker 57-60.

17: "you mean to plant among them." Mossiker 87.

17: "the two Armes of the Crosse signified king Powatah ..." Mossiker 60.

17: "Hee asked mee the cause of our coming." Mossiker 87, 343.

17: "distinctly each others successors." Mossiker 120.

17: "shott cleane through his bearde" "the naturall necessity." Mossiker 61-62.

18: 50 out of 100 died: Mossiker 66. One cause of death was foul water: Rountree (*Pocahontas's People*) 34-35.

18: "Had we been as free from all sinnes ...." Mossiker 64.

18-19: "send but thirty Carpenters ...." Mossiker 117.

19: "the very excrements of a full, swelling State." Mossiker 143.

19: "changed the harts of the Salvages... " Mossiker 68.

19: Smith was chosen by lot: Mossiker 69.

Chapter 2: The White Feather

21: "I am the daughter of the king...." From William Makepeace Thackeray, *The Virginians: A Tale of the Last Century,* 1904, Charles Scribner's sons, quoted in Mossiker 328.

23: Capture of John Smith. Mossiker 73-81.

23: Torturing captives to death. Rountree (*Pocahontas's People*) 54.

25: "the Circle of meale signified their Country..." Mossiker 76.

25: "many of their heads [were] bedecked with the white downe of Birds...". Mossiker 79, quoting Smith. Meaning of white feathers: Allen 31, 39, 58, 295.

25: "Pocahontas the Kings dearest daughter, when no intreaty could prevaile, got his head in her armes" Mossiker 81, quoting Smith.

25: A father's identity did not determine status in Algonquin society. Allen 72, and Rountree (*Three Indian Lives*), generally.

25: Cartwheels: Mossiker 96, quoting Strachey.

26: "A True Relation of Such Occurrences and Accidents of Noate as Hath Hapned in Virginia since the First Planting of That Collony" (1608).

26: "[A]t the minute of my execution, she hazarded the beating out of her owne braines to saue mine....," Mossiker 83, 122, 230-232, quoting Smith's recollection of a letter he wrote Queen Anne. John Smith recited the contents of his 1616 letter in his 1624 work, *The Generall Historie of Virginia, New-England, and the Summer Isles,* Fourth Booke, p.121-123. Portions of the *Generall Historie* are quoted verbatim in the annotated *Narratives of Early Virginia, 1606-1625,* by Lyon Gardiner Tyler, published by Barnes & Noble, New York, 1907. The letter is set forth beginning on p.325 of the *Narratives.* A facsimile of the *Generall Historie* portion of the *Narratives* was accessed April 7, 2015, at the "American Journeys Collection," http://www.americanjourneys.org/pdf/AJ-082.pdf, Wisconsin Historical Society Digital Library and Archives, Document #AJ-082, www.americanjourneys.org and www.wisconsinhistory.org, 2003.

27: Midewewin: Allen 71-72.

27: "Father-daughter" relationship was not necessarily biological. Allen 21, 287.

27: "Since a white feather...always signifies a Beloved Women..." Allen 31.

27: Others waited on her. Mossiker 99-100, based on Strachey.

27: Commoner husband. Allen 58.

27: "Lady Pocahontas." Mossiker 91.

27: "The Powhatan princess" and her "royal red blood." Mossiker 318-320.

29: "if she has enough to eat and a few trinkets to wear" Devoto 171.

29: "live to make him hatchets, and her bells, beads, and copper..." Mossiker 81.

29: "toyes" and "presents." Mossiker 88-89.

29: "And this reliefe, most Gracious Queene, was commonly brought us by this Lady Pocahontas." Mossiker 89-91.

29: Compassionate heart. Mossiker 147.

30: "a perpetuall league and friendship." Mossiker 103-104.

30: "Bid Pokahontas bring hither two little Baskets" Mossiker 103-105.

31: "Thirtie young women." Mossiker 108-113.

31: Mattaponi oral tradition about "take me": Custalow 35.

31: Corn Maidens. Mossiker 111-113.

32: "Your Father is to come to me, not I to him...." Mossiker 108, 115-116.

33: "My countrie is large enough to goe from you." Mossiker 121.

33: No more Mississippis....Beckwourth and Bonner 347.

33: "For Pocahontas his dearest jewell and daughter, in that darke night came through the irksome woods." Mossiker 122.

34: Affection to our nation. Mossiker 147.

34: Smith forced Opechancanough to load the boat with corn. Mossiker 118-127.

34: Indians lived at the fort; colonists boarded with tribes. Mossiker 127-130, 153 n.17.

34: Three English youths. Mossiker 101, 153.

35: "he that will not worke shall not eate." Mossiker 127-129.

35: The Starving Time. Mossiker 134-139, 142.

Chapter 3. The Tempest

37: "But God that would not this Countrie should be unplanted ...." Mossiker 140-141, quoting an anonymous chronicler.

39: *Sea Venture* and Rolfe family. Mossiker 141.

39: Lord De La Warre. Mossiker 142.

39: Gentlemen and scum. Mossiker 143.

39: Brutal warfare. Mossiker 144-145.

40: "marryed to a private Captayne called Kocoum" Mossiker 147, quoting Strachey.

40: Sir Thomas Dale. Mossiker 145-146.

41: Pocahontas captured from among the Potomacs. Mossiker 155-157.

42: *Counter-Blaste to Tobacco.* Mossiker 202.

43: Letter from Rolfe to Dale. Mossiker 344.

43: Disapproval of Rolfe's marriage. Personal communication with Arica L. Coleman, based on her then-forthcoming book, published in 2013 as *That the Blood Stay Pure: African Americans, Native Americans, and the Predicament of Race and Identity in Virginia.*

44: Baptism and marriage. Mossiker 189-194; Rountree (*Pocahontas's People*) 60.

45: Voyage to England. Mossiker 209 and following.

49: Reunion with Smith. Mossiker 273-274, quoting Smith.

50: "'tis enough that the child liveth." Mossiker 279, quoting a letter by Rolfe.

51: Eastern shore of Chesapeake Bay. Rountree (*Pocahontas's People*) 79, 83, 92, map 90.

52: Attack in 1622 and peace treaty of 1632. Rountree (*Pocahontas's People*) 75-81.

53: Anglicized Nansemond. Rountree (*Pocahontas's People*) 84.

53: Thomas Rolfe returned to the New World in 1635. Rountree (*Pocahontas's People*) 64.

53: Attack in April 1644 and treaty of 1646. Rountree (*Pocahontas's People*) 84-88.

54: Bacon's Rebellion in 1675. Rountree (*Pocahontas's People*) 96-100.

54: 1677 Treaty of Middle Plantation. Rountree (*Pocahontas's People*) 100-105.

54-55: "we had to have something to present to the governor" Waugaman 12-13.

Chapter 4: Mother of Presidents

Information on the Cherokee in this and the following chapters is from Perdue, the Museum of the Cherokee Indian (Cherokee, NC) and the National Museum of the American Indian (Washington DC).

59: Virginia discussed an end to slavery. Kelly 73-58.

59: "began to think of themselves as a culture apart." Kelly 40-41.

60: Marriages and descendants: Bolling, generally; Robertson 49; Mossiker 319; Randall 5; Edith Wilson 230; Smith 23.

61: Signers of the Declaration of Independence: Richard Henry Lee and Frances Lightfoot Lee, two of Virginia's representatives in the Continental Congress. Generals: Henry Lee III ("Light Horse Harry" in the American Revolution) and his son Robert E. Lee, confederate general in the American Civil War.

61: Jefferson was a friend of the families of Lewis and Clark. Jones 24.

61: Pocahontas, Powhatan and Matoaka showed up as names: Robertson 35 (Powhatan Bolling 1767-1802), 41 (Powhatan Archer), 42 (Powhatan Bolling), 42 (Pocahontas Rebecca Bolling), 44 (Pocahontas Anne Robertson Bolling, 1805-1838), 51 (Powhatan A. Gay and Pocahontas V. Gay), 52 (Pocahontas Ferguson Vaughan and Matoaca Gay), 55 (Powhatan Bolling Whittle).

61: Duelist Powhatan Bolling. Robertson 69.

61: General Zachary Taylor incident. Meltzer 94.

61: Armstrong Archer. Coleman, Prologue (note 1) citing Archer, Armstrong, *A Compendium of Slavery as it Exists in the Present Day in the United States of America,* published in 1844 in London by J. Haddon Printers.

61: British and French population. Wexler 1.

62: "If the French claim all the land on one side of the river" Biggers 28.

62: Iroquois neutrality. Udall 22-23.

62: "will you sleep with me?" Jones 20 n.8.

63: "do not conceive that Government has any right" Jones 23 n.15.

65: George Washington traveled the Ohio River around 1770. Morgan 119.

65: George Rogers Clark, heading for Kentucky in 1773. Jones 24-25.

65: Frederick Jackson Turner, "The Significance of the Frontier in American History," *Report of the American Historical Association,* pp.199-227, 1893, quoted in Morgan 96.

65: Rock pyramid. Perdue 11.

65: "two darling sons" Morgan 335.

66: Killed at most three Indians. Morgan 46.

66: Quaker agent Kirk, "our friend" Nabokov 78-79.

66: "wandering about seems engrafted in their nature...." Morgan 135.

66: "Back water" ... "Even taters wouldn't freeze" Morgan 68-70.

66-67: Treaties of 1768. Morgan 88-89.

67: A buck, or buckskin, meant a dollar. Faragher 32.

67: "wasps and yellow-jackets" Morgan 103.

67: Cherokee headmen visited London in 1730. Perdue 15.

67-68: "Ah, Wide-Mouth, I have got you now" Morgan 71-72.

68: "War is their principal study" Ehle 14; Brands 84.

68: Five Civilized Tribes and slavery. Doran 335.

68: Black slavery. Perdue 35.

68: Sequoyah. Biggers 26-43; Morgan 42, 67.

70: Torture and murder of James Boone. Morgan 136-139.

70: Torture and murder of Chief Logan's family. Jones 25-28; Faragher 96. There are slight variations in the telling of this atrocity: hung by her thumbs (Jones) or wrists (Faragher).

70: Treaty of Sycamore Shoals. Jones 29.

70: Nancy Ward. Bataille 272-73; Hoig 26, 59-64.

72: "compelled to seek a retreat in some far distant wilderness." Jones 30 n.12.

72: "Our cry is all for peace...." National Museum of the American Indian.

72: George Washington "the Town Destroyer." Nabokov 93.

73: "The father has called on his Indian children" Nabokov 92.

73: George Rogers Clark traveled from Kentucky to petition the governor of Virginia. Wexler 4-6; Jones 31.

Chapter 5: Father of Waters

77: Kidnapping of Boone's daughter. Morgan 203-209.

77: Female sharpshooters. Morgan 220-222.

77: Cornstalk. Morgan 150; Jones 27, 32-33.

78: George Rogers Clark during Revolution. Jones 33-39.

78: Boone's capture and adoption by Shawnees and defense of fort. Morgan 226. Boone's biographers have to rely on oral accounts, which, of course, vary. Faragher suggests that the cries of the Shawnee women when Boone escaped were cries of warning to the Shawnee warriors; he notes that the story of Boone's adoptive mother begging him not to go includes a long conversation that isn't plausible under the circumstances of a hasty escape. Morgan and Faragher agree that the adoption bond was mutual and genuine, in Boone's case and in several other incidents of Indians capturing and adopting whites.

80: Boone guided Lincoln's grandfather. Morgan 282.

80: Death of Lincoln's grandfather. Sandburg 21.

81: The Hard Winter. Morgan 286.

81: "their extermination, or their removal." Jones 41.

81: Killing of settlers' children. Jones 42, 51.

81: Battle of Blue Licks. Morgan 325-327; Jones 44.

83: "I am afraid to lose sight of my house" Morgan 291.

83: William Clark in 1784. Jones 47.

83: Treaty of Hopewell. Perdue 23.

83: "I hope you have now taken us by the hand in real friendship." *Gazette of the United States,* July 25, 1789, in *Journal of Cherokee Studies,* Spring 1979, 4(2)-54-56.

83: Trade and Intercourse Acts of 1790. Perdue 27.

83: $500 reward. Jan. 7, 1793. *Journal of Cherokee Studies,* Spring 1979, 4(2):59.

84: Moluntha, McGary, Kenton. Morgan 365.

84: Clark as Indian fighter. Jones 55-79.

84: The Algonkian word for woman. Mossiker generally; Allen generally; Colby 40, 42 n.49.

84-85: Shawnees and Miamis slaughtered the wounded. Jones 10-11.

85: Battle of Fallen Timbers. Jones 78.

85: "We raised corn like the whites" Jones 79.

85: "Cut a number of antick tricks" Jones 82.

86: "One makes shoes, another hats" Jones 86.

86: "we have met often in war-never before in peace" Jones 154.

86: "The utmost good faith shall always be observed" Northwest Ordinance of 1787.

86: Henry Knox. Langguth 411; Perdue 20-27.

86: Civilization policy. Perdue, generally.

87: "your blood will mix with ours" Wexler 58.

87: Cherokee cousins married white women. Perdue 46-47.

87: Auguste and Pierre Choteau. Jones 157-158; Ambrose 125; Ronda 10.

88: Killed the officers; cunning of the rattlesnake; Clark's mission. Jone 70-71.

88: Clark family and travels. Jones 93-112.

89: Kentucky considered abolishing slavery. Jones 107.

89: The Louisiana purchase included all or part of the present states of Arkansas, Missouri, Iowa, Oklahoma, Kansas, Nebraska, Minnesota, North Dakota, South Dakota, New Mexico, Texas, Montana, Wyoming, Colorado and Louisiana.

89: American flag raised in St. Louis. Ambrose 129-130.

Chapter 6: A Voyage of Discovery

91: "friendly and conciliatory manner" Ronda 1.

93: Bird Woman; Boat Pusher. John W.W. Mann 191.; H. Howard 16 n.1. Lewis' journal entry of May 20, 1805 noted "this stream we called Sah-ca-gah-we-ah (or bird woman's River) after our interpreter the Snake woman." Irving Anderson ("A Charbonneau Family Portrait") 58.

93: Saka Tza We Yaa. George, http://www.trailtribes.org/lemhi/agaidika-perspective-on-sacajawea.htm Rozina George, a self-described great-great-great niece of Sacagawea, was a reviewer for John W. W. Mann, *Sacagawea's People*.

93: Hidatsa or Shoshone: Baker in Josephy (*Lewis and Clark through Indian Eyes*) 125-136.

93: "Your observations are to be taken with great pains" "writingest" Cutright 9.

93: "[W]hat will become of his paprs?" Clark to his brother Jonathan, Jones 179; Cutright 56. In Clark's letter to his brother about the tragedy, "my" papers is crossed out and changed to "his."

93: Biddle: Cutright 53-57.

94: "the principal guide" Cutright 220-21. According to Irving Anderson, "Eva Emory Dye was the first to romanticize the deeds of the expedition's Indian woman in her novel *The Conquest*, published in 1902. Dye portrayed Sacagawea as the guide to the expedition...." Anderson ("A Charbonneau Family Portrait") 9. However, the story of the woman with a baby on her back was not unknown earlier. For example, in 1844, William M. Boggs, son of Missouri's governor L.W. Boggs, met Jean-Baptiste Charbonneau at Bent's Fort and identified him as "the small Indian papoose, or half-breed of the elder Charbenau that was employed by the Lewis and Clark Expedition as guide...." Hafen 217.

94: Jefferson broached an expedition with George Rogers Clark. Jones 48.

94: Captain Robert Gray. Dary 9-10.

94: Jefferson secretly asked Congress to appropriate $2,500. Jones 111.

95: Peace medals and gifts. Ronda 5, 8-9, 57.

95: "The same world would scarcely do for them and us." Jones 40.

95: Lewis had served under Clark. Jones 93.

95: "it's fatiegues, it's dangers and it's honors" Jones 113.

98: Prepared for expedition Jones 114-21.

98: Maps. Ronda 13.

98: Cultivated friendships with Rene Auguste Choteau and Jean Pierre Choteau. Ronda 10; Ambrose 125.

98: "paths already well established" DeLoria in Josephy (*Lewis and Clark through Indian Eyes*) 7.

98: A French explorer met the Mandans in 1738. Colby 15, 24 n.8.

98: Size of Corps. DeVoto 2-3, 93. This is a round number; the size of the Corps fluctuated during the first year.

98: York was Clark's "servant" since childhood. Jones 17, 142.

99: Keelboat and pirogues. Colby 54; DeVoto 3.

99: Effect of horses on Sioux (Johnson 110), Cheyenne (Ronda 56), and Crow (Johnson 123). The remains of ancient cousins of the modern horse have been found in North America, but there were no modern horses here when the Spanish arrived.

99: George Drouillard. Ronda 15.

99: Encounters with tribes along Missouri River from Omahas to Mandans. Ronda generally; Deloria in Josephy (*Lewis and Clark through Indian Eyes*) 5-23.

99: "traveling medicine show" Ronda 32.

99-100: "[T]he great chief of the Seventeen nations" Ronda 57.

100: "Bad birds" Ronda 19.

100: Sioux were respected for military might and sought after as allies and partners. Ronda 28-31.

100: Yankton Sioux had interactions with British, French, and Spaniards. Deloria in Josephy (*Lewis and Clark through Indian Eyes*) 7.

100: Teton Sioux politics and near-confrontation. Ronda 35-36; Devoto 35-36; Josephy (*Lewis and Clark through Indian Eyes*) xvi.

102: "the captains were able to persuade the Sioux to back off" Josephy (*Lewis and Clark through Indian Eyes*) xvi.

102: "The way was open...." Josephy and Marc Jaffe, p. xvi, *Lewis and Clark through Indian Eyes*

102: Arikaras. Ronda 46-97. There is debate whether the Arikara and Pawnees separated before or after European contact with the New World. Ronda 43-44; Johnson 131.

103: Winter among Mandans. Colby 20-21; DeVoto 76; Ronda 88-105.

103: The Hidatsa are also called Minatarees. Colby 27, n.11.

103: Provided medical care for Indians. DeVoto 73, 76-77, 85-86.

104: Louis Veneri. Devoto 315.

104: Olivier Charbonneau; Toussaint Charbonneau. Colby 10, 15, 27.

Chapter 7: A Baby on Her Back

107: "diserved a greater reward" Colby 64.

107: Lemhi, also known as the Salmon Eaters or Agaideka. Colby 37, 39; John W. W. Mann (*Sacagawea's People*), generally.

107: Disadvantage relative to other tribes: Colby 39. There is debate about whether the bands now called the Lemhi lived in an environment of scarcity or relative plenty before the effects of European migration were felt. John W.W. Mann xx-xxiii. By 1805, however, their food resources were limited, due to indirect rather than direct effects of European contact.

107: "suffered much by the small pox" DeVoto 209.

107: Small pox and trading networks. Trahant in Josephy (*Lewis and Clark through Indian Eyes*) 53-54.

107: Sacagawea captured. Colby 15, 37.

107: Hidatsa oral history. Colby 40 n.45; Baker, "Mandan and Hidatsa of the Upper Missouri," in Josephy (*Lewis and Clark through Indian Eyes*) 125-136.

107: Sold, won, or arranged marriage? Colby 40-47.

108: Jessaume. Colby 22, Ronda 80.

108-109: Birth of Baptiste: Colby 19-20.

109: From Mandan to Sacagawea's reunion with Lemhi. DeVoto 120-216, Ronda 144-152.

109: Toussaint signed on as interpreter. Colby 20-21.

109: canoes to replace the keelboat. DeVoto 86 n.8.

109: A 55-day-old baby; 33 people. Colby 49.

109: "united in one family with our red brethren" Jones 152.

109: Sacagawea's knowledge of plants. Colby 51-52; Jones 134; DeVoto 93.

109: cooked intestines. DeVoto 107.

110: Game was plentiful. DeVoto 103.

110: "the white bear" DeVoto 95.

110: "seens of visionary inchantment" Ronda 134-135.

110: "caught and preserved most of the light articles" DeVoto 111.

110: Judith River and Julia Hancock. Jones 142.

110: The moccasins were not of her nation. DeVoto 120.

110: Disgust at buffalo jump. DeVoto 120.

110: Choosing the correct river. DeVoto 125-133.

110-111: Great Falls and Sacagawea's illness. DeVoto 134-143.

111: Flash flood. DeVoto 152.

111: prickly pear DeVoto 155.

111: "the gates of the Rocky Mountains." DeVoto 158-164.

111: "The Indian woman recognizes the country...DeVoto 163.

111: Arrived at the Three Forks. DeVoto 165.

111: Camped where Sacagawea had been kidnapped. DeVoto 171.

112: No buffalo in the mountains. DeVoto 163, 176.

112: "if any Indians can subsist" DeVoto 169.

112: The Lemhi were close to starvation. Ronda 140-41.

112: Need for horses: Ronda 137, Thwaites 2:279, DeVoto 168-69.

112: Raids by Hidatsa (Ronda 108, DeVoto 192), Blackfeet (Ronda 140, DeVoto 161) and Atsina (Gros Ventre) (Ronda 140).

112: "we were not Indians, nor their enemies." DeVoto 164.

112: "a lame crew" DeVoto 173.

112: Beaver's Head: DeVoto text.

112: "tab-ba-bone" DeVoto 186-87, Ronda 140.

112: The dogs wouldn't cooperate. Ronda 141.

113: "most distant fountain" DeVoto 188-189.

113: Lemhi interactions with Corps; Sacagawea's reunion. DeVoto 186-216; Ronda 144-152.

115: From Lemhi camp to Pacific Northwest. DeVoto 233-292; Ronda 155-86.

115: Some of the worst roads that ever horses passed. DeVoto 233.

115: Peter Clarke of the Flathead-Salish. Jones 138.

116: "the most terrible mountains I ever beheld" Ronda 157, citing the journal of Patrick Gass.

116: "as cold in every part." DeVoto 240.

116: Nez Perce. Ronda, 157-163.

116: British, Spanish, Russian, and Yankee ships in Pacific Northwest. Josephy (*Lewis and Clark through Indian Eyes*) 7; Deloria in Josephy (*Lewis and Clark through Indian Eyes*) 5-23; Ronda 169, 182-83.

116: "a woman with a party of men is a token of peace." DeVoto 250.

116: Tribes feared "the Snake Indians," probably the Bannocks. DeVoto 269.

117: Wet and disagreeable...rained verry hard...horriable.... DeVoto 278-292.

117: "Tremendious gusts of wind..." Ronda 182.

117: Skilled canoe navigators. DeVoto 282.

117: Clatsop meant dried salmon. Ronda 186.

117: York was polled. Ambrose 311. "Janey in favour of a place where there is plenty of Potas." Colby 59. "Potas" might have meant *wappato* roots, which Clark called "equal to the Irish potato" (DeVoto 292) but Ronda (176) uses *wappato* in a different context, as does DeVoto (275).

117: Clark's brother owned two slaves named Janey. Jones 200.

117: Sacagawea let Clark trade her belt of blue beads for a robe of sea otter skins. DeVoto 289.

117: "The Squar, gave me a piece of Bread..." Jones 135.

117: "two Dozen white weazils tails." DeVoto 294.

118: Sacagawea visited the beach and saw the dead whale. DeVoto 301.

118: Indians knew enough English to trade (DeVoto 306-07) and explorers learned some Chinookan (DeVoto 348).

118: Coboway; theft of canoe. Ronda 210-211.

118: Warned that snow inland would remain deep for months. DeVoto 310.

118: Left record and departed. DeVoto 332-43.

118: The journey home: Ronda 214-51.

119: Walla Walla. DeVoto 367.

119: From Walla Walla to Nez Perce. DeVoto 369-74.

120: Sacagawea went with Clark when Corps divided. Jones 144.

120: "pore defenceless Snake Indians." Ronda 247.

120: Honeybees (Jones 146) and cows (Thwaites, vol. 5, 339).

Chapter 8: My Little Dancing Boy

121: "I will educate him and treat him as my own child" Colby 64; Jones 146.

123: Slave names. Jones 17.

123: Clark used the nickname Pompey for one of his own sons. Jones 176.

123: "offered to take his little son" "willing provided the child had been weened" Thwaites (vol. 5) 344.

124: "men of the Enlightenment" "all men should be given the opportunity" Colby 65, 67.

125: General Jackson adopted a Creek boy. Jones 296.

125: Lewis brought Jessaume's son to St. Louis. Colby 67.

125: Lewis appointed governor; Clark appointed Indian agent. Jones 155.

125: "musty, fusty, rusty old bachelor" Jones 163; shared meals, Colby 78.

125: York. Larry Morris 141-144.

126: "I gave him a Severe trouncing" …"the hero of the Missouri expedition." Larry Morris 141, 144.

126: Clark routinely whipped his slaves. Jones 164.

126: "the Red-Headed Chief." Jones 256.

126: Peaceful Shawnees and Clark's letter to Madison. Jones 197.

126: "nine out of ten of the Indian Traders have no respect for our Laws." Jones 197.

126: Factory system. Jones 164-65, 263-64.

127: Sauk and Fox concessions. Jones 150, 156-157.

127: "vicious" Great Osages" Jones 166-167.

127: Theft, murder, robbery. Jones 167.

127: The validity of the 1808 treaty was soon disputed; not all chiefs had been present, and those who were there believed they were agreeing to share the land. A treaty was finalized in 1809. Jones 167-169, 176.

127: "if he was to be damned hereafter" Jones 332.

127: Attack by Arikaras; Shannon's leg amputated. Larry Morris 82; Jones 161.

127: Choteaus, Lisa and fur trade. Jones 157-58; Colby 74-76, 89, 101.

128: Lewis' belongings were sent to Clark. Cutright 56.

128: Charbonneau family in Missouri. Colby 67-79.

128: "We have on board a Frenchman named Charbonet, with his wife…" Colby 74.

128: "the Wife of Charbonneau a Snake Squaw, died…." Colby 85-86.

128: Clark became guardian for Baptiste and Lisette. Larry Morris 117; Colby 88-89; Jones 249.

129: Elizabeth Carboneau. Colby 90.

129: "Se-car-ja-we-au dead" Larry Morris 115. Clark made the note sometime between 1825 and 1828 in a list of the fate of members of the Corps of Discovery.

129: Charbonneau hit Sacagawea. Colby 32; Jones 129.

129: Wind River Reservation in Wyoming; Eastern Shoshones (eastern bands of Northern Shoshones): Johnson 158-60.

129: Spoke French, told stories of a great fish by the western sea, and kept a medal with the likeness of Thomas Jefferson. H. Howard 179-180.

129: Porivo died in 1884. Her grave in Wyoming is marked as Sacagawea. H. Howard 195.

129: Porivo, Bat-tez, Bazil, Toussaint. Howard 175-191; Larry Morris 210-211. The two researchers were a Dakota Sioux physician, Dr. Charles Eastman, and an American professor, Grace Hebard.

129: "Bazil's mother" enrolled in Wind River in 1877. George, http://www.trailtribes.org/lemhi/agaidika-perspective-on-sacajawea.htm.

129: Northern Shoshone: Madsen 18, 30, 53; Johnson 163.

130: Bazil was the ancestor of Indian and white families: personal communication with Eric Walquist, January 3, 2012.

130: Mark of "Bazeel" on 1868 treaty. Madsen 242. The Northern Shoshone were called the Eastern Shoshone in the treaty and by Rozina George, and the Northern Shoshoni by Madsen. Either description is distinct from the Lemhi. Madsen 13.

130: A Lemhi who signed the treaty was mistakenly identified as a Bannock. John W.W. Mann (*Sacagawea's People*) 28; Madsen 243.

130: Lemhi family history: George, http://www.trailtribes.org/lemhi/agaidika-perspective-on-sacajawea.htm.

130: Bat-tez, semi-literate and taciturn, died in 1885 in Wyoming. H. Howard 182, 184. In 1971, Irving Anderson presented additional evidence that the son of the woman on the Wind River Reservation was not Jean-Baptiste Charbonneau. Bat-tez or Baptiste of Wind River knew little English. ("J.B. Charbonneau" 257). In addition, Anderson searched Wind River Reservation records, including treaty documents of 1868 and 1872, and found no evidence of a signature or mark with the name "Baptiste." ("J.B. Charbonneau" 262, 264.)

130: Jean-Baptiste Charbonneau's gravesite in Oregon is a Registered National Historic Place. Colby 179-181. The site is in Danner, Oregon, in Malheur County, at a site known as Inskip Station or Ruby Ranch. 255.

130: Anastasia: The last tsar of Russia abdicated in 1917; the Bolsheviks took power in 1918 and eventually ordered the execution of the royal family. There is strong evidence that all of them were killed, but Anastasia's body cannot be accounted for among the skeletal remains. King, Greg and P. Wilson 311-322, 470.

130: Hidatsa oral tradition. Baker in Josephy (*Lewis and Clark through Indian Eyes*) 125-136; Allen 103-104; H. Howard 191.

130-131: "taking with him all of his family and twenty-two negroes" Beckwourth and Bonner 14.

131: Beckwourth. Elinor Wilson 11-22.

131: "harrowing spectacle of my little murdered playmates" Beckwourth and Bonner 15-16. Beckwourth recorded that he was born in 1798, but Elinor Wilson believes it was about 1800. There were few massacres in the St. Louis area when Beckwourth was a young child there, around 1809, and none recorded that matches the facts he recalled. Perhaps Beckwourth was conflating an incident from his early childhood in Virginia with the trouble to come in Missouri.

132: War of 1812 and Indian alliances. Wexler 59-72. Jackson went on to defeat the British in the Battle of New Orleans on January 8, 1815, unaware of a peace treaty between the U.S. and the UK.

132: Britain cultivated Indians allies in order to limit American power near British Canada. Jones 190.

132: Clark provided military help to the Osages, his treaty partners, against an alliance of Shawnees, Delawares, and the new community of western Cherokees. Jones 189, 214-215, 236-248.

132: "into the great waters whose accursed waves brought them to our shores" Brands 192.

132: Delegation to Washington in May 1812. Jones 206.

133: Baptiste lived at a boarding house; Clark paid for tuition at St. Louis Academy. Colby 93-94; Jones 260.

133: "a son of Captain Clarke...." Colby 142, from Smith, E. Willard, Journal, in L.R. Hafen and Ann W. Hafen, eds. To the Rockies and Oregon, 1839-42, The Far West and Rockies Series, vol. 3, Glendale, CA, Arthur H. Clark Co. 1955.

133: "the gates were shut against us" Jones 78.

133: Tecumseh and Red Sticks. Perdue 48.

133: Jackson had Choctaw allies against Creeks (Johnson 67) and Creeks allied with Jackson against Seminoles during the Seminole War of 1817-1818 (Brands 327).

133: "The Americans we must fight, not the English" Wexler 76.

133: Clark was appointed governor of the Missouri Territory in 1813. Jones 212-213.

133: "the Cherokees...were no better than the Virginians." Jones 215.

133: Cherokees attacked Osage village. Jones 244.

133: "hair-buyer" Jones 219.

133: 80-year-old Daniel Boone joined the Missouri militia. Jones 224.

134: Aftermath of War of 1812. Jones 224; Colby 95.

134: Jean-Baptiste's record of baptism dated December 28, 1809. Colby 72.

134: Children in household baptized on August 8, 1814. Colby, 90 n.34

134: 1815 treaty conference; 51 million acres of land concessions. Jones 226-238.

134: "be kept in a good humor for two or three years" Jones 234.

134: "extend its protection to the Native inhabitants" Jones 236.

134-135: The election for governor was held in 1820, in preparation for Missouri's admission to statehood in 1821. Jones 254-255.

135: "undue partiality to Indians." Jones 253.

135: Julia Hancock Clark died in 1820. Jones 254.

135: Coboway's document thrown into the fire. Ronda 213.

135: Fur trade. Wexler 44, 93, 97.

135: Baptiste worked for the Missouri Fur Company. Colby 101.

135: Duke Paul. Colby 101-13.

136: Anton Fries, child of "the American." Colby 110-11 n.22.

Chapter 9: The Sons of the Red-Headed Chief

137: "justice and humanity require us to cherish and befriend them." Jones 286.

139: Fair-haired Clark of the Nez Perce. Jones 138.

139: Clark remained Superintendent. 259, 265, 279.

139: Factories and forts, Jones, 165-166. Factories were not manufacturing sites. "Factors" were government-licensed traders.

139: Beaver trade, licenses, associated fighting. Jones 157-58, 161, 172, 263-275; Colby 127-136.

141: "To remove them .. by force.. would be revolting to humanity…" Wexler 103, citing *The Writings of James Monroe.*

142: "treason against the motherland" Perdue 39.

142: Doublehead was killed. Perdue 37. Doublehead was not beloved among his own people; he was known as a murderer of both whites and Indians.

142: Sequoyah moved west in 1818. Perdue 149.

142: Sauk and Fox concessions and encroachment on Shawnee and Delaware land. Jones 150, 156-157.

142: 1825 concessions of Sauk, Shawnee, Delaware, Osage, Kansas. Jones 280-283.

142: "wonderfully adapted to an Indian population" Jones 281.

142: "humain feeling" Jones 285.

143: "of right it ought to yield" Jones 279.

143: Paternalist rationale; "debased" Jones 259, 264.

143: "meliorate the condition" Jones 284.

143: Baptiste return from Europe and appearance. Colby 109, 112, 116-117.

143: "His mind...was well stored"..."the best man on foot" Colby 113-114.

143: Indian war dance (Colby) 136-37, comfort a friend (Colby 161), stabbed a man (Colby 137), bullwhip (Colby 114).

144: *rendezvous* Wexler 97; Dary 83; Colby 128-129.

144: Pine Leaf (or Woman Chief). Beckwourth and Bonner 202, 205, 401-03; Elinor Wilson 51-53.

145: "A war of Extermination should be waged against them" Jones 313.

145: "it will only make me add one to the few scalps I am going to take...." Letter dated July 6-7, 1832, from Whitney, Ellen M. (ed.) The Black Hawk War, 1831-32, Springfield, Illinois State Historical Society, 1970, p.745, accessed at www.wisconsinhistory.org/.

145: Clark appealed for release of Black Hawk. Jones 325.

145: Inoculation against smallpox. Jones 329-332.

145: 1827 Cherokee Constitution. Perdue 40.

146: Pressure on and removal of other "civilized tribes:" Johnson 61; Perdue 73; Jones 304; Museum of the Cherokee Indian.

146: "passed them in the chase" "some progress" President Andrew Jackson to Congress, 1829, Wexler 110, citing James D. Richardson (ed.), *Messages and Papers of the Presidents,* Washington, D.C., U.S. Government Printing Office, 1896.

147: Indian Removal Bill. Jones 297; Perdue 76 and generally.

147: Squatters took over Sauk and Fox cornfields. Jones 299.

147: 1830 treaty council. Jones 300.

147: Refugees displaced from east. Jones 299-05; Perdue, 38, 51, 73, 12-22.

147: "it is impossible to refuse clothing to many women and children." Jones 305.

148: Liquor permits. Jones 298, 305, 307, 316.

149: "the most orderly and sober Indians" Jones 320.

149: Cherokee cases. Perdue 69-115.

149: Georgia sovereignty showdown. Perdue, 55, 70-71, 76-89, and generally.

149: Georgia "hoist[ed] the flag of rebellion against the United States" Perdue 79.

149: "Our federal union: it must be preserved." Brands 446.

149: "the Union…will soon fall and crumble into atoms." Perdue 79.

150: "John Marshall was a Virginian…." Stites 2.

151: "John Marshall has made his decision…." Horace Greeley, quoted in Brands 493.

151: Jackson told John Ridge that the United States would not enforce the decision. Perdue 59, 94.

152: "an unbending necessity tells us we must leave" The Museum of the Cherokee Indian, Cherokee, North Carolina.

152: "[W]e can't be a Nation here" Perdue 102.

152: We "will never consent to be citizens of the United States" Perdue 47, 106.

152: "forcibly if we must" Perdue 100.

152: Strange family sitting at his dinner table. Perdue 105.

152: 1835 Treaty of New Echota. Perdue 112.

152: John Ridge said that he was signing his death warrant. Perdue 114.

152: Assassination of John Ridge, Major Ridge and Boudinot. Perdue 150.

152: Signed a petition rejecting the treaty. The National Museum of the American Indian and other sources give different counts of the number of signers.

153: Eight babies died. Perdue 123.

153: Death of Harriet Boudinot. Reported in the New York Observer, Nov. 26, 1836; *Journal of Cherokee Studies,* 4(2):102-107, Spring 1979.

153: Death of Harriet Clark. Jones 308.

153: Smallpox. Jones 207, 329-332. With Clark's authorization, Indian agent Joshua Pilcher and Dr. Joseph R. De Prefontaine went looking for the Lakota Sioux, who met them along the Missouri, desperate for vaccinations. The doctor used his personal supply of the vaccine when the government supply ran out, and fell ill while on this mission.

153: Deaths on the Trail of Tears. Museum of the Cherokee Indian; Perdue 125-128.

154: A man over 100 years old. Perdue 125.

154: Ninety-year-old former slave and her children. Perdue 129-130.

154: Clark died on September 1, 1838. Jones 333.

154: Tsali and Thomas. Perdue 133; *Journal of Cherokee Studies,* Vol. 14, generally; Museum of the Cherokee Indian. The story of the Eastern Cherokee is fictionalized by Charles Frazier in *Thirteen Moons.*

Chapter 10: Baptiste and Beckwourth

155: "There are no more Mississippis to drive him beyond." Beckwourth and Bonner 347.

157: The buffalo jump. Cushman 48-49.

157: "Let them kill, skin, and sell until the buffalo is exterminated" Hine 317-318.

159: "The men at the fort had taught him to swear quite fluently" Beckwourth and Bonner 341.

159: "one of the most infernal practices" "I am now about to fight my brother" Beckwourth and Bonner 444-461; Elinor Wilson 102.

160: Cherokees during the Civil War. Confer 46-51; Perdue 161.

160-161: Nez Perce and Flathead were curious about religion. Wexler 119-120.

161: "he did not say anything about white men wanting to settle" Nabokov 130.

161: Santa Fe Trail; St. Helena and mint juleps. Colby 139-140, 145-147.

163: Cherokees traveled the Oregon Trail. Dary 131.

163: Baptiste guided Clark family members on Oregon Trail. Dary 86; Colby 150-151.

163: Henderson Luelling. Dary 172-173.

163: Provisional government of Oregon Territory. Dary 110.

164: Captain Truckee and Fort Hall. Dary 106, 126-127, 236.

164: First wagon trains had peaceful encounters. Dary 135-139.

164: Kearney and Clark families. Jones 301-02; Sides 34; Dary 176.

164: Stephen Watts Kearney relations with tribes. Dary 134-135; Sides 34.

164: Dispute over Canadian border. Wexler 152; Dary 128, 147.

165: George Washington Bush. Dary 118.

165: Donation Land Act of 1850. Dary 251-253.

165: Background to Mexican War. Wexler 93-94.

165: Cherokee planters in Texas. Wexler 94.

166: Meriwether Lewis Clark served as an artillery officer; Baptiste served as a scout. Colby 157-159. Beckwourth was a guide and interpreter. Elinor Wilson 107-109.

166: "Diggers," horror at white cannibalism: Canfield xii, 5-6, 121.

166: Indian hunts. Nabokov 101.

167: Baptiste as *alcalde*. Colby 160-161; California Archives, Unbound Documents, 364-365 and San Diego Archives, Documents, vol. II, 328, the Bancroft Library, U.C. Berkeley.

167: Shoshonean dialects. http://multitree.org/codes/shh; http://www.britannica. com/EBchecked/topic/541836/Shoshone.

167: Payomkawichum: Mission San Luis Rey Museum, Oceanside, California.

167: Antonio Peyri and Pablo Tac. Nabokov 61-63; Mission San Luis Rey Museum.

168: Janitin forcibly converted. Nabokov 58-60.

169: Baptiste fathered a Luiseno child: The Oceanside Historical Society's "Facebook" site confirmed postings dated July 21, 2011 and Feb. 23, 2012 by Rainer Mueller, in which Mr. Mueller discussed the child's birth and baptism (baptism entry #1884, May 28, 1848). Mueller further reports that the mother, Margarita Sobin, later married Gregory Trujillo, and inherited land that is now called Rancho Cucamonga. It is possible that Sobin-Trujillo descendants are part of the surviving Luiseno community. There is currently no information on the fate of the baby girl. The baptism certificate is catalogued in the Early California Population Project of the Huntington Library with an "LA" church baptism number 1884. These records extend only until 1850. A search of death records suggests that she did not die in infancy. This child is not mentioned in the meticulous research by Susan Colby, Baptiste's biographer.

169: Sentencing order in Baptiste's handwriting, ledger of indebtedness, and explanation for Charbonneau's resignation. Engelhardt 147-152. Other documents apparently written by Charbonneau include a brief note in Spanish (Furtwangler 304) and a note stating "No water, January 2- Charbonneaux," recorded by the commander of the Mormon Battalion in 1847 (Irving Anderson ("J.B. Charbonneau") 259.

170: "regarded by the people as favoring the Indians more than he should do" Colby 161-62.

170: "distasteful for a decent man" Engelhardt 151.

170: Gold Rush. Dary 187-95.

170: "house-keeping" on Murderer's Bar on the American River. Colby 164-165; Elinor Wilson 127.

170: Duke Paul visited the Gold Country. Colby 169-171.

170: Massacre at Whitman mission. Dary 178-186.

171: Rising tensions between wagon trains and Indians. Dary 195-230.

171: Starvation among Indians. Dary 209.

171: Sioux and Pawnee fighting each other and emigrants. Dary 210, 258, 260.

171: American doctor. Dary 212.

171: Smallpox, Sauk and Fox. Dary 244.

172: Treaty Council in 1851. Dary, 246-251.

172: "understand which band of a tribe he is commissioned to punish...." Beckwourth 529-531.

172: Renewed fighting in 1853-54: Dary 258-261.

172: Corruption. Nabokov 199-202; Brown (*Bury My Heart*) 176.

172: Grattan incident and Battle of Blue Water Creek. Dary 260-263.

173: Mormon settlement named Limhi. John W.W. Mann 24.

173: Coalescing of Lemhi bands; Cameahwait family's leadership. John W.W. Mann 15-37.

173: Charbonneau as a surveyor ... PO Secret Ravine...hotel clerk in Auburn. Colby 163-174.

174: Sioux uprising. Akipa, in Howe 10-11.

174: "I went to save the lives of two particular friends...." Brown (*Bury My Heart*) 44.

175: Dakota were farming. Finkelman in *William Mitchell Law Review* 415, 419. This source notes research suggesting that Dakota farmers brought in a good crop shortly after the food crisis, and that anger at white arrogance was as much a cause of the uprising as actual starvation. See Finkelman 419 n.54.

175: "I could not afford to hang men for votes:" Finkelman 405.

175: One of the men hanged by mistake had saved the lives of whites. Finkelman 414 n.34.

175: Murder of Snag; Tendoy became chief. John W. W. Mann 25-26

175: Massacre Rock and Bear River Massacre. Dary 285-289.

175: Washakie: Madsen generally; O. Howard 313-21; Brown (*The American West*) 270-272.

177: Sand Creek massacre; "a few hours of madness...turned to their war leaders." Brown (*Bury My Heart*) 67-98. See also Dary 292-294.

177: Beckwourth's testimony. Elinor Wilson 174-180.

179: Railroad workers killed. Dary 301.

179: Death and burial of Baptiste. The cause of death might have been pneumonia or "mountain fever." Colby 174-181. "Metaphorically speaking, he had a case of the latter all his life...." Colby 181.

179: "My heart turns naturally to my adopted people" Beckwourth 533-535.

180: Fort Laramie Treaty of 1868. Dary 301-303.

Chapter 11: The Paiute Princess

181: "If I could tell you but a tenth part of all she willingly did ..." O. Howard 237.

183: The Winnemucca and Truckee families and the Northern Paiutes: Canfield generally; Knack and Stewart generally; Hoxie, Ch. 4.

183: Quotations from Sarah Winnemucca are from her book, *Life Among the Piutes: Their Wrongs and Claims*. This book is listed in the bibliography under her married name, Hopkins. Sarah was married to a white man named Lewis Hopkins in the early 1880s. They parted ways after he repeatedly gambled away money she had accumulated to help her people.

185: "Rag Friend." Canfield 6.

185: Star-Spangled Banner. Canfield 37.

185: "one who looks after." Canfield 3.

186: "angel" Canfield 7.

186: Growing up in California. Canfield 7-11.

186: Washo, Ormsby, and Captain Jim. Canfield 11-13.

186: Washo Indians starved. Canfield 20.

188: Death of Truckee. Canfield 29-30.

188: Inconsistent accounts. Canfield 30-31.

188: Dodge. Canfield 15, 18-20, 28.

188: "Chief Winnemucca." Canfield 20.

188: Theatrical performance. Canfield 36-42.

189: Pyramid Lake War. Canfield 15-28.

189: Ely Parker: Brown (*Bury My Heart*) 171-186; Nabokov 202-204; Hoxie, Ch. 4.

189: "subordinate embryo-general." Nabokov 203.

190: "We are all Americans." http://www.nps.gov/apco/parker.htm.

190: "professed Christian whites." Nabokov 204.

190: "Who slew Custer?" Nabokov 236.

191: Young Winnemucca died. Canfield 74.

192: Samuel Parrish. Canfield 94-110.

192: Oytes. Canfield (generally).

192: Wovoka. Canfield 68, 100, 159: Dee Brown (*Bury My Heart*) 390.

192: Annie Parrish. Canfield 97, 104-105.

192: Old Winnemucca asked for land on the Owyhee River. Canfield 115.

192: Washakie. Madsen 30, 36, 53 and generally; Dee Brown (*The American West*), Chapter 19; Montana State Capitol historical exhibit.

193: "Thus began a long friendship ... no Nez Perce had ever killed a white man." Brown (*Bury My Heart*) 300-301.

193: Threw away his Bible. Josephy (*500 Nations*) 411.

193: The Nez Perce forced to flee. Brown (*Bury My Heart*) 300-314; Josephy (*500 Nations*) 409-418; Josephy (*Chief Joseph's People and their War*) generally; O. Howard 184-198.

194: Fort Fizzle Historical Site, Montana.

194: Tzi-kal-tza. Jones 138.

194: Sending "our mother" to Washington, DC. Canfield 125.

194: Bannock War. Canfield 123-149.

194: General Crook. Canfield 135.

195: "Her name is everywhere." Canfield 149.

195: Lemhi helped settlers but were under pressure to leave. John W.W. Mann 29-37.

195: Statement of Natchez to *Daily Silver State.* Canfield 118.

195: Removal to Yakima. Canfield 150-159.

196: "Princess Sarah." Canfield 162-167.

196: "Very forgetful." Canfield 175.

196: Quote attributed to Sheridan. Brown (*Bury My Heart*) 166.

197: Death of Old Winnemucca. Canfield 196-199.

197: Dawes Act. Canfield 209, 248-249; Nabokov 237.

197: "Gumbo with greasewood...." Nabokov 259.

198: "Egypt had its locusts...." Nabokov 256-257.

198: "God damn a potatoe." Nabokov 237.

198: Ely Parker's comments on allotment. Nabokov 234.

198: "seat of barbarism." Nabokov 233.

198: DeWitt Clinton Duncan's comments on allotment. Nabokov 265-267.

199: Martin Charlot's comments on allotment. Nabokov 267-271.

199: John Stands in Timber's comments about allotment. Nabokov 244-246.

199: Peabody school. Canfield 238-255.

200: *Silver State* editorial. Canfield 250.

200: Elma and John Smith; Sarah's death. Canfield 257-259.

200: Ghost Dance: Nabokov 253-255.

200: Wounded Knee: Brown (*Bury My Heart*) 413-418.

Epilogue

205: "Indelible thread of red." Waugaman and Moretti-Langholtz 1, quoting the late Thomasina Jordan, Chair of the Virginia Council of Indians.

206: "We are not a people of the past...." Perdue 164.

206: Mandan-Hidatsa-Arikara. Johnson 130-31; http://minotdailynews.com/page/content.detail/id/564391/Tex-Hall--Proposed-fracking-regs-will-hurt-energy-development-on-reservations.html?nav=5010, accessed March 31, 2012.

206: Expulsion of Lemhi, modern Lemhi. John W.W. Mann xix, xxiii, 35-36 and generally; also, www.lemhi-shoshone.com.

206: Luiseno scholar. *This Week in Indian Country Today* (Sept. 19, 2012) 18.

207: Paiutes' legal struggles. Knack and Stewart generally.

207: "a broken heart." Josephy (*500 Nations*) 417.

List of Maps and Illustrations

Front Cover

Friendly Indians Watching a Wagon Train, painting by Oscar E. Berninghaus. Courtesy of Sotheby's New York and of Barbara Brenner, granddaughter of Mr. Berninghaus.

Statue of Pocahontas. Historic Jamestowne. Jamestown, Virginia. National Park Service/Colonial National Historical Park and Preservation Virginia. Courtesy of the National Park Service.

Statue of Sacagawea. *Sacagawea and Jean Baptiste,* by Glenna Goodacre, 2001, 9' 5" high, edition of 15. Photo courtesy of Glenna Goodacre Ltd. © Daniel Barsotti.

Chapter 1: The Invasion of Virginia

Page 12: Map. *North America divided into its III principall [sic] parts.* Philip Lea, 1685. Courtesy of the Library of Congress.

Page 12: Coastal Grass – Virginia. © crystalseye/Dollar Photo Club.

Chapter 2: The White Feather

Page 24: Captain John Smith. After an early portrait by Simon van de Passe, 18th century, detail of John Smith from an illustration in *The Generall Historie of Virginia, New England, and the Summer Isles; with the names of the Adventurers, Planters, and Governours from their first beginning, Ano: 1584, to this present 1624.* Engraver uncertain. In the public domain.

Chapter 3: The Tempest

Page 47: Pocahontas. Engraving by Simon van de Passe, 1616. In the public domain.

Chapter 4: Mother of Presidents

Page 64: Blue Ridge Mountains. © John Keith/Dollar Photo Club.

Page 64: Map. *The United States of America laid down from the best authorities, agreeable to the Peace of 1783.* John Wallis, 1783. Courtesy of the Library of Congress.

Page 69: Sequoyah. *Se-Quo-Yah* by R.T. Hand-colored lithograph, I.T. Bowen's Lithographic Establishment, ca. 1838. Courtesy of the Library of Congress.

Page 71: Map. *A map of the British and French dominions in North America, with the roads, distances, limits, and extent of the settlements, humbly inscribed to the Right Honourable the Earl of Halifax, and the other Right Honourable the Lords Commissioners for Trade & Plantations,* John Mitchell, 1774. Courtesy of the Library of Congress.

Page 71: Corn Field – Ohio River Valley. © neveemilia/Dollar Photo Club.

Chapter 5: Father of Waters

Page 77: Cornstalk. Drawing of Cornstalk from *Frost's Pictorial History Of Indian Wars And Captivities: From The Earliest Record Of American History To The Present Time* (1872) Paperback, by John Frost and Samuel G. Drake. http://en.wikipedia.org/wiki/Cornstalk

Page 79: *Daniel Boone.* Anonymous, 19th century, after Chester Hardin painting. Courtesy of the National Portrait Gallery, Smithsonian Institution/Art Resource, New York.

Page 82: Map. *A Map of the United States and part of Louisiana.* Benjamin Davies, 1805. Courtesy of the Library of Congress.

Mississippi River Vista – Wisconsin. © johnsroad7/Dollar Photo Club.

Page 85: Chief Little Turtle. Early 19th century lithograph. http://commons.wikimedia.org/wiki/File:Little_Turtle.jpg

Chapter 6: A Voyage of Discovery

Page 96-97: Map. *A map of Lewis and Clark's track, across the western portion of North America from the Mississippi to the Pacific Ocean: by order of the executive of the United States in 1804, 5 & 6.* Samuel Lewis, 1814. Courtesy of the Library of Congress.

Page 96: Lemhi Pass, Beaverhead-Deerlodge National Forest, Montana. Courtesy of the Forest Service of the United States Department of Agriculture. In the public domain.

Page 97: Columbia River Gorge – Oregon. © RG/Dollar Photo Club.

Chapter 7: A Baby on Her Back

Page 108: Sacagawea. Obverse of the Sacagawea dollar coin. Design by Glenna Goodacre. http://en.wikipedia.org/wiki/File:Sacagawea_dollar_obverse.png.

Chapter 8: My Little Dancing Boy

Page 124: *William Clark*. Portrait by Charles Willson Peale, 1810. http://commons.wikimedia.org/wiki/File:William_Clark.jpg. In the public domain.

Chapter 9: The Sons of the Red-Headed Chief

Page 140: Tzi-Kal-Tza. *Tzi-Kal-Tza of the Nez Perce seated with a rifle across his lap*. The original photo is attributed to the William Henry Jackson collection. In that collection, there is no mention of William Clark. A ca. 1890s reproduction of the original image includes some biographical information that claims that Tzi-Kal-Tza was the son of Captain William Clark of the Lewis and Clark expedition. This claim was made by Nathaniel Pitt Langford and he claimed it was verified by Granville Stewart, Historical Society of Montana. All this information is printed on the verso of the photo. Photo reprinted with the permission of the Wisconsin Historical Society.

Page 148: *John Ridge, a Cherokee*. Hand-colored lithograph, I.T. Bowen's Lithographic Establishment, ca. 1838. Courtesy of the Library of Congress.

Page 148: Elias Boudinot. http://commons.wikimedia.org/wiki/File:Boudinot.jpg. In the public domain.

Page 150: John Marshall. Henry Inman, 1832. http://commons.wikimedia.org/wiki/File:John_Marshall_by_Henry_Inman,_1832.jpg. In the public domain.

Chapter 10: Baptiste and Beckwourth

Page 158: *James P. Beckwourth in Hunter's Costume*. Engraving courtesy of the Bancroft Library, University of California, Berkeley. Call number: Beckwourth, James P. – POR 1

Page 162: Map. *Map of the United States, Territory of Oregon, west of the Rocky Mountains, exhibiting the various trading depots or forts occupied by the British Hudson Bay Company, connected with the western and northwestern fur trade.* Washington Hood, 1838. Courtesy of the Library of Congress.

Page 162: The Oregon Trail, South Pass, Wyoming. Courtesy of the National Park Service.

Page 168: A sentencing order written by Jean-Baptiste Charbonneau. Image is reproduced with the permission of the Santa Bárbara Mission Archive-Library. Image # CMD 4084. A facsimile of the sentencing order was printed in *San Luis Rey: The King of the Missions,* by Father Zephyrin Engelhardt. Published by The James H. Barry Co., San Francisco, 1921. *San Luis Rey* can be accessed on open archive, http://www.archive.org/stream/cu31924020157560#page/n0/mode/1up.

Page 176: Chief Washakie. *Portrait of Chief Washakie in Native Dress with Feather Headdress and Pipe n.d.* Photo by Baker and Johnston. http://en.wikipedia.org/wiki/Washakie. In the public domain.

Page 178: Captain Silas Soule. Photo ca. 1863-1864. Courtesy of the National Park Service.

Chapter 11: The Paiute Princess

Page 184: Map. *Map of an exploring expedition to the Rocky Mountains in the year 1842 and to Oregon & north California in the years 1843-44.* John C. Fremont, 1845. Courtesy of the Library of Congress.

Page 184: Independence Lake, Tahoe National Forest. © David Frissyn/Dollar Photo Club.

Page 187: *Sarah Winnemucca.* Albumen silver print by Norvell H. Busey, Baltimore, Maryland, 1883. Reprinted with permission of the National Portrait Gallery, Smithsonian Institute/Art Resource, New York.

Page 191: Ely Parker. Photo by Mathew Brady, ca. 1860-1865. Courtesy of the National Archives Online Public Access.

Epilogue: "We're Still Here."

Page 205: Statue of Pocahontas. Historic Jamestowne. Jamestown, Virginia. National Park Service/Colonial National Historical Park and Preservation Virginia. Courtesy of the National Park Service.

Page 205: The Pamunkey Reservation today. Photo courtesy of the author.

Page 207: Chief Joseph and Oliver Howard, 1904. The copy of this photo in the archives of the Cumberland County Historical Society is signed "To General R. H. Pratt from his friend John Wanamaker, November 22, 1909." A copy of a newspaper article is attached, with the headline "An Historic Picture." The article explains that the photo was reproduced from the Commencement edition of the *Red Man and Helper,* the school newspaper at the Carlisle Indian School. This edition of the school newspaper, dated March 18, 1904 (vol. xix, no. 33) can be found at http://home.epix. net/~landis/joseph.html, a collection of material related to the Carlisle Indian School and its alumni.

Back Cover

Statue of Pocahontas. Historic Jamestowne. Jamestown,Virginia. National Park Service/Colonial National Historical Park and Preservation Virginia. Courtesy of the National Park Service.

Map. *Map showing the location of the Indian Tribes within the United States. Prepared to accompany the Manual of Missions.* G.W. & C.B. Colton & Co., 1868. Courtesy of the Library of Congress.

Statue of Sacagawea. *Sacagawea and Jean Baptiste,* by Glenna Goodacre, 2001, 9' 5" high, edition of 15. Photo courtesy of Glenna Goodacre Ltd. © Daniel Barsotti.

Index

About the Author

Cyndi Spindell Berck received her Bachelor of Arts with a major in history from the University of California, Los Angeles. She went on to earn graduate degrees in law and public policy at the University of California, Berkeley, and has worked in both fields, as well as in journalism and academic editing. Born in New York and raised in Los Angeles, she now lives in Berkeley, California, with her husband, Peter, and their youngest son, Joe.